Labour Law, Vulnerability and the Regulation of Precarious Work

For Laura

Labour Law, Vulnerability and the Regulation of Precarious Work

Lisa Rodgers

Law School, University of Leicester, UK

Edward Elgar
PUBLISHING

Cheltenham, UK • Northampton, MA, USA

Published by
Edward Elgar Publishing Limited
The Lypiatts
15 Lansdown Road
Cheltenham
Glos GL50 2JA
UK

Edward Elgar Publishing, Inc.
William Pratt House
9 Dewey Court
Northampton
Massachusetts 01060
USA

A catalogue record for this book
is available from the British Library

Library of Congress Control Number: 2015957858

This book is available electronically in the Elgaronline
Law subject collection
DOI 10.4337/9781784715755

ISBN 978 1 78471 574 8 (cased)
ISBN 978 1 78471 575 5 (eBook)

Typeset by Columns Design XML Ltd, Reading
Printed and bound in Great Britain by TJ International Ltd, Padstow

Contents

Abbreviations

BERR	Department for Business Enterprise and Regulatory Reform
BIS	Department for Business, Innovation and Skills
DTI	Department of Trade and Industry
ILJ	Industrial Law Journal
ILO	International Labour Organization
MLR	Modern Law Review

Table of cases

UK CASES

EUROPEAN UNION CASES

ILO COMMITTEE OF EXPERTS REPORTS

Table of legislation

EUROPEAN UNION PROPOSED DIRECTIVES

ILO INSTRUMENTS

LEGISLATION FROM OTHER JURISDICTIONS

1. Introduction

1.1 CONTEXT

A few years ago it was announced that '[L]abour law is widely considered to be in crisis'.[1] That crisis was deemed to have both external and internal dimensions. The external dimension concerned a number of attacks against the dominant provisions of labour law. There was the suggestion that labour law no longer fit with the reality of either economic conditions or the way in which labour relationships were constructed. It no longer covered those individuals in need of protection, in particular those left bereft by changes in economic conditions. Labour law had not moved with the (economic) times. Well-worn arguments that labour law provided an obstacle to efficiency, flexibility, and economic and social progress could be reasserted and they gained momentum. The internal dimension was characterised as an introspective process within labour law and amongst labour lawyers. In the face of changing economic and social conditions questions were raised about whether traditional labour law concepts still met the needs of labour. It was also questioned whether the inherited concepts which were used to explain the position of labour and the constitution of labour relationships continued to display conceptual coherence. The justifications for labour law needed to be rethought and reconsidered.

One of the main responses to this 'crisis' has been to suggest that labour law needs to be constructed around the idea of precarious work. As precarious work has been a major feature of the economic and social changes identified, there needs to be more thinking about how the phenomenon of precarious work has been created and what this means for labour law institutions. Indeed, regulations have been introduced at various geographical levels to attempt to tackle the problem of precarious work. As precarious work has been largely associated with non-standard

---

[1]   G Davidov and B Langille, 'Understanding Labour Law: A Timeless Idea, a Timed-Out Idea, or an Idea Whose Time Has Now Come?' in G Davidov and B Langille (eds), *The Idea of Labour Law* (Oxford University Press 2011) 1

working outside the traditional 'standard employment relationship' (full-time work for a single employer), regulations have focussed on certain vulnerable groups: part-time workers, fixed-term workers and temporary agency workers. For each of these groups legislation has been created to ensure that they are treated 'equally' with the standard workforce. It was hoped that in providing this legislation for precarious work groups, labour law would be meeting a practical need, but it would also regain its legitimacy. It would be seen as responsive to dominant economic (and social) forces, demonstrating its efficiency and flexibility. Indeed, 'flexibility' has been the watchword of many of these kinds of regulations.

It is in the context of this 'crisis' and the associated regulation for precarious work that this book lies. The book investigates in detail the trend towards the regulation for precarious work, what this means and how it should be understood. However, this book goes beyond this pure exposition of the 'phenomena' and regulation of precarious work. It takes the 'crisis' as an opportunity for greater thinking about the whole concept of 'vulnerability' in employment relationships. In the literature on precarious work, vulnerability has been considered in its links with the notion of precarious work. Indeed, the terms 'precarious' and 'vulnerable' have been used more or less interchangeably. This is particularly the case in the literature concerned with the determination of the factors which constitute 'precarious' work, and the social effect of this phenomenon. For example, Eyraud and Vaughan-Whitehead identify a number of risks in the 'new economy' which 'put workers in more uncertain or vulnerable situations'.[2] When these risks combine, workers enter into 'vulnerability vectors' which mean that workers are trapped in work of poor quality, and are at increased risk of experiencing other social problems. Non-standard work is cited as a point of entry into such a 'vulnerability vector', particularly for women and younger workers.[3] The width of the term 'vulnerability' also means that it is used to develop the 'dimensions of precariousness' identified by Rodgers as constituting precarious work. Rodgers' model identified that precarious work should be defined according to four elements:

(1) temporal (degree of certainty over the continuity of employment);
(2) organisational (working conditions, pay, individual and collective control over work);

---

[2] F Eyraud and D Vaughan-Whitehead, *The Evolving World of Work in the Enlarged EU: Progress and Vulnerability* (ILO 2007) 31

[3] Ibid 39

(3)   economic (sufficient pay and salary progression); and
(4)   social (legal and social protection).[4]

This model has been developed by Grimshaw and Marchington to suggest seven features of jobs that carry a risk of vulnerability, and 'four dimensions of vulnerability' created by the UK employment model (flexibility, insecurity, under-valuation and poor working conditions).[5]

   The aim of this book is to consider the concept of 'vulnerability' much more closely, and the relationship of the notion of vulnerability to a number of different theoretical perspectives and standpoints (including the notion of precarious work). Indeed, the notion of 'vulnerability' is chosen precisely because it is flexible enough to allow this exposition of the relationship between different theoretical perspectives on the need for regulation in the employment relationship, while still within the context of the trends towards the regulation of precarious work. The notion of vulnerability is chosen for an additional reason: the importance of *vulnerability theory* to the arguments in this book. This vulnerability theory has not been traditionally associated with labour law, but it is argued in this book that it provides a really useful framework for a more in-depth examination of the need for regulation in employment relationships. It is especially useful because it puts the labour subject centre stage. It takes the focus away from the economic and social processes which affect the labour market (in general or at a specific moment) and moves the focus towards thinking about the individuals affected by the institutions. But it is not limited to a consideration of the external effect of economic processes on individuals or groups in the labour market. It is concerned with the complex and ever-changing nature of the individual, and the multi-factoral and multi-dimensional processes involving those individuals and groups.

   In the section that follows, there will be an exposition of the story of labour law in response to the 'crisis', and particularly the development of the notion of precarious work. Section 1.3 will highlight some of the limitations of this narrative, and Section 1.4 will outline the alternatives and counter-arguments which will be explored more fully during the course of this book. In Section 1.5, there will be an explanation of the structure of the book and the reasons for the choice of that structure.

---

   [4]   G Rodgers, 'Precarious Work: The State of the Debate' in G Rodgers and J Rodgers (eds), *Precarious Jobs in Labour Market Regulation: The Growth of Atypical Employment in Western Europe* (ILO 1989) 3
   [5]   D Grimshaw and L Marchington, 'United Kingdom: Persistent Inequality and Vulnerability Traps' in F Eyraud and D Vaughan-Whitehead (eds), (n 2) 550

1.2   FROM CLASSICAL LABOUR LAW TO REGULATION FOR PRECARIOUS WORK

Arguably the link between vulnerability and labour law can be discerned in the foundational argument that labour law is 'not a commodity'.[6] The attempt here is to recognise that workers are first and foremost people rather than simply commodities to be bought and sold on the labour market. This recognition determines that regulation should aim to imbue the human subject of labour law with 'dignity' so that 'all forms of work … can be a source of personal well-being and social integration'.[7] Of course, this reference to the decommodification of the subject of labour law represents only half of labour law's traditional theory of justice.[8] The second half is not about labour *per se*, but about the relationship between that labour and the employers of labour. The argument is that employees are in need of protection because they suffer from an 'inequality of bargaining power' vis-a-vis their employers. This means that the 'normal' set of rules of market ordering needs to be limited to ensure that the worst excesses of labour market exploitation are avoided (either through law or collective bargaining processes).

Recently, these foundational aspects of labour law have been challenged. The notion that the 'inequality of bargaining power' between employers and employees should be the foundation for labour law regulation has been criticised. It is argued that this notion is outdated for two reasons. Firstly, it is based on certain assumptions about the position of work in society, namely, that work or employment is simultaneously the site of:

(1)   the greatest social oppression;
(2)   the greatest inequality of bargaining power;
(3)   the most revolting excesses of power; and
(4)   the greatest social conflict.[9]

---

[6]   This formulation is cited specifically as the 'fundamental principle' of the International Labour Organisation in paragraph I (a) of the Declaration of Philadelphia which is annexed to the ILO Constitution. The Constitution is available at <http://www.ilo.org/public/english/bureau/leg/download/constitution.pdf> accessed 1 August 2012

[7]   G Rodgers, E Lee, L Swepston and J van Daele, *The ILO and the Quest for Social Justice 1919–2009* (International Labour Office 2009) 7

[8]   B Langille, 'Labour Law's Theory of Justice' in G Davidov and B Langille (eds), *The Idea of Labour Law* (Oxford University Press 2011) 105

[9]   A Hyde, 'What is Labour Law' in G Davidov and B Langille (eds), *Boundaries and Frontiers of Labour Law* (Hart Publishing 2006) 46

This is simply no longer the case.[10] Secondly, it is based on the stereotype of the 'standard employment relationship' (full time, year round work for a single employer) under which inequality of bargaining power may be taken for granted.[11] The reality is that this 'standard employment relationship' no longer exists (if it ever did), so that regulation based on this principle fails to capture those most in need of labour market protection. There are also problems with embedding the foundation of labour law in the *link* between 'inequality of bargaining power' and the recognition that 'labour is not a commodity'. It has been argued that this link constrains the possibilities of labour law, because worker protection is limited to addressing the lack of bargaining power experienced by workers in the negotiation of their terms and conditions of employment. This means that labour law tends towards paternalism and does not properly consider the assets, capabilities and potential of workers as human beings. Essentially, the foundation of labour law in an understanding of the unequal relationship between employee and employers means that the range of human vulnerabilities inherent in the assertion that 'labour is not a commodity' is not explored: '[d]ignity will not provide the required moral ammunition if it is understood as merely providing a set of reasons as to why humans must be protected when they meet the wheels of commerce.'[12]

The literature on precarious work develops some of these criticisms of the traditional theory of labour law, and provides further context for the arguments made in this book. The starting point for this literature is the deterioration of the 'standard employment relationship', and the set of institutions and work practices which served to underpin this relationship. It is argued that for a time, between the end of the Second World War and the mid-1970s, the development of institutions (including labour law) around this 'standard employment relationship' made some sense. The 'Fordist' model of industrial production (large industrial enterprises

---

[10] For example, persistently high levels of *unemployment* can be seen to pose the greatest social threat. This is well represented by the comments of Eyraud and Vaughan-Whitehead that: 'From our analysis of the labour market we can distinguish between different types of risk with regard to employment and working conditions that may threaten workers ... We would consider the greatest risk as *remaining excluded from the labour market* because this often leads more quickly to social exclusion.' F Eyraud and D Vaughan-Whitehead, 'Employment and Working Conditions in the Enlarged EU: Innovations and New Risks' in F Eyraud and D Vaughan-Whitehead (eds), (n 2) 31

[11] M Freedland, 'From the Contract of Employment to the Personal Work Nexus' (2006) 35 *ILJ* 1, 28

[12] Langille (n 8) 111

engaged in mass production based on a narrow specialisation of skills and a clear management hierarchy) and the male-dominated nature of the workforce supported the 'standard employment relationship', which, because of its dominance, became the foundation of an 'occupational status' around which labour law and other social institutions (social security law) were established. Under these (industrial and social) conditions, a particular social compromise was reached whereby the (male) worker 'conceded dependency' in return for a secure livelihood for himself and his family.[13] The upshot was a 'core of social stability' which both protected workers and also provided a basis for economic growth and stability.[14]

However, there are a number of economic and (related) social processes which have undermined this standard employment relationship and its institutions. The economic processes are cited in the literature as:

(1)   technological innovation (in the fields of information technology);
(2)   increased competition stemming from globalisation; and
(3)   the considerable increase in the dominance of the service sector over that of manufacturing.[15]

Social changes have included ageing societies and changing consumer demand, as well as the 'crumbling' of the gender contract[16] (the male head of the household working to provide for his family). The buzz-word of both industrial and social organisations has therefore become not 'stability' but 'flexibility'. Companies have come to organise themselves on a more flexible basis to meet the demands of increased competition, employing 'dislocating strategies' such as outsourcing, networking and subcontracting.[17] At the same time, the organisation of work has changed significantly.[18] There has been a dramatic increase in more flexible forms

---

[13]   A Supiot, 'The Transformation of Work and the Future of Labour Law in Europe: A Multi-disciplinary Perspective' (1999) 138 (1) *International Labour Review* 31, 33

[14]   Rodgers (n 4) 1

[15]   Supiot (n 13) 34

[16]   L Vosko, *Managing the Margins: Gender, Citizenship and the International Regulation of Precarious Employment* (Oxford University Press 2009) 81

[17]   M Weiss, 'Re-inventing Labour Law?' in G Davidov and B Langille (eds), *The Idea of Labour Law* (Oxford University Press 2011) 45

[18]   Burchell B, 'The Prevalence and Redistribution of Job Insecurity and Work Intensification' in B Burchell, D Lapido and F Wilson (eds), *Job Insecurity and Work Intensification* (Routledge 2002)

of work, which both meet the needs of capital to enhance 'competitive advantage', and also the need of workers to combine work and family responsibilities in the light of the increased labour market participation of women.[19] These more flexible forms of work are often referred to as 'non-standard' or 'atypical' and include: part-time work, fixed-term work, temporary agency work, homeworking and self-employed or economically dependent work.[20]

The literature on precarious work highlights the disadvantages for workers employed on these non-standard contracts. Firstly, it is argued that jobs created on the basis of 'flexibility' are simply a vehicle through which labour market risk is shifted from employer to worker: the 'gains to employers in matching supply and demand have been translated directly into costs for workers'.[21] Secondly, there is no incentive for companies to invest in workers in these kinds of jobs, given that these jobs have only peripheral or marginal importance to the company. The result is jobs which are not only insecure, but are also characterised by low pay, low status and little in the way of promotion or training prospects.[22] Thirdly, there is also a question mark about the level of 'choice' that labour market participants have in selecting flexible employment. It is argued, for example, that women's continued primary responsibility for childcare leaves them with comparatively few options for paid work, and forces them to accept terms and conditions which are to their detriment and disadvantage. Thus part-time work or other non-standard work is not a 'choice' at all.[23] Finally, there is the problem that labour market institutions are still tied to the model of the 'standard employment relationship'. This means that non-standard workers have great difficulties in obtaining the protections and benefits associated with employment law.[24] This position continues despite specific protection for atypical workers through statute.[25] Although these statutes create equal treatment

---

[19]   Weiss (n 17) 46

[20]   Vosko (n 16) 1

[21]   S Fredman, 'Precarious Norms for Precarious Workers' in J Fudge and R Owens (eds), *Precarious Work, Women and the New Economy* (Hart Publishing 2006) 177

[22]   Ibid 177

[23]   Ibid 180

[24]   KVW Stone, 'Legal Protections for Atypical Employees: Employment Law for Workers without Workplaces and Employees without Employers' (2006) 27 (2) *Berkeley Journal of Employment and Labour Law* 251, 269

[25]   Examples from the European Union include Directives covering part-time work, fixed-term and temporary agency work: Council Directive 97/81/EC of 15 December 1997 concerning the Framework Agreement on Part-time work

rights for non-standard workers, they do not determine their employment 'status' (in terms of being an employee or worker for example). Consequently, these workers still encounter problems in qualifying for many labour law rights.

However, the theoretical strength of the precarious work analysis can be viewed as hampered by the association of precarious work with non-standard work. The empirical reality is that non-standard work is extremely heterogeneous and not all non-standard work can be designated precarious.[26] A good example is the phenomenon of temporary agency work. Although some of this work is characterised by low pay and poor working conditions, it is also adopted as a strategy by 'gold-collar' workers to maximise their market power.[27] These gold-collar workers often have greater bargaining power than 'standard' workers, and so it is difficult to consider this group 'precarious'. The association of precarious work and non-standard work is not only an empirical problem, but is also normative. It means that the frame of reference for analysing and for regulating for precarious work remains the 'standard' employment relationship in contrast to 'non-standard' forms. This means that regulation covering non-standard work can be limited to situations where that work deviates only slightly from the standard employment relationship. Vosko refers to the ILO Convention on Part-Time Work, which demands that the situation of part-time workers only differs from their full-time equivalent according to the number of 'normal hours' carried out. This, in fact, allows for the exclusion of a range of part-time workers who have contracts which differ significantly from the norm: those workers engaged on a casual, seasonal or temporary basis.[28]

The transformative power of labour law based on the theory of precarious work is limited for another reason. This theory is underpinned by economic understandings about the transformation of work, and

concluded by UNICE, CEEP and the ETUC, OJ [1999] L14/9; Council Directive 1999/70/EC of 28 June 1999 concerning the Framework Agreement on Fixed-term work concluded by ETUC, UNICE and CEEP, OJ [1999] L 175/43; Directive 2008/14/EC of the European Parliament and the Council of 19 November 2008 on temporary agency work, OJ [2008] L327/9

[26]   R Gomez and M Gunderson, 'Non-standard and Vulnerable Workers: A Case of Mistaken Identity' (2005) 12 *Canadian Labour and Employment Law Journal* 177, 178

[27]   P Leighton, M Syrett, R Hecker and P Holland, *Managing Self-employed, Agency and Outsourced Workers* (Butterworth-Heinemann 2007) 57

[28]   ILO Convention 175 'Convention Concerning Part-time Work' (International Labour Office 1994); Vosko (n 16) 101

ultimately the *desirability* of non-standard work as emerging from sound and inevitable economic processes. Precarious work is treated as the problem encountered by individuals, which needs to be managed (for example, by equal treatment mechanisms) to ensure that the traditionally poor working conditions associated with this kind of work are addressed. It docs not say anything about the *elimination* of precarious work, understood as non-standard work forms.[29] This is perfectly compliant with a liberal or neo-liberal understanding of the function of labour law, and therefore cannot engage with debates about whether it is this neo-liberal dominance which is one of the problems when it comes to understanding labour law regulation. It cannot consider whether the problem is systemic: part of a greater shift in the division of national income between workers and owners of capital.[30]

1.3 LIBERAL THEORY AND THE UNDER-THEORISATION OF THE LABOUR SUBJECT

It is the argument in this book that the theories surrounding precarious work tend to *under-theorise* the notion of vulnerability in employment relationships. Although 'precarious' or 'vulnerable' workers are referred to often in this literature, the literature on precarious work makes a set of assumptions about what vulnerability means in employment relation-ships. Those assumptions are essentially based on liberal characteris-ations of the nature of the labour subject. The first of those assumptions is that vulnerability in employment relationships is created externally to the labour subject. Labour subjects are acted upon by a set of (primarily economic) processes which justify some level of regulation. The second assumption is that vulnerability is a pathological or negative state. It is damaging to individuals, just as it is ultimately damaging to economic processes. Vulnerability denotes a subject of powerlessness and depend-ency; a subject failing to take advantage of all the benefits that the economic system has to offer. It is argued in this book that it is the combination of these two elements which has resulted in the *under-theorisation* of the nature of vulnerability in employment relationships and of the labour subject. It has meant that labour law does not consider sufficiently the complexity of the labour subject, and therefore is

---

[29] Vosko (n 16) 2

[30] This is the argument made by Fudge in J Fudge, 'Beyond Vulnerable Workers: Towards a New Standard Employment Relationship' (2005) 12 *Canadian Labour and Employment Law Journal* 151, 172

ill-equipped to promote the autonomy, resilience and agency of individuals or groups in the labour market.

Indeed, it might also be argued that labour law's classical theory of
justice also tends to under-theorise the nature of the labour subject. It is
possible to argue that some of the classical arguments are complicit with
the liberal view of the labour subject identified above. Care must be
taken in this assertion, as is clear from the analysis of the writings of the
two 'founding fathers' of the classical labour law position (in Europe):
Hugo Sinzheimer and Otto Kahn-Freund.[31] For a start, it is not possible
to assert that either author was complicit in a liberal view of *law*. In fact,
both authors were profoundly sceptical of a number of liberal legal
institutions. They both expressed unease with the notion of freedom of
contract in relation to the conclusion of the employment relationship.
They were convinced that the inequalities of bargaining power in
existence in the capitalist system meant that the employment relationship
could never be an institution created by free and equal partners. As a
result of his/her economic position the employer was always in a better
position to determine the terms of the employment contract, and used the
contract as a tool to aid in the suppression and subordination of working
individuals. The reliance of workers on the contract of employment for
their livelihood meant workers were forced to agree to the terms of the
employment contract and remained constrained and limited by those
terms. Furthermore, both were influenced by the social law tradition
expounded by Gierke, Ehrlich and Renner.[32] This tradition will be
discussed further in the next section, but this tradition offers a scathing
critique of the institutions of liberal law (and particularly the separation
between public and private law). Both Sinzheimer and Kahn-Freund were
convinced of the limited usefulness of liberal 'state' law in the furthering
of the needs of labour. That state law was too divorced from social
processes to properly or fully represent the needs of labour.[33] At most,
state law should act to cement the autonomously created norms of the

---

[31] R Dukes, 'Constitutionalizing Employment Relations: Sinzheimer, Kahn-
Freund, and the Role of Labour Law' (2008) 35 (3) *Journal of Law and Society*
341, 341
[32] For a discussion of these influences see R Lewis, 'Kahn-Freund and
Labour Law: An Outline Critique' (1979) 8 *ILJ* 202 and R Dukes, *The Labour
Constitution: The Enduring Idea of Labour Law* (OUP 2014)
[33] According to Sinzheimer: 'Die Gemeinschaft kann nicht mehr darauf
vertrauen, dass ihr Wohl passiv aus den Selbstbestimmungen der einzelnen folgt'
(Society can no longer passively rely on the self-interest of individuals – my
translation) H Sinzheimer, 'Die Reform des Schlichtungswesens' (1930) in H

social sphere.[34] Kahn-Freund also pointed out the limited usefulness of the courts as a means for the resolution of labour disputes. Those courts dealt only with the 'marginal' and the 'sporadic', and could not hope to create an ordered system of industrial relations (on their own).

However, despite the rejection of the institutions of liberal law, Kahn-Freund and Sinzheimer put forward a view of the liberal *subject* of labour law: workers as autonomous, independent and rational beings. Indeed, this view of the liberal subject was central to the development of Sinzheimer's idea of dependent labour at the heart of his labour law theory. To promote this theory, Sinzheimer relied on Marx's ideas about the position of labour under the capitalist system. He argued that the capitalist system distorted the central value of human activity in favour of the promotion of individual ends.[35] The insertion of individuals into the capitalist system meant that individuals were separated from their own labour: they no longer had control over their own work and merely served the ends of others. Under the capitalist system, labour was directed and controlled by the profit-seeking aims of capitalists. As a result, work no longer fulfilled a social or personal function for workers. It no longer enabled them to develop their own autonomous ends. The capitalist system was a threat to the liberal subject of labour. Indeed, Sinzheimer referred to the work of (the liberal theorist) Kant in this regard: the insertion of workers in the capitalist system reduced those workers to 'things' with a price with no purpose but to serve the needs of others. Instead workers should be viewed as elements of dignity, they belong to the world of 'spiritual beings' who have their own autonomous purposes and should be allowed to pursue those purposes with the independence and rationality they naturally possess.[36] Sinzheimer's views were echoed by Kahn-Freund who argued for the promotion of the dignity of labour outside the excessive constraints of the capitalist owners of production.[37]

Sinzheimer, *Arbeitsrecht und Rechtssoziologie: Gesammelte Aufsätze und Reden (Band 1)* (Otto Brenner Stiftung 1976) 237

[34] H Sinzheimer, 'Zur Frage der Reform des Schlichtungswesens' (1929) in H Sinzheimer (n 33) 226

[35] H Sinzheimer, *Grundzüge des Arbeitsrechts* (2nd ed Gustav Fischer Jena 1927) 8 ff

[36] H Sinzheimer, Grundzüge des Arbeitsrechts (1927) in H Sinzheimer, *Arbeitsrecht und Rechtssoziologie: Gesammelte Aufsätze und Reden* (Band 1) (Otto Brenner Stiftung 1976) 8

[37] P Davies and M Freedland, *Kahn-Freund's Labour and the Law* (Stevens 1983) 69

Kahn-Freund and Sinzheimer were also convinced about the external creation of vulnerability. Again the ideas of Marx were promoted here, to argue that workers were made vulnerable by the operation of the capitalist system. That capitalist system not only created labour as 'commodities' to be bought and sold on the labour market, it also created an inequality of bargaining power between employers and workers. That inequality of bargaining power was promoted and maintained by the institutions created by the controllers of labour (for example, the contract of employment). The problem with this view, for the purposes of the arguments in this book, is that it tends to categorise workers in uni-dimensional terms. Particular individual vulnerabilities for the meaning of those vulnerabilities are not specifically theorised or considered. They are also presented as acted upon by the capitalist system in a uniform way, which does not represent the experience of workers in practice. It is argued in this book that there is a need to consider the complex and multi-faceted vulnerability of workers more seriously. There is a need to put this vulnerability centre stage: to start with the subject of labour itself. This subject is not the liberal subject of classical liberal theory. This is the 'vulnerable subject' of sociology and (feminist) philosophy. These ideas will be discussed in the next section.

1.4 PUTTING VULNERABILITY CENTRE STAGE

The concept of 'vulnerability' is very wide. It is used in a great many contexts, both within and outside the law, most of which are beyond the scope of this book.[38] In terms of law, it is interesting that the concept of 'vulnerability' has previously been used as a foundational legal principle in areas other than labour law. 'Human vulnerability' is mentioned as one of Hart's 'truisms'. According to his argument, these 'truisms' provide the law with a certain minimum content; they explain the voluntary submission of subjects to law (and morals). Hart's argument is that the

---

[38]   There are many examples which could be cited here. One example is the discussion in political, social and healthcare literature about the challenges faced by 'vulnerable adults'. These are defined as 'people who are at greater than normal risk of abuse. Older people, especially those who are unwell, frail, confused and unable either to stand up for themselves or keep track of their affairs, are vulnerable.' See NHS, 'Vulnerable Adults' (11 May 2011) <http://www.nhs.uk/CarersDirect/guide/vulnerable-people/Pages/vulnerable-adults.aspx> accessed 15 August 2014

vulnerability of humans to each other, in the sense of physical susceptibility to bodily attack, gives reason for submission to (criminal) legal
rules.[39] He explains that: 'If men were to lose their vulnerability to each
other there would vanish one obvious reason for the most characteristic
provision of law and morals: Thou shall not kill.'[40] Moreover, the idea
that 'human vulnerability' is at the foundation of legal rules is seen in an
area of law more closely associated with issues of employment or labour
law, that of human rights. For example, Turner argues that the ontological
vulnerability of human subjects is the 'common basis' of human rights.[41]
The definition of 'human vulnerability' here is wider than that used by
Hart: vulnerability can stem from physical threats (both natural and
social), but can also refer to human susceptibility to psychological, moral
or spiritual suffering.[42] In any event, human vulnerability is the universally shared experience which forces human beings to institute legal
rules, and specifically universal human rights.[43]

The wide scope of 'human' vulnerability, in terms of its physical,
moral and psychological elements, has crept into some corners of labour
law. For example, it is possible to argue that the understanding of the
scope of this vulnerability has extended the duties imposed on employers,
particularly in the field of health and safety at work. An example is the
reasoning in relation to stress at work cases; here it is understood that
employers should take some responsibility not only for the physical but
also the psychological well-being of their employees.[44] However, the
potential of this term in the context of labour law theory has rarely been
discussed. For example, in the case of the classical labour law position,
the term 'vulnerability' appears rarely: the language is of subordination,
oppression and other terms relating to the imbalance of power between

---

[39] HLA Hart, *The Concept of Law* (Oxford University Press 1961) 190
[40] Ibid 190
[41] B Turner, *Vulnerability and Human Rights* (Pennsylvania University Press
2006) 1
[42] Ibid 28
[43] Ibid 6
[44] In the case of *Walker* v *Northumberland County Council* [1995] IRLR 35
the Court formulated a test to determine the liability of employers in stress cases.
This included the 'threshold question' about whether the kind of harm was
reasonably foreseeable. This threshold question would depend on a number of
factors, including a consideration of the particular 'vulnerability' of the Claimant
(paras 23–29). See also MJ Davidson and J Earnshaw, 'Vulnerable Workers: An
Overview of Psychosocial and Legal Issues' in MJ Davidson and J Earnshaw
(eds), *Vulnerable Workers: Psychosocial and Legal Issues* (1st Edition, John
Wiley and Sons 1991)

labour market participants. In the case of the more recent literature on precarious work, the complexity of human vulnerabilities has also been neglected as the foundational or organisational principle for the constitution of labour law. The reasons for this failure are introduced above and discussed through the course of this book.

The argument in this book is that this failure actually reduces the effectiveness of labour law. A failure to consider in detail the vulnerabilities to which individuals are subject means that labour law does not properly respond to labour's needs. Two theories are introduced which do attempt to deal with this vulnerability more centrally and more fully. The first of these theories has already been mentioned in the context of its influence on the classical labour law scholars: that of social law. It is my argument that the ideas of social law are usefully considered outside the context of classical labour law. It is useful to reconsider these theories in the light of a specific analysis of their take on vulnerability and to build a critique of current labour law based on that analysis. This might, in fact do more justice to these theories than was achieved in the context of classical labour law theory.[45] Furthermore, it is useful to consider authors within this tradition whose works were not considered in depth by the classical labour law scholars as examples of ways in which this tradition could be developed in an alternative way. Indeed, more modern takes on the function and legal position adopted by social law will be considered as part of this analysis (including the work of Francois Ewald).

However, it is also argued in this book that, although social law is useful in shifting the analysis of labour law in a more sociological direction, it does not encapsulate all of labour law's vulnerability. Although it does draw out a number of the problems associated with the acceptance of liberal political theory and liberal legal institutions, it does posit certain pre-conceived ideas about the nature of vulnerability itself. Vulnerability is connected to social position (for example, in the division of labour as asserted by Durkheim). As laws emanate from the interaction

---

[45]   Indeed, although both Sinzheimer and Kahn-Freund were influenced by social law in the development of their ideas, the practical application of those ideals did not always meet social law ends. For example, Kahn-Freund's framework of the proper functioning of the industrial relations system was developed in the context of liberal political thinking, within which Kahn-Freund was seemingly complicit. His framework reflected and contributed to the notion of industrial pluralism and 'voluntarism' which underscored the Donovan Royal Commission's findings. This appears to run counter to the social law tradition of the rejection of liberal political ideas and the institutions of the liberal political state. This will be discussed further in Chapter 2.

between individuals then it follows that group position is fundamentally important on this scheme. It is groups who have the ability to be recognised as worthy of protection by the state. As a result, vulnerability is counteracted by the development of strong groups who can fight for rights at a higher level; the achievement of group rights denotes a level of escape from vulnerability for individuals. Of course the reality of our labour market demonstrates that the legal recognition of groups is not sufficient to counteract vulnerability in its entirety. The development of group law (such as that pertaining to precarious workers) is influenced by forces other than the group itself and is not always constructed in a way which either includes all members of the group or ensures group protection. There is also the problem on the social law scheme that rights are never fixed: they are continuingly shifting according to changes in power relations in society.

This book asserts that it is *vulnerability theory* which has the most potential for the development of labour law. This theory puts the labour subject (in all its complexity) at the heart of labour law. It allows for an analysis of the labour subject which goes beyond the constraints of liberal theory, a theory which has been so influential in the development of our labour law. Instead of considering workers as a set of autonomous, independent and rational beings, acted on unilaterally and uni-dimensionally by economic forces, vulnerability theory allows workers to be considered as 'vulnerable subjects': complex, multi-dimensional actors within a complex multi-dimensional institutional space. This holds potential for labour law because it allows greater thinking about the whole concept of the *agency* of workers and the sustainability of labour law. It also allows greater thinking about the importance of identity in the experience and structure of labour. However, perhaps most of all, it offers to investigate how disadvantage and inequality is created, maintained and perpetuated, and what that means for the vulnerability of the labour subject. In a sense then, it brings together a number of insights to social law and even some of the concerns of the classical labour law scholars without being constrained by their particular context. It suggests that precarious work will not be tackled without a profound examination of all the institutions which create vulnerability and the position of workers within that. Until these structures are addressed (for example, the constraints of the need to show an 'employment relationship' for access to legal rights, and the need to conform to a particular legal identity, such as domestic worker, temporary worker, and so on), then individuals cannot build the resilience and autonomy which should be the aim of any legal system of labour rights.

1.5   STRUCTURE OF THE BOOK

Following the introduction, Chapter 2 outlines the context of vulnerability in employment relationships. The first half of Chapter 2 sets out the series of external pressures which are brought to bear on employment relationships, and how those pressures have been theorised. Economic pressures are discussed in terms of the systemic pressure of the capitalist system, which forms the heart of the classical labour law position on the nature of vulnerability in employment relationships. They are also discussed in terms of more modern economic changes, which, it has been argued, have created a specific set of work arrangements. Those new work arrangements have, in turn, determined a layer of 'precarious workers' in the labour market. These precarious workers display a set of particular vulnerabilities (and need to be regulated in a particular way as a result). Chapter 2 then moves to discuss legal and social changes which have been brought to bear on employment relationships, and how those have affected the vulnerability of workers. The second half of Chapter 2 sets out the problems with this external theorisation of vulnerability, namely that it fails to really theorise vulnerability at all. The alternative 'internal' constructions of vulnerability are then discussed and their potential value for widening the 'external' perspectives outlined in the first half of Chapter 2.

   Chapter 3 builds on this contextualisation of vulnerability in employment relationships. It outlines how the contextualisation and conceptualisation of vulnerability in employment relationships leads to the theorisation of particular legal solutions. Four theoretical positions (introduced in Chapter 2) are discussed: (1) classical labour law theory, (2) efficiency theory, (3) social law theory and (4) vulnerability theory. Practical examples of the application of those theories are discussed. For example, classical labour solutions are discussed in relation to the promotion of collective bargaining, efficiency theories are linked to the phenomenon of precarious work and its regulation, and social law is discussed in the context of the promotion of (substantive) equality. The potential of vulnerability theory for widening the reach and scope of current labour laws (in relation to vulnerability) is discussed. These themes are taken up more specifically in Chapter 4. This chapter provides an in-depth analysis of the regulations and policy relating to precarious work at different geographical levels. The relationship of these instruments with the different theoretical perspectives introduced in the introduction and developed in Chapters 2 and 3 are discussed. In particular, there is an assessment of the fit of each of these policies with the aims and aspirations of vulnerability theory, and some tentative suggestions are made about the direction of the aims of this legislation in the future.

Chapters 5 and 6 present two case studies on temporary agency work and domestic work respectively. These case studies are chosen as these groups are widely considered to be particularly precarious or vulnerable in the labour market. In each of these case studies there is an overview of the legal instruments pertaining to them. There is then a discussion of how the vulnerability of these groups would be characterised in the different theoretical perspectives introduced in this book, and how far the current regulations relating to these groups meet the regulatory goals of these different perspectives. Finally, criticisms of the different theoretical perspectives are made. At the end of each section, there is a particular section on the potentiality of vulnerability theory for re-thinking and re-assessing the needs of these groups, and what that means in terms of potential regulations for these groups.

2. Vulnerability in context

2.1 INTRODUCTION

The aim of this chapter is to investigate the 'context' of vulnerability in relation to the labour subject. This 'context' may be seen as a set of external pressures which act on the labour subject to create disadvantages. These external pressures can be characterised broadly or narrowly in terms of both subject matter and timeframe. For example, it can be argued that, in economic terms, it is the capitalist system which creates problems for workers and exposes them to vulnerability. On the other hand, it can be argued that it is not the capitalist system as a whole which creates vulnerability, but rather specific economic processes determined by a particular mode of organisation of the capitalist system at a particular moment. Likewise, it is possible to relate social changes to those in the economic sphere, and argue that changes in the gender organisation of work have created a set of vulnerabilities for those working in the system. This 'context' of vulnerability is rather familiar in the literature on labour law and so is a good starting point for the consideration of vulnerability in the labour relation.

However, it is the argument in this book that this particular 'external' characterisation of vulnerability tends actually to result in an *under-theorisation* of the vulnerability of the labour subject. This external characterisation is complicit with the (liberal) proposition that workers are naturally autonomous, rational, atomised beings. They are homogenous in this sense. Individual vulnerabilities are not, therefore, relevant to a consideration of how to deal with external forces. It is the external forces which require theorisation and comment rather than the labour subject itself. Of course, the problem with this under-theorisation is that it actually detracts from thinking about the experience of individual workers and, ironically, how best to create and promote autonomy. As a result, the argument presented here is that there is a need to consider theorisations of vulnerability which start from the subject of labour itself. The benefit of these theories is that they provide greater scope for thinking about identity (not constrained by the liberal imaginings of these categorisations, or by 'class-based' economic determinism) and how that affects the employment relationship. They also provide a greater possibility for the consideration of the *agency* of labour, and how autonomy can be produced by and through vulnerability. Labour actors become not just unwilling pawns subject both to vulnerability and the external forces which create it. They become vulnerable subjects whose capacities and capabilities cannot be developed to allow them to pursue their own ends.

This chapter will proceed as follows. After this introduction, the 'external' characterisation of vulnerability will be discussed. Within this external characterisation there will first be an examination of the theorisation of the capitalist system as the creator of vulnerabilities for labour. This will be linked to the work of Karl Marx being adopted (wholly or partly) by the classical labour law scholars. Second, there will be an examination of the processes of 'globalisation' as the creator of vulnerability. The argument here is that specific processes within the capitalist system can create problems for (precarious) workers, although there is no overall failure of the system itself. Within this external characterisation of vulnerability there will also be a brief examination of the social changes associated with these modern patterns of capitalism, and the influence of these on the creation of vulnerability. Following an examination of the external characterisation of vulnerability, there will be a focus on accounts which emphasise the personal or 'internal' nature of vulnerability. There is an introduction to the 'vulnerable subject' theorisations according to which individual, institutional and group vulnerability is the starting point for considering all the economic, social and cultural processes which flow from it. It is argued in the final section that the social law approach can be used to further the preoccupations of this vulnerable subject approach for the purposes of labour law. The subject of labour can be more precisely considered. The implications of all these approaches for finding labour law 'solutions' to labour problems and, particularly, the problems of precarious work will be considered in the next chapter.

2.2 THE EXTERNAL CREATION OF VULNERABILITY

2.2.1 Vulnerability in the Capitalist System

It is possible to view workers as having been made vulnerable by the operation of the capitalist system as a whole. This is the enduring narrative of classical accounts of labour law, which draw inspiration from the writings of Karl Marx on the functioning of capitalism. On this (Marxist) view, labour is made vulnerable by a number of processes at work under the capitalist mode of production. Two processes can be singled out in particular. The first process is that of commodification, which determines that human beings are reduced to goods which can be exploited for profit. This process involves the alienation of human beings from both the means of production and also themselves, resulting in a stifling of human potential and creativity. The second process is the function of the capitalist system in creating an inequality of bargaining power between employers and employees. This inequality of bargaining power is created by employers' ownership of the means of production and is maintained by the reliance of employees on their engagement in the capitalist system to meet their subsistence needs.

The process of commodification determines that, under capitalism, human beings are reduced to goods which can be exploited for profit. As Marx explains in *Das Kapital*, when workers becomes involved in the labour process, those workers change not only the object of labour, but also themselves: '[L]abour has incorporated itself within its subject: the former is materialised, the latter transformed.'[1] This constituting function of work makes workers particularly vulnerable within the capitalist system of production. It means that the capitalist system has the potential to control the humanity and personality of individual workers. Furthermore, this system threatens the 'physical integrity and moral dignity of the individual'[2] because it acts to alienate workers from both the process of working and the fruits of their work. The workers lack control over what they produce, and anything that they do produce is appropriated by others, so that the workers do not benefit from it. This includes their own labour: 'Labour produces not only commodities; it produces itself and the workers as a commodity – and does so in the proportion in which it produces commodities generally.'[3] Furthermore, the more that the commodified workers produce, the cheaper they become, and ultimately the less value they have (and the less they have to consume). Finally, labour is alienated from the work task, which is structured so as to stifle

---

[1]   K Marx, *Das Kaptial: A Critique of Political Economy* (Pacifica Publishing Studio 2010) 84

[2]   P Davies and M Freedland, *Kahn-Freund's Labour and the Law* (Stevens 1983) 69

[3]   K Marx, *Economic and Philosophic Manuscripts of 1844*, 1871–2 quoted in H Spector, 'Philosophical Foundations of Labor Law' (2005–2006) 33 *Florida State University Law Review* 1119, 1137

creativity and mental and physical energy.[4] The result is that the humanity of workers is compromised.

The capitalist system creates further vulnerability for workers through the inequality of bargaining power between employers and employees. In Marxist terms, this inequality of bargaining power is created by employers' ownership of the means of production and is maintained by the reliance of employees on their engagement in the capitalist system to meet their subsistence needs. According to the Marxist analysis there are essentially two classes in the capitalist system of production: the bourgeoisie and the proletariat. The bourgeoisie own the means of production and control the surplus value created by the labour of the proletariat class. The accumulation of this surplus value (profit) by the bourgeoisie allows the proper functioning of the capitalist system, but means that the proletariat class are maintained in a permanent position of subordination, as they have no realistic alternative to working in the capitalist system and no means of increasing their control over either the means of production or their own labour.[5] Kahn-Freund points out that this class relationship of control and subordination reflects the reality of all employment relationships. For Sinzheimer, too, this idea of subordination is central. He explains that the subordination of the worker by the employer is symptomatic of the subordination of labour to property in liberal capitalist societies.[6] In these societies, property rights are absolute and are the source of managerial power. The employer as proprietor becomes the only economic agent and therefore has unlimited power to manage labour, which serves to increase the powerlessness and vulnerability of the worker.[7]

Both Kahn-Freund and Sinzheimer point out that the inequalities inherent in the employment relationship are maintained by the different interests and aims of both workers and managers in the employment system. Whereas management's priority is to maximise investment (and represent the welfare of future generations), labour's is to maximise

---

[4] A Giddens, *Capitalism and Modern Social Theory: An Analysis of the Writings of Marx, Durkheim and Weber* (Cambridge University Press 1971) 12

[5] R Bellotti, 'Marxist Jurisprudence: Historical Necessity and Radical Contingency' (1991) 4 (1) *Canadian Journal of Law and Jurisprudence* 145, 146

[6] O Kahn-Freund, 'Hugo Sinzheimer 1875–1945' in R Lewis and J Clark (eds), *Labour Law and Politics in the Weimar Republic* (Basil Blackwell, Oxford 1981) 91

[7] There is a very good commentary on this in R Dukes 'Constitutionalising Employment Relations: Sinzheimer, Kahn-Freund, and the Role of Labour Law' (2008) 35 (3) *Journal of Law and Society* 347

consumption (and the maintenance or improvement in the immediate standard of living).[8] The labour/capital relationship is therefore not only unequal but inherently conflictual: '[I]n labour-management relations conflict is very much the "father of all things".'[9] However, it is in the interests of the dominant class, and the law it produces, that this conflict and subordination inherent in all employment relationships is obscured. One method of obscuring this subordination is by 'that indispensable figment of the legal mind known as the contract of employment.'[10] This institution rests on the idea that the parties to the employment contract freely negotiate its terms; that there is equality of bargaining power between the parties. Kahn-Freund argues that this idea of freedom of contract is a 'verbal symbol' rather than a 'social fact'. It is a 'conceptual apparatus', which has been created to see 'relations of subordination in terms of coordination'.[11] He argues that the 'social fact' of 'freedom of contract' usually represents only the freedom to restrict or give up one's freedom.[12] The lack of social power of all workers means that the ability of workers to actually negotiate in the conclusion or performance of the terms of the contract of employment is severely limited.[13]

In fact, this analysis can also be said to have Marxist roots. Marx argued that class domination is not just present in the industrial sphere. Rather, the class which owns the means of production also has the means to disseminate and enforce *ideologies* (expressed in law, politics and religion), which function to legitimate its dominance.[14] The corollary is that legal concepts, such as freedom (of contract) and equality, cannot be taken at their face value. These concepts do not, in any way, represent social reality; they are merely constructs which serve particular political and economic ends. The import of this discussion is the conviction that the inequality of bargaining power which exists between employers and employees does not stay confined to the industrial sphere. It is reinforced by law and by the ideology of the ruling class, and means that dominance is not only material but also intellectual: '[T]he ideas of those who lack the means of intellectual production are subject to it.'[15] This view of

---

[8]   Kahn-Freund in Davies and Freedland (n 2) 66
[9]   O Kahn-Freund, 'Intergroup Conflict and Their Settlement' (1954) *British Journal of Sociology* 193, 195
[10]   Kahn-Freund in Davies and Freedland (n 2) 18
[11]   Ibid 25
[12]   Ibid 25
[13]   Ibid 17
[14]   Giddens (n 4) 41
[15]   Marx, *The German Ideology* 61 quoted in Giddens (n 4) 41

vulnerability thus captures the idea that it is not only all workers which are subject to domination, but *all of* workers, because of the complicity of employers with the political and legal ideology of dominance.

That said, for Marx and those adopting his ideas, while capital (and capitalism) might control many aspects of the material (and even legal and political) existence of workers, there is a core of humanity which is separate from the effects of capitalism. Workers have a 'dignity' which belongs to their sphere of spiritual life and which is outside the control of the material life of capitalism. On this point, Sinzheimer refers to the Kantian distinction between things that have a price (commodities) and those that have dignity. The capitalist system attempts to reduce workers to things which have a price: they serve the ends of others, and can be replaced at any time by anything with equivalent value. However, workers are, in fact, elements of dignity. They have independent value which is irreplaceable.[16] This theoretical standpoint is important for the purposes of the characterisation of the (vulnerability) of the labour subject. It suggests a complicity with the (liberal) idea that ultimately workers are rational autonomous beings. Capitalism can act to threaten autonomy but it cannot compromise the moral truth of its existence.

The problem with this position, which will be exposed throughout this book, is that it suggests vulnerability as a negative state: autonomy rather than vulnerability is the natural state of human beings. The focus is on the external factors rather than the characterisation of individual workers, because that characterisation is assumed, and deemed unworthy of further theoretical consideration. This means that classical labour law can be co-opted to a certain extent within the liberal project and (it is argued in this book) this dilutes the force of some of the classical arguments. Alternative approaches to the liberal subject view are discussed in Section 2.3 of this chapter.

2.2.2 Vulnerability and Economic Change

A number of more modern theories have also attempted to theorise the context of worker vulnerability in terms of the operation of economic systems. These theories suggest, in contrast to classical labour law, that the context of vulnerability is very specific. It is specific in terms of the economic processes which produce it, and it is specific in terms of the labour market actors that it effects. For example, particular vulnerabilities

---

[16] H Sinzheimer, Grundzüge des Arbeitsrechts (1927) in H Sinzheimer, *Arbeitsrecht und Rechtssoziologie: Gesammelte Aufsätze und Reden* (Band 1) (Otto Brenner Stiftung 1976) 8

experienced by workers, it is theorised, are as a result of the pressures of globalisation which act on different individuals differently.[17] The argument proceeds as follows. Prior to the globalisation phenomenon, and after the two world wars, it was possible to identify a distinct and stable employment relationship between employers and workers.[18] This 'standard employment relationship' (full-time, year-round employment for a single employer) was a function of the 'Fordist' model of production in existence at the time and also the social compromise which had grown up around it. This 'Fordist' model consisted of manufacturing production in large factory units run by one company. The employment structure was male dominated, with the male employee functioning as the 'breadwinner' for his family. Tasks were closely defined, and the structure of the enterprise was characterised by a clear structure of hierarchies. While it was possible to identify 'subordination' within these enterprises, and a distinct power on the part of the employer to command and control the workforce, the trade-off was a certain amount of stability and security within the employment relationship. This stability and security was reinforced both by the operation of the social security system,[19] which guaranteed an income for the incapacitated worker and his family outside employment and by the operation of (labour) law based on the notion of the contract of employment.[20]

However, this system of industrial organisation (and social compromise) started to break down with the processes of globalisation. The

---

[17] This is not the only theory of economic change which can be said to create worker vulnerability. Indeed, there is now the suggestion that the digitalization and expansion of the internet is profoundly affecting worker vulnerability. One particular problem which has been identified is 'crowd sourcing', by which individuals are recruited via the internet and which falls outside regulatory regimes. This kind of sourcing is in its infancy and will not be considered in detail in this book. For further information on economic and industrial change see M Risak and J Warter, 'Decent Crowdwork: Legal Strategies for Fair Employment Conditions in the Virtual Sweatshop'. Paper presented to the Regulating for Decent Work 2015 conference <http://www.rdw2015.org/uploads/submission/full_paper/373/crowdwork_law_RisakWarter.pdf> last accessed 22 July 2015

[18] G Rodgers, 'Precarious Work in Western Europe: The State of the Debate' in G Rodgers and J Rodgers (eds), *Precarious Jobs in Labour Market Regulation: The Growth of Atypical Employment in Western Europe* (ILO 1989) 1

[19] A Supiot, 'The Transformation of Work and the Future of Labour Law in Europe: A Multi-disciplinary Perspective' (1999) 138 (1) *International Labour Review* 31, 35

[20] S Deakin, 'Does the "Personal Employment Contract" Provide a Basis for the Reunification of Employment Law?' (2007) 36 (1) *ILJ* 68, 68

increased speed of transport and communication meant a growth in international trade and investment. Transnational companies proliferated, aided by a political commitment to the deregulation of economies and the opening up of international borders. At the same time, the nature of production changed. There was a shift away from the manufacturing sector towards the service sector.[21] Information and knowledge became commodities in their own right, and these commodities were not tied to geographical location like the traditional 'raw materials' of production. Furthermore, the increase in global competition meant that companies had to become more 'flexible' in the way they organised production. This was true for the global transnational corporations just as much as the new 'micro-enterprises', both aiming to meet the spiralling upward demand for new products in innovative ways. The result was a series of industrial arrangements which no longer complied with the 'Fordist' model of production. Industrial organisation became characterised by a whole range of disaggregative practices such as subcontracting, franchising, networking and outsourcing. Vertical integration was replaced by flat hierarchies.[22] Links *between* companies became more important than links within them, as firms seeking specialisation came to rely increasingly on other firms in the production chain.[23]

The argument continues that these globalisation processes have resulted in a profound change in employment patterns and the way in which the workforce operates. On the one hand, there has been the emergence of 'knowledge workers': high functioning entrepreneurs who can build their own networks and profit from the reliance of enterprises on managerial, professional and technological expertise.[24] On the other hand, there are the 'precarious' or 'vulnerable' workers who are forced into 'flexible' work, but do not have the skill set to guarantee employment security. The prospects for these workers are generally assessed negatively; these jobs are described as typically poorly paid, unstable and outside the scope of collective representation.[25] In neither case do these

---

[21] J Fudge and R Owens, 'Precarious Work, Women and the New Economy' in J Fudge and R Owens (eds), *Precarious Work, Women and the New Economy: The Challenge to Legal Norms* (Hart Publishing 2006) 4

[22] M Weiss, 'Re-Inventing Labour Law?' in G Davidov and B Langille (eds), *The Idea of Labour Law* (Oxford University Press 2011) 45

[23] Fudge and Owens (n 21) 7

[24] J Fudge, 'The Legal Boundaries of Employer, Precarious Workers, and Labour Protection' in G Davidov and B Langille (eds), *The Boundaries and Frontiers of Labour Law* (Hart 2006) 296

[25] Ibid 296

workers fit the traditional employment pattern under the 'standard employment relationship'. Knowledge workers have significant labour market power because their skills constitute highly desirable 'human capital'. In Marxist terms, these workers own the means of production (knowledge), so that the dividing line between these workers and the businesses for which they work is increasingly blurred. It is no longer the case of a worker in a subordinate position working for an employer who has complete control over the person and the work. Furthermore, these knowledge workers are not reliant on job security or permanent positions. They are independent risk-takers who are highly mobile and are not tied down by geographical location. These high status workers have sufficient employment security to enable them to take the risk of periods of unemployment, so they desire neither the old occupational status nor the institutions which surrounded it. In the same way, 'precarious' workers do not fit the traditional or standard employment models. These precarious workers are required to meet the demands of firms for 'flexible forms' of labour, and so positions are 'atypical' in the sense of being part-time, temporary or for a fixed term only. There may be very little commitment on either side to receive or accept work (casual or 'zero-hours' contracts being good examples), or workers may be operating outside the formal labour market completely. In any case, none of these forms of work fit with the 'standard employment relationship': full-time, year-round employment for a single employer.

2.2.3   Legal Precariousness

It is possible to argue that the change in economic forms of work following processes of globalisation have created particular legal problems for precarious workers. The argument proceeds that, traditionally, employment laws have been built around the 'standard' employment relationship and the assumption of long-term relationships between employees and firms.[26] As those standard employment relationships have broken down, they no longer provide the framework for individuals to take advantage of legal protections. For example, precarious workers may not qualify for employment law as a result of the fact that they fall outside the boundaries of the status required by the legislation. They may not qualify as 'employees' or 'workers' because they are unable to show sufficient commitment or 'mutuality of obligation' between themselves

---

[26]   K Stone, 'Legal Protections for Atypical Employees: Employment Law for Workers without Workplaces and Employees without Employers' (2006) 27 (2) *Berkeley Journal of Employment and Labor Law* 251, 254

and their employers. As a result they are not able to take advantage of employment rights and are 'left to fend for themselves without a safety net to protect them'.[27] Individuals are left in not only an economically precarious position, but also a legally precarious one.

The identification of this problem has invited a number of responses amongst labour lawyers, which stem from a number of theoretical backgrounds. For example, it is possible to argue that the problems of precarious work are simply another moment in the systemic problems created by the capitalist system, and so the extension of traditional methods of regulation to all workers is therefore required to meet the problem. A number of innovative methods have been suggested to affect this extension.[28] Another response is to suggest that precarious or atypical work requires special regulation which takes account of its particular economic features. A more extreme view of the need for economic efficiency in meeting the needs of this new group might lead to suggestions for very targeted regulation for only the most precarious workers, or may view deregulation as the best approach to allow individuals the space to achieve their goals and to take better advantage of the benefits offered by economic change.[29] On these models, vulnerability is viewed very narrowly. Vulnerability is seen as an inefficiency or market failure in relation to certain workers who are not able to take advantage of all the benefits of the operation of the capitalist system. For some workers, the flexibility engendered by non-standard working is a choice and that choice should be respected. Vulnerability is not a systematic problem of the capitalist system (as might be argued in classical labour law) and it does not attach to all workers, or even all non-standard workers. As a result, care needs to be taken to ensure any 're-regulation' under the new economic conditions matches and responds to real and actual disadvantage and respects individual choice.

It is important to point out at this stage that this 'regulation for efficiency' has been viewed in some quarters and by some labour lawyers as part of the 'context' of vulnerability. The argument proceeds that efficiency modes of regulation *create* increasing and expanding levels of precarity as they leave that regulation to market forces, or favour regulation which provides only minimum levels of protection. The result

---

[27] Ibid 254

[28] A Goldin, 'Labour Subordination and the Subjective Weakening of Labour Law' in G Davidov and B Langille (eds), *Boundaries and Frontiers of Labour Law* (Hart 2006)

[29] The detail of these theories and how they view the structure of regulation is considered in more detail in Chapter 3.

of efficiency modes of regulation can therefore be seen as the 'dilution of the norms' of labour law and as a practical disadvantage for workers.[30] An example might be the failure to set minimum wage laws (on the basis that the market is in the best position to fix the optimal wage level) or the creation of minimum wage laws which fail to make a real difference to workers in 'precarious' employment relationships. Those minimum wage laws may have an inappropriate personal scope or they may be poorly enforced. Furthermore, the level of the minimum wage may be set too low to allow workers on that wage to escape poverty. For example, the UK has instigated a minimum wage regulation, but the level of that wage is (purposefully) set at a level which can be easily absorbed by the market. It is argued that the minimum wage is therefore not a living wage, but merely provides a threshold for the operation of the benefits system.[31] As a result, those working in precarious jobs find that the minimum wage does not significantly improve their position. Indeed, the level of the minimum wage in the UK has been criticised by the European Committee of Social Rights for its inconsistency with the obligations under Article 4 of the European Social Charter 1961 (the right to a fair remuneration).[32]

Indeed, it has been argued that the recent economic crisis has merely exacerbated the trend towards regulation for 'efficiency' and the deregulation of labour markets.[33] This has served both to increase the ranks of the precarious workforce and to subject those in precarious economic relationships to further disadvantage. In the EU, a number of member states have introduced measures to increase the flexibility of labour markets. This has involved reducing restrictions on the use of fixed-term contracts and increasing their maximum length. There have also been a number of member states who have amended rules on dismissal to ease the flexibility of companies in the management of their staff. For example, in Greece, the notice period required in relation to dismissal has been decreased to six months, and that notice period is only required

---

[30]   S Fredman, 'Precarious Norms for Precarious Workers' in J Fudge and R Owens (eds), *Precarious Work, Women and the New Economy* (Hart 2006) 185

[31]   B Simpson, 'The National Minimum Wage: Five Years on: Reflections on some General Issues' (2004) 33 *Industrial Law Journal* 22, 24

[32]   N Countouris, 'The Legal Determinants of Precariousness in Personal Work Relations: A European Perspective' (2014) 34 *Comparative Labor Law and Policy Journal* 21, 33

[33]   V De Stefano, 'A Tale of Oversimplification and Deregulation: The Mainstream Approach to Labour Market Segmentation and Recent Responses to the Crisis in European Countries' (2014) 43 (3) *Industrial Law Journal* 253

after 12 months of service.[34] Furthermore, in the UK, the qualification period for dismissal has been increased from one to two years.[35] It was hoped that this would significantly improve the efficiency of the operation of the labour market in this country.[36] It is also worth noting that a number of member states have significantly reduced their support for collective bargaining processes, or have promoted the decentralisation of that collective bargaining to enterprise level.[37]

While this analysis is useful in exposing the problems with the efficiency view, it is still possible to argue that there is a failure in this criticism to really engage with the notion of vulnerability and how those notions affect the regulation of (precarious) work. The 'external' foundations of vulnerability (in economic and social conditions) are accepted in this literature. Legal regulation is criticised for its consequences: failing to deal adequately with the problem of precarious work. However, there remains the question of whether it is the constitution or theorisation of vulnerability itself (under the economic view) which is part of the problem of the failure to deal adequately with the 'problem' of precarious work. In particular, there is a need to consider the constitution of vulnerability in efficiency theory as underlain by liberal theories of the nature of individuals as rational, atomised and independent beings. This is a fact that is central to efficiency theory and is actually at the heart of the problem of efficiency theory itself. Indeed, this view of vulnerability under efficiency theory means that the efficiency account is very little about vulnerability at all. The concept of vulnerability is not explored or theorised of itself. There is little examination of how individual experience or agency is important in shaping or counteracting vulnerability because that agency is already assumed as a 'natural' feature of every labour market participant. This element of efficiency theory needs to be discussed in more depth, not from an 'external' but an 'internal' or personal perspective. This 'internal' perspective will be discussed in more detail in Section 2.3.

---

[34]   Acts 3863/2010 and 3899/2010
[35]   The Unfair Dismissal and Statement of Reasons for Dismissal (Variation of Qualification Period) Order 2012, SI 2012/989
[36]   BIS, *Employment Law Review Annual Update* (March 2012) 5
[37]   S Marshall, 'Shifting Responsibility: How the Burden of the European Financial Crisis Shifted Away from the Financial Sector and onto Labor' (2013–2014) 35 *Comparative Labor Law and Policy Journal* 449

2.2.4   Vulnerability and Social Change

It has been argued that the economic changes of globalisation identified in the 'Vulnerability and economic change' section above have been associated with deep changes in the 'gender contract'. The argument proceeds that in the period after World War II, there was a particular sexual division of labour which determined the way in which work was organised and the way in which work was institutionalised and regulated.[38] The gender contract involved women having responsibility for 'socially necessary, but generally unpaid' labour in the home, while men were responsible for earning a wage which supported dependent wives and children.[39] The institutions which built up around this sexual division of labour focussed on the 'public' (male) wage earner and privileged paid work; domestic work was barely recognised as 'work' at all. It has now been suggested that there has been a weakening of this gender contract caused by a range of economic and social factors. The improved education of women and falling fertility rates, along with an increase in marital breakdown has allowed an increase in labour market participation among women. At the same time, the flexible nature of employment (associated with technological changes) and the growth in public services have facilitated their labour market entry.[40]

However, it has been argued that the entry of women into the labour market has not eradicated structures of male dominance or the institutions which surround it. While it is true that an increase in non-standard jobs has enabled women to enter the labour market and to balance caring and work responsibilities, it is also the case that good quality jobs still tend to be associated with the 'standard employment relationship' (full-time, permanent jobs with one employer). As it remains difficult for many women with caring responsibilities to undertake these jobs, their employment tends to be concentrated in 'precarious' employment, with little or no job stability and low wages. The result is that those women may still have partial dependence on a man or struggle to make ends meet. The alternative is that caring responsibilities are contracted out to domestic workers in the home or to other care providers. This creates another layer of precarity, as domestic work remains an instance of

---

[38]   J Fudge, 'Feminist Reflections on the Scope of Labour Law: Domestic Work, Social Reproduction and Jurisdiction' (2014) 22 *Feminist Legal Studies* 1, 4

[39]   J Fudge, 'Rungs on the Labour Law Ladder' (1996) 60 *Saskatchewan Law Review* 237, 262

[40]   Fudge (n 38) 4

'private' employment and so outside the bounds of much regulation. Therefore, despite the increase in labour market participation by women, liberal structures continue to create considerable vulnerability for women or men with caring responsibilities and those involved in the provision of care. This will be discussed in more detail in the case study on domestic work in Chapter 6.

While this kind of analysis does expose problems with certain liberal structures (the gender contract), it does not explain or seek to explain vulnerability more generally. Furthermore, it tends to constrain thinking about identity to one particular dynamic, rather than all the possible constituents of personal vulnerability. As a result, this approach may be useful in certain sectors (for example, in the analysis of the problems faced by domestic workers), but it may not be able to explain precarious work or vulnerability more generally. It is argued in this book that, in order to understand precarious work more generally, there must be a shift in focus away from 'external' notions of vulnerability, which rely on an analysis of economic or social change towards the personal constitution of vulnerability (albeit in relationship with those external forces). The next section will discuss two possible avenues to explore this personal nature of vulnerability: the social law and the vulnerable subject approach. It is argued that these two approaches are related and may provide greater insight into the vulnerability of workers, and how best to deal with or tackle that vulnerability.

2.3 THE PERSONAL NATURE OF VULNERABILITY

So far in this analysis, the vulnerability of the labour subject has been considered according to a set of external social and economic processes. However, there are a number of problems which are identified with this kind of approach for the labour subject. The first problem is that these external approaches tend either to disregard the identity of the labour subject (in line with understandings of the atomised, free, autonomous liberal subject), or they tend to focus on one kind of identity (gender, race, and so on) which corresponds to the kind of designation of identity for the purposes of liberal discrimination law (this will be discussed in more detail in the next chapter). Second, the external impact view of influences of economic and social systems could be seen to have a disenfranchising effect on the actors within the labour system. According to external approaches, labour subjects can have little involvement in changing the economic/social and ultimately legal systems to which they are bound. This will be seen in the next chapter in terms of the legal solutions which are suggested to 'tackle' precarious work. The aim of the following section is to consider alternative approaches which suggest a greater theorisation of the labour subject itself and how that labour subject is affected by, but may also influence, institutional structures and structure of regulations to improve their own position.

2.3.1 Social Law as the Sociology of Law and Group Vulnerability

The first approach that will be considered in this section is that of 'social law'. The idea of social law is understood in a number of different ways, and a 'social law' approach has been adopted by a number of different authors for different reasons and to achieve different ends. For some, social law has no particular theoretical meaning: it stands simply for the collection of all labour and social security laws.[41] Others have been influenced by the theoretical potential of social law. For example, Sinzheimer (one of the classical labour law scholars) was influenced by Gierke's work on the need to embed private law with public law concerns.[42] However, the approach in this book will be to develop a social law approach independently of the commentary of the classical labour law scholars. The idea is to explore this sociological approach to law as a personal approach to labour law scholarship. This requires that works are explored that may not have been explored in detail by the classical scholars, or that parts are emphasised which were not empha-sised in the classical tradition. It is argued in this book that the social law approach is useful because according to this approach, the starting considerations are not external economic and social changes which then determine the direction of the law. Rather, under this approach, society is the force which directs the law. It follows then that the capacities and capabilities of individual subjects as well as the relations between them become central to both the need for and design of the law. Law and vulnerability have a dichotomous relationship. Individual vulnerabilities determine the form of sociality, or collection of relationships that individuals form.[43] Law itself can direct these relationships but those relations can never be entirely bound by the law. This suggests a level of

---

[41]   J Shaw, J Hunt and C Wallace, *European Social Law of the European Union* (Palgrave MacMillan 2007); M Dawson, *New Governance and the Transformation of European Law: Coordinating EU Social Law and Policy* (Cambridge University Press 2011)

[42]   O van Gierke, *Die Soziale Aufgabe des Privatrechts* (Berlin 1889)

[43]   G Gurvitch, 'The Problem of Social Law' (1941) 52 (1) *Ethics* 17, 21

independence and agency for individuals which moves us beyond vulnerability as a negative powerless state. It provides a promising starting point for thinking about vulnerability as a progressive tool of analysis. It moves the consideration away from the creation of vulnerability through external economic social and legal forces to the creation of social and legal processes by the operation of individual agency.

The focus of this section will be on those theorists within this aspect of the social law tradition who specifically consider the application of this element of theory to labour, in particular Emile Durkheim and Francois Ewald. The particular concern will be how the vulnerability of labour is constructed in this view (if at all). The next chapter will discuss in particular how this social law theorisation could be useful in the design and creation of labour laws. In Durkheim's work, one of the central starting points is the *value* of work to individuals and to society as a whole. Employment gives workers the opportunity to gain personal self-fulfilment, and most importantly, gives workers a sense of membership to the social system. This means that external pressures are neither necessarily negative (commoditising) nor positive (economically productive), as might be asserted in the classical or economic efficiency views of labour law respectively. Already at this point there is the idea of the importance of 'agency' to the experience of workers in the field of employment. In Durkheim's work, the best functioning social system exists in conditions of 'organic solidarity'. This 'organic solidarity' develops where the specialisation of work activities develops into a particular 'division of labour'. This 'division of labour' allows people to find their 'fit' in the (capitalist) system according to their particular strengths and weaknesses.[44] This is fundamental to the sustainability of the system of organic solidarity: the personal fulfilment that people gain through work gives them an incentive to constantly reinforce the social order and also find freedom.

However, although this division of labour is fundamental to the development of a sustainable social order, it is not sufficient in itself. Work does not always provide the value to workers that it should (for example, there may be work stoppages or a mismatch between workers' skills and the jobs in which they finds themselves). Something more is needed. In particular, there is a need to mediate between workers and the state where the work relation fails. This mediation is provided by groups or 'associations' which are essential to the experience of labour in two

---

[44] Durkheim, *The Division of Labour in Society* (Macmillan Press Limited 1984 [1893]) 311

ways. First, they have their own norms attached to them which allow their members a sense of belonging (which is important, for example, where that work relation is unsatisfactory). More importantly, these associations are the main way in which individuals attain visibility vis-a-vis the state. This visibility is fundamental to workers, because it is only through this visibility that workers can have their interest recognised as part of the general (state) interest. Once this particular (group) interest becomes part of the general interest then it is necessarily protected through state legislation and reinforced by the courts (whose role is to 'create the means and methods to effectuate the ends of society').[45] That group then takes all the benefits which society can afford.

With this view, worker identity in all its different forms is fundamentally important. As has been mentioned, social lawyers reject the Marxist idea of the existence of just two classes in society: (1) the proletariat and (2) the bourgeoisie. It is argued that although it may be possible to identify these two groups in broad terms, empirical analysis reveals that society is much more complex than the Marxist scheme implies. Social lawyers argue that Marx misunderstood the way in which society was constituted. Under Marx, all identity was economically constituted; Marx addressed neither gender nor race discrimination in his theory of capitalism and was not concerned with the subordination of women *per se* (although he did recognise that this might result from capitalist exploitation).[46] For social lawyers, this view is damaging to workers and actually creates vulnerability. It is damaging because it denies a voice to groups constituted on other grounds.[47] It serves to exclude groups from participation in both the social and legal system, and to mask the

---

[45]   NO Littlefield, 'Eugen Ehrlich's Fundamental Principles of the Sociology of Law' (1967) 19 (1) *Maine Law Review* 1, 19
[46]   D Neacşu, 'The Wrongful Rejection of Big Theory (Marxism) by Feminism and Queer Theory: A Brief Debate' (2005) 34 *Capital University Law Review* 125, 127
[47]   Ibid 136. Some authors do however suggest that group vulnerability cannot be considered without reference to economic subordination. See for example the comments of M Crain 'Between Feminism and Unionism: Working Class Women, Sex Equality and Labor Speech' (1993–1994) 82 *The Georgetown Law Journal* 1903, 1906–1907: 'I argue that attacking class oppression is integrally connected to achieving sex equality. Economic subordination lies at the core of women's political and social disempowerment, and mobilizing women therefore requires intermingling economic and political concerns. Consciousness-raising and organising of working class women *in the workplace* is essential to the feminist project of elevating women as a group from our subordinated position in society.'

different inequalities which in fact exist in society, through which different social groups can gain recognition and a properly functioning social order can be established.

This is not to suggest that vertical inequality of bargaining power between employers and workers can never exist on the social law scheme. Indeed, in Durkheim's work, he recognised that the locus of wealth in the hands of capitalists could cause a problem for social development and for the life chances of workers.[48] But he also recognised that the conflict between capital and labour was not the only source of vulnerability. Rather, there was a great diversity of tastes, aptitudes and skills within the 'working class', and not all workers were equally, or indeed inevitably vulnerable.[49] As a result, vulnerability could be just as easily created by the inequality of bargaining power *between* groups of workers, as between capital and labour itself. For example, Durkheim's scheme of 'organic solidarity' relied on an understanding of inequality of bargaining power between workers. Durkheim identified that, as societies develop, labour functions become increasingly specialised. This process of specialisation leads to the creation of a division of labour in which specific tastes, aptitudes and capacities held by workers develop. These talents and aptitudes are not distributed equally in society and are only possessed by certain individuals and/or groups. With the increase in specialisation of functions brought about by the division of labour, these groups must increasingly interact with each other. This interaction is necessary because of the narrow remit of their functions which dictates an increased need for exchange. However, despite the need for this increased interaction between groups, it is also a source of conflict as a result of the different interests of those at different levels of the occupational strata.[50] For Durkheim, these inequalities could only be managed through a system of 'organic solidarity'. This organic solidarity is the ultimate aim of all industrial societies, because it represents that all groups in the division of labour recognise their own function and their place in society. It represents a social morality which recognises how inequality of bargaining power between groups can be managed to the benefit of all.

Other theorists in the social law tradition have reinforced Durkheim's visions of the way in which society operates and therefore should be regulated. For example, Ewald argues that under the modern welfare

---

[48]   Durkheim (n 44) 302
[49]   Durkheim (n 44) 311
[50]   Giddens (n 4) 103

state, society could be viewed as constituted through relationships of interdependence and solidarity between groups. Rather than one 'social contract' based on invariable terms, there was a series of 'solidarity contracts' which contained the compromises reached between the parties. In terms of the labour market, the employment contract itself was conceived in solidaristic terms. The contributions of workers and employers were seen as not only equally necessary, but also interdependent, such that one could not exist without the other.[51] According to Ewald, this notion of interdependence means that individual subjects of labour are not viewed as vulnerable individuals acted upon by all-powerful employers. Rather, labour subjects are viewed as having a level of agency in the direction of the employment relationship. The question is, however, whether the law recognises this solidaristic nature of employment contracts, or simply acts according to principles which ignore this solidarity completely. What is required is a law which looks at the 'vulnerabilities' of employees in employment relationships and sees these in multi-dimensional and multi-directional terms. Only this way can there be any kind of social law approach to labour.

The next section considers how this very specific approach to vulnerability (in employment relationships) might be developed. It considers the 'vulnerable subject' theorisation which attempts to put vulnerability at the heart of the operation of law and society. It is argued that this vulnerable subject approach builds on the insights under social law in the sociological tradition by putting the multi-dimensional nature of individuals and their relations at the centre of the determination of any law. It considers how the interdependence of the vulnerable subject can be harnessed to provide progressive law.

2.3.2   The Vulnerable Subject and Labour Law Theory

Martha Fineman has been central in suggesting that the notion of vulnerability provides an important and revolutionary theoretical basis for considering legal and social institutions. Her starting point is that the Western legal tradition is built up around the notion of the 'liberal subject'. Liberal subjects are presented as rarefied autonomous beings with all the attributes to function fully and independently in society. They are social actors 'capable of playing multiple and concurrent adult (formerly all-male) societal roles: the employee, the employer, the

---

[51]   F Ewald, 'A Concept of Social Law' in G Teubner (ed), *Dilemmas of Law in the Welfare State* (Walter de Gruyter Berlin 1986) 43

spouse, the parent, the consumer, the manufacturer, the citizen, the taxpayer and so on'.[52] The problem is that this presentation of the liberal subject is 'reductive' and 'fails to reflect the complicated nature of the human condition'.[53] The idea of the liberal subject creates a set of institutions which only serve to create and recreate disadvantage and inequality. Fineman provides a number of examples of this phenomenon. For example, the reliance on the liberal subject leads to a concern for regulation which supports and encourages human autonomy. The regulation which results tends to be non-interventionist. Vulnerability is associated with dependency which carries negative connotations and thus is only accounted for where it is 'deserving' in the sense of being developmental or biological dependency. Dependency which is derivative (socially created) is largely ignored or seen as outside the boundaries of state intervention.[54] This leaves the majority of vulnerability situations untouched. Another example might be the categorisations associated with particularly vulnerable populations under anti-discrimination law and the formal equality paradigm through which these relationships are regulated. These categorisations are socially divisive and the scheme of formal equality does little to help those eradicate inequality for affected persons/ groups.

Fineman suggests that the liberal subject needs to be replaced by the 'vulnerable subject'. This idea of the vulnerable subject is a recognition that vulnerability is a 'universal, inevitable, enduring aspect of the human condition'.[55] It has at least two aspects. The first aspect is that of embodiment or ontological vulnerability. Each and every person is susceptible to harm, injury and misfortune, and many of the events that condition these harms are outside human control.[56] The second aspect is institutional vulnerability. This recognises that, although each person is ontologically vulnerable, the actual experience of vulnerability varies depending on an individual's economic and social relationships. The key to challenging vulnerability is not to aim for invulnerability, as this is impossible and smacks of the liberal assertions of the attainability of

---

[52] M Fineman and A Greer, 'Introduction: An Invitation to Future Exploration' in M Fineman and A Greer (eds), *Vulnerability: Reflections on a New Ethical Foundation for Law and Politics* (Ashgate 2013) 17

[53] Ibid

[54] M Fineman, 'The Vulnerable Subject and the Responsive State' (2010) 60 *Emory Law Journal* 251, 264

[55] M Fineman, 'The Vulnerable Subject: Anchoring Equality in the Human Condition' (2008) 20 (1) *Yale Journal of Law and Feminism* 2, 8

[56] Ibid 9

individual independence, autonomy and self-sufficiency. The key is for the state to build resilience through responding to vulnerability, and this would involve actively supporting redistribution and mechanisms that lessen institutionalised disadvantage.

For our purposes, this analysis is significant because it suggests that economic and social structures do not act in one way on equally autonomous individuals (as might be implied in the analysis in Section 2.2 of this chapter). The relationships of interaction and the creation of establishment of vulnerabilities is much more complex than that, affecting different people in different ways. Precarity must be considered in a multi-dimensional way, right from individual vulnerability to group vulnerability to institutional vulnerability. Vulnerability cannot be viewed as created by social and economic forces to which the state reacts. It is true that the state has a major role in tackling vulnerability, but it also has a major role in creating it. An example which will be discussed in the following chapters is the governmental reaction to the financial crisis of 2008. It has been argued by a number of authors that despite the fact that '[n]o legitimate explanations focus on labour as the cause' of the crisis, labour has consistently been targeted in measures to reduce indebtedness and rebalance national budgets.[57]

However, there have been significant criticisms of the 'vulnerable subject' approach which it is worth raising here. Some authors have criticised this approach on the basis of its presentation of the relationship between vulnerability and autonomy. It has been suggested that in Fineman's analysis, autonomy and vulnerability are set in opposition to each other. Autonomy is understood according to the libertarian conception of the ability to lead one's life as one sees fit. Understood in this way, autonomy is opposed to vulnerability: the less vulnerable one is to changing circumstances, the more autonomous one would be.[58] MacKenzie argues that autonomy should be understood in a much wider sense, as the 'capacity to lead a self-determining life and the status of being recognised as an autonomous agent by others'.[59] Autonomy should not be viewed as a sui generis condition of humanity, but as 'relational': developed through relationships and through social capacities (some

---

[57]   Marshall (n 38) 451

[58]   J Anderson, 'Autonomy and Vulnerability Entwined' in C Mackenzie, W Rogers and S Dodds, *Vulnerability* (Oxford University Press 2014) 134

[59]   C Mackenzie, 'Relational Autonomy and Capabilities for an Ethics of Vulnerability' in C MacKenzie, W Rogers and S Dodds, *Vulnerability* (Oxford University Press 2014) 41

social relationships are hostile to the development of autonomy). According to this viewpoint, individual self-identity is continually negotiated in and through particular social, geographical and historical contexts and conditions.[60] As a result, responses to vulnerability should be guided by obligations to respect and promote autonomy. This would avoid the tendency to excessive paternalism which has been associated with the vulnerability approach, and it is this approach which is adopted for the purposes of this book. It is argued that this paternalistic approach is itself pathogenic as it reinforces a sense of a subject's loss of agency and therefore makes that subject more susceptible to future harm.

It is my contention (while mindful of the criticisms of these theories) that personal approaches to the labour subject adopted in the social law and vulnerable subject theorisations hold a number of benefits for thinking about the best ways in which to regulate labour and particularly precarious work. The subject of labour law is considered more carefully, and the numerous dimensions of vulnerability can become part of the labour law scheme, rather than exist outside it. Furthermore, autonomy can be considered as a factor to be developed to promote resilience, rather than dictating that labour subjects should be left to their own devices. In the social law scheme work can be constitutive of autonomy, as it can enable individuals and groups to develop their own sense of self and their own particular set of capabilities. The same can be said of regulation. Rather than regulation stifling autonomy, law which responds directly and accurately to the experience of vulnerable subjects can help individuals reach their own goals. Finally, autonomy can be considered socially or relationally, leaving a space for the development of collective solutions to labour problems.

2.4 CONCLUSIONS

This chapter aimed to characterise theorisations of labour law according to their view of the subject of labour law. It emerges from this analysis that the subject of labour law is often under-theorised in these approaches. In the classical labour law scheme, the labour subject is treated as an autonomous being with an identity only so far as belonging to the 'working class'. The actions of the capitalist system and the bourgeoisie owners of the means of production act against that autonomy and make the subjects of labour vulnerable. Vulnerability is economically

---

[60]   Ibid 43

determined, and the economy has the ability to put all workers in a precarious position. The more modern theories of labour law often share this view of the economic determination of vulnerability, but present vulnerability as a failure of individuals to take advantage of the benefits of economic processes. Again, the subject of labour is an autonomous being, but under this theorisation the responsibility of the labour subject is paramount. By contrast, the responsibility of the state is to stand back from these economic processes and from interfering with the autonomy of labour. To a certain extent, this under-theorisation of the labour subject is exposed when considering theories that suggest that the economic processes of globalisation have not been identity-neutral. For example, in Section 2.2 of this chapter, the feminist characterisations of the gendered nature of economic changes suggest that there needs to be more thinking about the creation of vulnerability under this system.

However, it is the contention of this chapter that the under-theorisation of the labour subject will not be resolved by considering in more detail all the various ways in which vulnerability is created in employment relationships. This is a top-down approach to vulnerability which will miss all the various aspects which go to make up the vulnerable subject of labour. Therefore, in the third section of this chapter there is a suggestion of ways in which to better theorise the vulnerability of the labour subject. The initial part of this section introduces the 'social law' approach. This approach is critical of liberal imaginings at the heart of law and the failure of these theorisations to deal with identity. It also suggests that agency (or autonomy) should be the outcome of a well-functioning labour system. This agency may be individual but inevitably involves collective solutions to labour problems. The final part of this section discusses the 'vulnerable subject' approach. This vulnerable subject approach provides a particular critique of the classification of the 'liberal subject' as the foundation of law in liberal theory. It is suggested in the vulnerable subject approach that having the liberal subject at the heart of the law only serves to reinforce inequalities which the state is unwilling to address. As an alternative, it is suggested with this approach that the 'vulnerable subject' should be at the heart of the law, because this will lead to a more responsive state which realises that all are vulnerable and that dependency is an inevitable characteristic of all individual lives.

The next chapter will investigate in more depth the different theoretical constructions of labour law identified in this chapter:

(1)   the classical labour law position;
(2)   the economic efficiency approach; and

(3)   the personal theorisation of vulnerability in the vulnerable subject/
      social law approach.

In particular, that investigation will involve an exploration of the link
between the theorisation of vulnerability under those different modes of
thought and solutions to vulnerability under the different schemes. This
investigation is important in terms of the consideration of the regulation
of precarious work. It appears that very wide characterisations of
vulnerability under the classical labour law approach lead to solutions
which may be insufficiently flexible or responsive to changing conditions. Likewise, the very narrow approach to vulnerability under economic efficiency theories does not allow the full extent of precarity to be
regulated. Therefore, different approaches are required which engage
more fully with the nature of vulnerability in employment relationships
and engage with its complexity. Vulnerability should not be seen as
acting on autonomous, independent, rational beings, but being part of the
constitution of labour itself. Only then can solutions be devised which
respect the heterogeneity of labour and really promote dignity. Chapter 4
will address in detail the actual legal responses to precarious work in the
context of vulnerability, and Chapters 5 and 6 will provide two case
studies which expose the precise operation of these responses. It is hoped
that through these chapters it will become clear that a better understanding of the labour subject would aid the construction and enforcement of
solutions to precarious work.

3. The goals of the regulation of labour law for vulnerability

3.1 INTRODUCTION

This chapter builds on Chapter 2 which considered the 'context' of vulnerability. Chapter 2 explained how the context of vulnerability may be seen as 'external' or 'internal' (personal). Vulnerability may be seen as created by economic, political or social pressures acting on the subject of labour, or can be viewed as starting from the subject of labour itself. It was explained that this characterisation was not theoretically neutral; rather different characterisations of the nature of vulnerability attach to different theories of labour law. For example, classical labour law theory views vulnerability as created by the operation of the capitalist system and attaching to all workers, whereas other labour law theories explain vulnerability as a particular economic moment and associate that vulnerability specifically with the problems of precarious work. The aim of this chapter is to delve more deeply into the labour law theories introduced in Chapter 2 and to explain what the characterisation of vulnerability in these different theories means for the way in which solutions to labour problems are designed and developed. Four broad theoretical characterisations will be discussed in this chapter in line with the divisions of the previous chapter. The first characterisation will be classical labour law theory. The second characterisation will be that couched in the language of economic efficiency. The third will be the theory of social law, and the final characterisation of the regulation of the work relation introduced in this chapter is that based on the 'vulnerable subject' of labour law.

During the course of this chapter, labour law goals will be mapped against a particular theoretical construct: Davidov's classification of labour law goals according to a universalistic-selective spectrum.[1] Davidov's scheme draws on the classification of different (welfare) programmes within the welfare state literature. He uses this universalistic-selective

---

[1] G Davidov, 'The Goals of Regulating Work: Between Universalism and Selectivity' (2014) 64 (1) *University of Toronto Law Journal* 1.

classification as a heuristic device to determine the aims of proposals under labour law. Under this scheme, labour law goals are considered selective if they deal with just the regulation of workers (outside wider social or economic concerns or values). These might be laws tailored only to those in employment or the instigation of trade union mechanisms within the labour law system. At the other end of the scale are labour law goals which aim to bring universalistic benefits; benefits to employers, employees and the wider society. Finally, there are labour law goals which might be considered within the 'mid-spectrum'. The aim of these mid-spectrum goals is to aid employees, but also to provide benefits for society at large. It is argued that this classification mechanism is a useful device for considering the aims of different labour laws, and clearly reveals where the particular vulnerabilities of labour are characterised and how best to deal with that vulnerability.

3.2 OVERVIEW OF CHARACTERISATIONS OF VULNERABILITY AND THEIR SOLUTIONS

The first characterisation of vulnerability in relation to the labour subject will be classical labour law theory. This theory situates vulnerability in the context of the operation of the capitalist system. It is argued on this theory that the operation of the capitalist system creates an inequality of bargaining power between employers and employees which is compounded by the commodification of all labour within this system. The operation of these processes means that labour is systematically vulnerable to both exploitation and the abuse of power. The goals of labour law in this scheme are selective: they aim to help employees specifically rather than any other group. A number of theorists within this scheme have favoured 'bottom-up' approaches, suggesting that trade union action could increase the social power of workers, and hence decrease their vulnerability (or increase their resilience). Other authors sympathetic to this approach have tended to favour strong (top-down) specific labour rights in order to counteract the alienating and subordinating processes of capitalism. From here labour law's 'traditional theory of justice' emerges: the combination of collective bargaining and employment legislation in order to construct a body of 'consumer protection' for the vulnerable in the labour market.[2]

---

[2] B Langille, 'Labour Law's Theory of Justice' in G Davidov and B Langille (eds), *The Idea of Labour Law* (Oxford University Press 2011) 106

The second characterisation of the proper design of labour law (discussed in Section 3.4) is that couched in the language of economic efficiency. This is a liberal framework which looks at how labour law can be designed to maximise business competitiveness. On the one hand, this kind of theoretical perspective can be used to suggest a deregulatory agenda. The argument proceeds that private law rules function perfectly well in regulating the employment relation. These rules maximise freedom of contract and forbid obstructions to competition.[3] On the other hand, there is a space for suggesting regulation where the benefits to businesses or employees exceed the costs (that regulation corrects market failures), or where current modes of private law regulation produce unacceptable distributary outcomes (for example, poverty). Regulation is acceptable where it is (on balance) of benefit to all groups (employers, employees and the wider society).[4] Under this scheme, regulation is almost exclusively top-down: there is real scepticism about the desirability of disrupting the general balance of power created by the market by increasing the power of workers through, for example, collective bargaining. It is argued in this book that understandings of the regulation of precarious work emanate from this efficiency paradigm.

The final characterisation of the regulation of the work relation introduced in this chapter is that based on the 'vulnerable subject' of labour law. This kind of approach does not fit with either of the first two approaches, and is a less familiar one within the law of employment.[5] It corresponds to the preoccupations of social law, namely that the experience of labour market participants is entirely *relational*. This relational aspect is personal (all people experience vulnerability in different ways at different times), inter-personal (between different labour market groups, for example), institutional (institutions can create as well as counteract vulnerability) and societal. This means that any regulation which ignores any of these elements will not address the needs of labour market actors generally, and precarious workers specifically. The regulation, which results from a vulnerable subject approach, thus attempts to combine 'bottom-up' approaches which build the resilience of workers with 'top-down' state action which supports those approaches as corresponding with the public interest. The ultimate goal is the alignment of personal and social ends.

---

[3]   H Collins, *Employment Law* (Oxford University Press 2003) 21
[4]   G Davidov (n 1) 5
[5]   Collins (n 3) 21

It will become clear during the course of this chapter that these different 'views' of the regulatory goals of labour law are not always completely distinct or mutually exclusive. For example, some of the concerns of authors in the classical labour law field are echoed in the social law stream, and some of the solutions may have overlapping characteristics. It is also not possible to separate the different views completely on the universalistic-selective spectrum. For example, although the aims of classical labour law might be largely selective, it is possible to determine mid-spectrum goals (such as a preoccupation with democracy) within this scheme. Likewise, efficiency theorists might suggest selective regulation in very narrow circumstances (for example for the most precarious workers). However, it is argued that the separation of the different theoretical characterisations of labour law is useful for deconstructing our current approaches to labour law, and building new approaches based on the 'vulnerable subject' of labour law.

3.3 GOALS UNDER CLASSICAL LABOUR LAW

3.3.1 Kahn-Freund and Sinzheimer: Towards Selective Goals

Both Kahn-Freund and Sinzheimer argued that there were two goals essential to any well-functioning industrial scheme. The first was the correction of the inequality of bargaining power to which employees were subject, and which forced employees into positions of subordination. The second (related) goal was to address some of the worst effects on employees of the commodification processes of capitalism. Both Kahn-Freund and Sinzheimer were committed to the idea that these goals could not be achieved simply through individual negotiation; nor could they be achieved through the instigation of individual rights. Rather, as the problems faced by labour were *socially* constituted (part of the wider commodification processes of capitalism),[6] it followed that the solution must also be social, and involve an increase in the social power of workers. They suggested that this increase in social power could best be achieved through the instigation of a robust and well-functioning system of collective bargaining. Through collective bargaining, workers had the opportunity to negotiate much more effectively with employers, who themselves represented 'collective power' in the form of the enterprise (an accumulation of material and human

---

[6] Kahn-Freund in P Davies and M Freedland, *Kahn-Freund's Labour and the Law* (Stevens 1983) 17

resources).[7] In turn, this system of collective bargaining would enable workers to be treated not as commodities but as fully functioning human beings. For workers, collective bargaining would allow them to meet their 'legitimate expectations'. It would not only ensure a certain level of job security in the shorter term, it would also guarantee 'a stable and adequate form of existence [and] as to be compatible with the physical integrity and moral dignity of the individual'.[8]

The theories of both Kahn-Freund and Sinzheimer were rooted in a deep commitment to pluralism, essentially that progress followed from the proper recognition and articulation of the different interests in industrial society.[9] This essentially meant that although both Kahn-Freund and Sinzheimer were committed to Marxist ideas about the sources of industrial conflict, they disagreed with Marx about the solutions to that conflict. For Marx, progress could only be achieved through the abolition of conflict between workers and management, and the dissolution of the capitalist system itself. By contrast, for both Kahn-Freund and Sinzheimer, this conflict was a necessary part of any properly functioning system of industrial relations, and to try to prevent this conflict could only be damaging.[10] However Kahn-Freund and Sinzheimer disagreed on how the balance between management and labour should be struck. For Kahn-Freund, the solution lay in exploiting the 'one interest which management and labour have in common': a set of 'reasonably predictable procedures'.[11] This procedural base would allow all negotiation options to be exhausted before one party resorted to radical action to change the status quo (for example, workers would go on strike). For Sinzheimer, the particular compromise to be struck was viewed as a function of the relationship of that compromise to the public interest. It was only where the public interest in the mediation of industrial conflict was recognised that there could be any lasting industrial peace.[12]

For Sinzheimer, the inequalities between management and labour created by the legal abstractions of 'property' and 'contract' could only be counteracted by giving labour a status equal to that of property. This

---

[7]   Ibid 17
[8]   Ibid
[9]   Ibid 27
[10]   H Sinzheimer, Zur Frage des Schlichtswesens (1929) in H Sinzheimer, *Arbeitsrecht und Rechtssoziologie: gesammelte Aufsätze und Reden (Band 1)* (Otto Brenner Stiftung 1976) 228
[11]   Kahn-Freund in Davies and Freedland (n 1) 27
[12]   Sinzheimer (n 10) 228

could be achieved through allowing collectivities of workers decision-making powers equal to that of employers in an 'economic constitution' consisting of employers' associations, trade unions, works councils and self-regulatory industrial councils.[13] This 'constitutionalisation' of the economic sphere would put an end to the control of markets by capital and to the control of the state by the propertied classes.[14] Central to Sinzheimer's theory was the idea that the creation of an economic constitution would create democracy in the economic sphere and would mirror the equalisation effects of democratisation of the political sphere. The economic constitution would ensure that each and every worker was involved (indirectly) in the direction of the economy (and society).[15] This empowerment would both counteract the inherent tendency of capitalist relations toward inequality, and would also mean that the economy was run much more effectively, both in terms of meeting economic and also social needs. Equality would therefore be achieved by two methods:

(1)   in the procedures for negotiation between the social partners, and
(2)   in the outcomes achieved through that negotiation.[16]

From the above analysis, it is clear that both Kahn-Freund and Sinzheimer were interested in the instigation of both universalistic and mid-spectrum goals through labour law. Both were interested in the concept of the democratisation of the industrial sphere (a mid-spectrum goal), and both were convinced that the proper regulatory (or de-regulatory) package would allow both industrial leaders and workers to achieve their goals. However, there were two features of their analysis which served to undermine these wider goals. The first feature was the conviction that the law should stay out of industrial relations (or provide only auxiliary supportive functions). This meant that their theories were unable to provide a vehicle for the capture of the value of law (in terms of worker protection). The second feature was the commitment within the theories to trade union action. This commitment to a particular selective method of regulation meant that the theories were unable to provide a means to provide long-term (mid-spectrum or universalistic) goals. The background to these problems and the limitations they presented are discussed in the following sections.

---

[13]   Sinzheimer (n 10) 226
[14]   H Sinzheimer, 'Das Rätessytem' (1919) in *Arbeitsrecht und Rechtssoziologie: gesammelte Aufsätze und Reden (Band 1)* (Otto Brenner Stiftung 1976) 327
[15]   Ibid 327
[16]   Sinzheimer (n 10) 227

3.3.2   Kahn-Freund and Sinzheimer: The Function of Law

In the work of Kahn-Freund and Sinzheimer there is the sense that law, in terms of state law, is a much less effective way of achieving worker goals than a properly functioning system of industrial relations involving equal and autonomous social partners. Indeed, for Sinzheimer, 'law' can only function properly if created and legitimised by autonomous means: '*die Entwicklung des Arbeitsrechts auf einer bestimmten Stufe die Notwendigkeit tarifträglicher Regelungen in sich schliesst*'.[17] The autonomous production and legitimisation of law is also in the state interest for a number of reasons. Firstly, state law can only be implemented effectively with the help of trade unions in consultation with management. These organisations are in the best place to be able to understand the implications of regulatory law in the whole range of different and changing industrial contexts, and therefore ensure the implementation of this law in a workable manner. Secondly, the autonomous production of law ensures the achievement of certain social aims for the state and for its workers. Finally, Sinzheimer viewed the relationship between the trade unions and management as forming the basis of an 'economic constitution' which would be the best means of achieving *economic* ends and meeting the aims of (economic) national policy. This economic constitution, and the economic democracy it involved, paralleled the political democracy already achieved in western society.

However, Sinzheimer did not advocate that the autonomous organisations of the economy should be totally free from state control. Rather, the economic constitution remained subordinate to the state and the political constitution. For Sinzheimer, the economy was a public matter, not a private one, and therefore should operate for the achievement of public and not private aims.[18] The economy should be run in the public interest, and that public interest would be defined by the organs of the economic constitution with reference to the needs of the population as a whole.[19] Indeed, the state remained free to intervene where that was deemed to be necessary for the achievement of fair terms and conditions of employment.[20] For Sinzheimer, this involvement was not problematic

---

[17]   'The development of labour law relies on the foundation of rules created by the social partners' (my translation) Sinzheimer (n 10) 226

[18]   Sinzheimer, 'Die Reform des Schlichtungswesens' (1930) in *Arbeitsrecht und Rechtssoziologie: gesammelte Aufsätze und Reden (Band 1)* (Otto Brenner Stiftung 1976) 236

[19]   Sinzheimer (n 10) 228

[20]   Sinzheimer (n 18) 239

because the state, as well as the autonomous organs of the economic constitution, also had an interest in the development of employment and social norms as part of the successful development of labour law.[21] However, Sinzheimer argued that in the economic sphere, the function of state law should be limited. State law should be subsidiary to 'autonomous legislation', as it was only the latter which would have sufficient flexibility and immediacy to be effective.[22]

In a similar way to Sinzheimer, Kahn-Freund viewed legal functions as secondary to the impact of the labour market (supply and demand) and 'the spontaneous creation of a social power on the workers' side to balance that of management'.[23] For Kahn-Freund, legal norms could only be enforced when backed by social sanctions: 'that is by the countervailing power of trade unions and other organised workers asserted through consultation and negotiation with the employer, and ultimately, if this fails, through withholding their labour.'[24] Furthermore, for Kahn-Freund, the regulation of terms and conditions through negotiation was a much more effective way of creating equilibrium between the parties of an employment relationship. He argued that this system of negotiation is much more flexible than legislation and represents a 'spirit of cooperation which cannot be engendered by the application of legal standards'.[25] The terms agreed through negotiation will also be more far reaching than legal standards: 'they are as manifold as they are subtle and do not lend themselves to enforcement by state-created machinery.'[26]

Kahn-Freund was particularly scathing about the possibilities of common law for the protection of workers in labour relations. He argued that the courts 'deal with the marginal, the exceptional, the abnormal, the pathological situations' and so cannot deal with the general protection of the worker.[27] More than that, the court is not interested in a balance of collective forces: '[i]t is (and this is its strength and weakness) inspired by the belief in the equality (real or fictitious) of individuals; it operates

---

[21]   Sinzheimer (n 10) 226

[22]   R Dukes, 'Constitutionalising Employment Relations: Sinzheimer, Kahn-Freund and the Role of Labour Law' (2008) 35 (3) *Journal of Law and Society* 347

[23]   Kahn-Freund in Davies and Freedland (n 6) 19

[24]   Ibid 20

[25]   O Kahn-Freund, 'Intergroup Conflict and Their Settlement' (1954) *British Journal of Sociology* 193, 204

[26]   Ibid 204

[27]   O Kahn-Freund, 'Hugo Sinzheimer 1875–1945' in R Lewis and J Clark (eds), *Labour Law and Politics in the Weimar Republic* (Basil Blackwell 1981) 53

between individuals and not otherwise.'[28] According to Kahn-Freud, there is no public interest represented in the civil courts. It is this and the personal background of the judiciary 'which explains the inescapable fact that the contribution which the courts have made to the orderly development of labour relations has been slight indeed'.[29] Indeed, as has been mentioned, both Kahn-Freund and Sinzheimer were concerned about the power relations inherent in the law itself, and the possibility for 'bourgeois society' to maintain power through legal abstraction. For both of these authors, the law could actually be a source of inequality in which the courts are complicit:

> The technique of bourgeois society and its law is to cover social acts and factors of social existence with abstractions: property, contract, legal person. All these abstractions contain within them socially opposed and contradictory phenomenon: property used for production and property between equal parties, capitalist and worker. Through abstraction it is possible to extend legal rules, which are appropriate to the social phenomenon for which they were originally developed, to other social phenomena, thereby concealing the exercise of social power behind a veil of law.[30]

3.3.3   Kahn-Freund's System of Collective Laissez-faire

Kahn-Freund labelled the British system of industrial relations in existence after the Second World War as 'collective laissez-faire'.[31] He characterised this system by the almost complete absence of the law: 'there is, perhaps, no major country in the world in which the law has played a less significant role in the shaping of [labour-management] relations than in Great Britain'. According to Kahn-Freund, this could be explained by the growth of the trade unions outside the parliamentary franchise after the First World War. This development meant that trade unions had not relied on the law to achieve their aims.[32] Instead, as trade unions grew in strength they had developed a preference for collective

---

[28]   Kahn-Freund (n 25) 12
[29]   Ibid 12
[30]   Kahn-Freund (n 27) 102
[31]   O Kahn-Freund, 'Legal Framework' in A Flanders and HA Clegg (eds), *The System of Industrial Relations in Great Britain* (Blackwell, Oxford 1954) 44
[32]   O Kahn-Freund, *Labour Law: Old Traditions and New Developments* (Clarke, Irwin and Company Limited, Toronto/Vancouver 1968) 7–8

bargaining and autonomous norm creation over and above state guarantees in the form of legislation.[33] Both unions and employers alike had come to see legislation merely as 'state interference' in their freedom of negotiation and 'from a worker's point of view, industrial action was far more promising an instrument of regulation than political action through legislation'.[34]

The system of collective laissez-faire was remarkable for the fact that it not only evidenced a low level of 'regulatory law', the auxiliary legislation in place was both 'marginal' and 'sporadic'.[35] This latter legislation, for example, did not seek to give rights or impose duties on the parties to negotiate with any particular opponent, neither did this specify the bounds within which those agreements needed to be reached.[36] Where the state did intervene, this was simply to give support to the autonomy of the collective parties, for example, by the 'general absence of direct legal sanctions in the State's efforts to encourage industrial peace by conciliation and arbitration and to extend collectively-agreed terms, and by the principle that the success of a statutory wages council was to be judged by its abolition in favour of collective bargaining'.[37] Perhaps the most supreme example of abstentionism was the absence in Britain of a positive legal right to strike and the establishment of the legal freedom to strike in the form of negatively expressed statutory immunities from judge-made liabilities,[38] which remains a feature of British labour law today. Furthermore, under the system of collective laissez-faire, collective agreements did not constitute legally binding contracts.[39] Routinely, terms of the collective agreements would be regarded as being impliedly incorporated into contracts of employment, but even where this was the case, these terms could be continually negotiated, even to the detriment of the employee.[40] To Kahn-Freund, this prevalence of norms over sanctions was not problematic, but even desirable: 'Legal norms and sanctions are blunt instruments

---

[33]   R Dukes, 'Otto Kahn-Freund and Collective Laissez-Faire: An Edifice without a Keystone?' (2009) 72 (2) *MLR* 245, 246

[34]   Kahn-Freund (n 32) 9

[35]   Ibid 7

[36]   Dukes (n 22) 355

[37]   R Lewis, 'Kahn-Freund and Labour Law: An Outline Critique' (1979) 8 *ILJ* 202, 209

[38]   Ibid 209

[39]   Kahn-Freund (n 25) 203

[40]   Dukes (n 22) 356

for the shaping of intergroup relations which have developed into a higher community.'[41]

Many criticisms have been levelled at the concept of collective laissez-faire, both as a description of the industrial relations system (in Britain) and as a prescriptive ideology in a normative sense. Kahn-Freund himself recognised that, towards the 1960s at least, the policy of abstention or non-intervention had become increasingly controversial, and greater recourse was being made to regulatory legislation.[42] He explained this development in terms of a number of factors:

(1)   He made reference to the growth in the labour force of the 'white collar element', which tended to 'falsify the assumption of a strong collective bargaining machinery'.[43]

(2)   He identified the growth of industry-wide collective bargaining far from the plant, which reduced the effectiveness of collective bargaining at plant level and introduced a greater need for regulatory legislation, particularly in the field of job security: 'it appears that … for the moment at least, our collective bargaining has stalled and legislation has to take its place.'[44]

He did not, however, abandon his conviction that collective bargaining was the best and most effective way to address vulnerability in the workplace. For Kahn-Freund, recourse to legislation was a temporary phenomenon to be replaced by collective bargaining once a suitable bargain was struck: '[Regulatory] legislation of employment in Britain is, like so much of our legislation, a response to needs as they arise and not informed by any desire for systematic order.'[45] Furthermore, he consistently argued that the common law was totally inadequate as a regulator of industrial relations, 'with its impracticable and unpredictable standards of "reasonableness" and its artificial concept of "intention of the parties", blanks which judges are able to fill as they choose'.[46]

It has also been argued that the representation of collective laissez-faire as a policy of state abstentionism served to mask the ideology which existed behind clear state policy. In other words, collective laissez-faire

---

[41]   Kahn-Freund (n 25) 204
[42]   Kahn-Freund (n 32) 10
[43]   Ibid 34
[44]   Ibid 34–35
[45]   Ibid 30
[46]   Ibid 34

was a particular kind of state intervention, both legislative and non-legislative, based on 'encouraging the establishment and maintenance of autonomous regulatory and dispute mechanisms'.[47] The evolution of voluntary institutions and rules under the guise of collective laissez-faire represented a distinctive ideology which was adopted by all sections of the industrial system, 'first by the trade unions and then by employers, the civil service and eventually even by the judges'.[48] This shared belief in the virtue of collective autonomy was connected to the growth of a broader social consensus. It fitted well with the British tradition of liberalism of the time, with its focus on the rights of individuals over and above the state.[49] According to Ramm, the notion of collective laissez-faire was useful to the government at the time, as the freedom of the individual to bargain was simply replaced by the notion of the collective to bargain: 'it replaced individual laissez-faire with collective laissez-faire'.[50]

It follows from the above discussion that the perfect separation of the 'political' from the 'industrial' envisaged by Kahn-Freund in his articulation of collective laissez-faire was not borne out in reality, and it is to be doubted whether this was (and is) ever an achievable aim. Indeed, Kahn-Freud's delimitation of what constituted the political and industrial spheres came itself to influence policy and to further the political ends of the state. According to Kahn-Freund's writing, the appropriate subject of collective bargaining was limited to the 'rules of the workplace' and 'to the question of the division of profits between re-investment and wages'.[51] This implied a rather restrictive idea of trade union function and legitimate areas of conflict.[52] In particular, Kahn-Freund disapproved of 'political' and 'national emergency strikes' which touched 'the borderline of what can legitimately be called industrial relations'.[53] He also disapproved of syndicalism and labour representation on company boards, which he saw as blurring the distinction between managerial functions and trade union functions (to act as a collective force in

[47]   Dukes (n 22) 358
[48]   Lewis (n 37) 210
[49]   Dukes (n 33) 236
[50]   T Ramm, 'Epilogue' in B Hepple (ed), *The Making of Labour Law in Europe: A Comparative Study of Nine Countries up to 1945* (Mansell, London 1986) 277
[51]   Dukes (n 22) 354
[52]   Lewis (n 37) 210
[53]   Kahn-Freund (n 32) 124

opposition to management).[54] Against this background, Kahn-Freund became involved in the drawing up of the Donovan report, which sought to set up new public agencies and laws designed to reform collective bargaining and protect management and trade unions from unofficial strikes, thereby allowing these bodies to regain control over workplace industrial relations.[55]

Ironically, the collective laissez-faire or voluntarist ideology has also been linked to the decline in trade unionism as a force in the UK and, paradoxically, as a force to protect workers against the excesses of management power. According to Rogowski, British trade union strength declined after the 1970s, precisely because it 'developed on the basis of procedural as opposed to substantive rules, which took the form of "gentleman's agreements" rather than legally enforceable contracts'.[56] As a result, the collective bargaining system had to develop its own institutional structures to protect itself, consisting of a wide variety of disparate organisations such as conciliation boards, arbitration panels and voluntary labour courts'.[57] This informal system proved unsustainable and resulted in 'largely informal, fragmented and autonomous shop-floor bargaining at the workplace [taking] control over many substantive issues'.[58] These arrangements lacked robustness and proved susceptible to the legal interventions and hostile campaigns of the Thatcher government in the 1980s. Furthermore, the British reliance on 'single channel' (worker representation by unions only) rather than 'dual-channel' (worker representation by unions and some other form, that is, works council) can also be traced to the voluntarist roots of the development of the industrial relations, and this too has undermined the effectiveness of collective bargaining in the UK.[59]

---

[54]   Dukes (n 22) 354

[55]   Lewis (n 37) 213

[56]   R Rogowski, 'Industrial Relations, Labour Conflict Resolution and Reflexive Labour Law' in R Rogowski and T Wilthagen (eds), *Reflexive Labour Law: Studies in Industrial Relations and Employment Regulation* (Kluwer Law International 1994) 64

[57]   Ibid 64

[58]   Ibid 64

[59]   R Dukes, 'Voluntarism and the Single Channel: The Development of Single-Channel Worker Representation in the UK' (2008) 24 (1) *International Journal of Comparative Labour Law and Industrial Relations* 87

3.3.4   Problems with the Choice of Selective Goals

The first main premise of the theories of Kahn-Freund and Sinzheimer is that collective bargaining is the best way to counteract worker vulnerability. The second related premise is that labour *law* is not well suited to achieving worker aims. The problem is that neither of these propositions match the experience of current labour market participants.[60] As far as the law is concerned, protective employment legislation has become an important way in which workers can challenge their treatment. There is now a suite of laws protecting workers from unfair dismissal, discrimination and so on (discussed in the next section). It does not, therefore, seem accurate to suggest that the law does not help workers achieve their ends, and that this achievement should be left to collective bargaining through trade unions. Likewise, the commitment to collective bargaining through trade union action brings into question the ability of this kind of classical labour law theory to address vulnerability in the workplace. Arguably, this view of the centrality of collective bargaining is context-specific and is not suited to helping current workers to achieve their ends. There are real difficulties faced by 'precarious' workers in both accessing and enforcing collective bargaining rights. Likewise, a conviction that legislation is of no use to precarious workers can actually serve to increase their legislative precariousness.

By way of illustration, underlying classical labour law theory about the centrality of collective bargaining is the assumption that there is both homogeneity of status and interest amongst workers. This assumption can be linked to the particular period of history in which the classical labour law scholars were writing. Indeed, it has been suggested that at the time

---

[60]   This approach has also been developed in the work of Freedland and Countouris on the personal employment contract. They suggest that labour law regulation should be informed by three foundational concepts. The first is 'dignity', which is a concept which ensures the 'protection of the person regardless of the specific arrangements for the performance of his or her work'. This concept aligns itself with the idea of human rights as a minimum standard for labour law. The second concept is 'capability', which Freedland and Countouris argue should act as a basis for the development of social rights in the labour law regime. This argument draws specifically on Deakin and Wilkinson's work. The final concept is that of 'stability' which has largely been rejected in the age of atypical work, but which has real economic benefits, and which, Freedland and Countouris argue, is the only way in which to guarantee the recovery of the economy after the recent economic downturn. See M Freedland and N Countouris, *The Legal Construction of Personal Work Relations* (Oxford University Press 2011)

Kahn-Freund was writing about the system of collective laissez-faire, a certain homogeneity of occupational status had developed among workers. This occupational status centred on three elements.

(1)   The prevalence, in the industrial sphere, of the manufacturing sector dominated by the Fordist production model (large companies engaged in mass production based on a narrow range of tasks).
(2)   The existence of the 'standard employment relationship', which consisted of permanent full time employment performed by the male breadwinner.
(3)   The linkage of social security benefits to work, which protected workers in times of difficulty.

All of these factors combined to produce a 'degree of regularity and durability in employment relationships' and was maintained by both the relative economic and social stability of the time.[61]

It could also be argued that, at this time, this homogeneity of status produced a certain homogeneity of interest among workers. Indeed, Kahn-Freund presented the interests of all workers as similar. He included within these interests the enjoyment of a reasonable level of job security, and 'the worker's interest in planning his and his family's life and in being protected against the interruption in his mode of existence, either through a fall of his real income or through the loss of his job'.[62] These interests were, of course, tied to the understanding that most jobs were for life (the Fordist mode of production) and that employees were men who brought home the family wage (under the 'standard employment relationship'). Most importantly, they were central to Kahn-Freund's understanding that collective bargaining in general and trade unionism specifically was the best means of achieving worker goals. Homogeneity of status and interest meant that, not only could trade unions develop a large membership base in the context of the grounding of work organisation in large enterprises with vertical hierarchies, they could also successfully represent the interests of their members in achieving, for example, a decent family wage.

Arguably it is not possible to characterise the modern labour market in terms of either homogeneity of interest or status. Both economic and social factors (discussed in detail in Chapter 2) have determined the

---

[61]   G Rodgers, 'Precarious Work in Western Europe: The State of the Debate' in G Rodgers and J Rodgers (eds), *Precarious Jobs in Labour Market Regulation* (ILO 1989) 1

[62]   Kahn-Freund in Davies and Freedland (n 6) 66

breakdown of the 'standard employment relationship' and its institutions. This creates two main problems for unions. The first is that work is no longer organised in a way which is conducive to the development of union membership. Indeed, in the UK, trade union density has almost halved since its peak in 1979.[63] The increase in service jobs means that workers interact more directly with clients, patients or customers, rather than reporting directly to a single 'employer'. This complicates the 'us and them' basis of union organisation.[64] Furthermore, the vertical integration of the firm in the Fordist mode of industrial organisation has broken down and been replaced by smaller and more decentralised work units. This has undermined the clear identification of the 'bargaining unit' upon which traditional trade unionism relies.[65] The second problem faced by trade unions is that both economic and social change has meant an increase in the diversity of interests represented by workers. The question is whether unions are equipped to deal with this diversification, or can maintain their attractiveness to all workers, given their traditional association with only a narrow set of interests.[66]

Therefore, it is to be questioned whether trade unions can deliver the equalisation of bargaining power for all workers as envisaged by Kahn-Freund and Sinzheimer. Certainly, the decline in trade union membership in many countries (in 2014, less than a third of workers in the UK (25.0 per cent) were actually a member of a trade union organisation[67]) means that it is difficult for trade unions to represent the interests of the entire workforce. There is also the problem of the increasing heterogeneity of worker interests which make it difficult for trade unions to capture all workers through their activities. Indeed, there are signs that unions are increasingly recognising the importance of representing the diversity of interests involved in the workforce. Trade unions have been strongly

---

[63] BIS, 'Trade Union Membership 2014' 5 <https://www.gov.uk/government/uploads/system/uploads/attachment_data/file/431564/Trade_Union_Membership_Statistics_2014.pdf > accessed 19 August 2015

[64] P Smith, 'Organizing the Unorganizable: Private Paid Household Workers and Approaches to Employee Representation' (2000) 79 *North Carolina Law Review* 45, 69

[65] Ibid 70

[66] A good example here is the relationship between trade unionism and domestic workers. Traditionally, unions ignored such workers because of the dominant vision of the status of domestic work and the work of women, and the fact that domestic work posed no competitive threat to male workers. This will be discussed in more detail in Chapter 6 on domestic workers.

[67] BIS (n 63) 5

involved in equal pay cases in recent years,[68] and have played a very important role in the promotion of (new) rights for particularly vulnerable groups. On the one hand, these activities represent a way forward for trade unions, and can be viewed as the modern solution to the problems experienced by the application of Kahn-Freund and Sinzheimer's theories. On the other hand, advocating particular interests is a difficult strategy for trade unions, given that these interests may conflict with the interests of the core workforce (which may still constitute a large part of their membership).

3.3.5   Employment Legislation to Counteract Market Forces

It became clear that if labour law were to achieve its classical aims, then the centrality of collective bargaining mechanisms had to be reconsidered. To a certain extent, the classical scholars recognised this position and Kahn-Freund in particular considered the possibility of using regulatory means to achieve a level of worker protection in conjunction with collective bargaining mechanisms. Despite this consideration, Kahn-Freund maintained his commitment to the fundamental and *a priori* position of collective bargaining in achieving worker goals. By contrast, other authors recognised to a greater extent the possibility of using employment legislation to improve worker status and protect workers against the vagaries of capitalism. Thus, there developed a second strand to the traditional theory of justice under labour law: the creation of employment legislation as a means of worker protection.

The second element of labour law's traditional theory of justice shares the same starting point as the first: vulnerabilities are created in employment relationships as a result of the operation of the capitalist system and the legal institutions which support it. If justice is to be achieved, there needs to be some check on the operation of this system, and some redistribution of power and resources from employers to employees. Labour law can provide this kind of check and redistributive effect because it has the power to set a series of minimum standards which all employers must meet, and it can also operate to modify the terms and conditions of employment contracts (that is, the operation of contract law) in favour of the employee. The logic here is that although contract

---

[68]   T Colling, 'What Space for Unions on the Floor of Rights? Trade Unions and the Enforcement of Statutory Individual Employment Rights' (2006) 35 (2) *ILJ* 140, 147–148

law is generally valid, the particular features of the employment relationship means that contract law needs to be limited or constrained in certain ways when the subject of the transaction is labour.

It is argued that, in employment contracts, the inequality of bargaining power between employee and employer dictates the structure of the contract of employment. As explained by Kahn-Freund and Sinzheimer, freedom of contract in employment relationships is a 'verbal symbol' rather than a 'social fact'.[69] The inequalities in the employment relationship mean that it is the employer who decides on the contractual terms and offers the contract on a 'take it or leave it' basis; it is not accurate to present the contract of employment as a freely negotiated and consensual agreement. The employee has little or no opportunity to negotiate contractual terms and is forced into accepting the contract of employment on the basis that the contract is necessary for his/her valued existence.[70] The result is that from the outset, contractual terms may be more favourable to the employer than to the employees. There is also the problem that a number of pressures act to force the employees to accept terms which are below their (theoretical) market value. There may be information asymmetries which mean that the employee is not aware of their market value, or they may experience geographical constraints which mean that they accept a less favourable offer.[71] Another problem is that employees may need a level of investment from the employer in order for them to reach their full market value, and in the absence of that investment is forced to take a lower set of contractual terms. Finally, there is an imbalance of power through the *conduct* of the relationship: the employer controls the operation of the contract over time. For example, while the employee accepts a permanent wage (changing only in line with prescribed limits), the employer is free to issue changing demands outside pre-agreed and circumscribed boundaries.[72] The employee has no defence to these changes in the context of the subordination of the employee to the employer's control in the capitalist system.

In this context, employment law can step in to modify contractual terms and thereby reduce some of the deleterious effects of subordination

---

[69]   Kahn-Freund in Davies and Freedland (n 6) 25
[70]   J Laws, 'Public Law and Employment Law: Abuse of Power' (1997) *Public Law* 455, 456
[71]   H Collins, 'Justifications and Techniques of the Legal Regulation of the Employment Relation' in H Collins, P Davies and R Rideout (eds), *Legal Regulation of the Employment Relation* (Hart 2000) 8–9
[72]   Davidov (n 1) 8

and commodification experienced by workers in the capitalist system. For example, unfair dismissal law can act to insert mandatory terms into employment contracts which dictate that an employee may only be dismissed for 'just' causes. This is necessary because of the particular 'trade-off' experienced by an employee when engaging in an employment relationship,[73] as when doing so, each employee has a level of interest in job security. This is because employees rely on the employment relationship to provide their means of subsistence and allow employees to follow their life plan. There are also social and emotional dependencies connected with work which employees have an interest in sustaining (at least in the short term). However, if the employment contract were allowed to operate without constraint, there would be no security guarantees. The employer's interest is in maintaining the maximum amount of flexibility in order to respond quickly to changing market conditions.[74] As the employer has a greater bargaining power than the employees, the employer's interests tend to prevail over those of the employees. The result is a lack of protection for employees under normal contractual conditions. In this situation the law steps in to protect the employees' interests against arbitrary, unfair or unjustified action by the employer.[75]

In theory then, unfair dismissal law protects workers against the vagaries of the market by providing them with a level of security. However, there are a number of reasons why unfair dismissal law has not fulfilled its potential in the context of social and economic changes. Unfair dismissal is 'selective' in the sense of applying only to employees and correcting only the inequalities which exist for those already employed. As a result, unfair dismissal law can *increase* inequalities which exist between different sets of workers, or between workers and society as a whole. A trade-off can be envisaged between an increase in security for the 'core' set of workers who fulfil the qualification criteria for unfair dismissal law, and a decrease in security for contingent workers outside this core, or for those who are unemployed. This might be seen as

---

[73]   G Davidov, 'In Defence of (Efficiently Administered) "Just Cause" Dismissal Laws' (2007) 23 (1) *The International Journal of Comparative Labour Law and Industrial Relations* 117, 123

[74]   Ibid

[75]   It is also possible to see this kind of employment law intervention as a 'redistribution' of power and resources from employees to employers. This is often the justification for minimum wage laws which ensure that the lowest paid workers (those subject to the greatest subordination pressure) receive a minimum level of resources.

an inefficient outcome (it protects those least in need of protection). Furthermore, the courts have struggled with their interpretive obligations outside the area of dismissals which are deemed 'automatically' unfair. For example, in the UK, the legitimacy of a decision to dismiss is considered against a 'bank of reasonable responses' test which takes into account the necessity for a level of managerial discretion. In order to be reasonable under this test, an employer's action does not have to accord with actions which the members of the court (tribunal) might have taken in the circumstances. Rather, in considering the reasonableness of the action, the tribunal must consider that 'there is no correct way to manage a business and employers may legitimately and fairly adopt different disciplinary standards'.[76] This standard has been criticised on the basis that it necessarily gives too much weight to managerial prerogative and provides only a very minimum standard of reasonableness.

3.4 GOALS UNDER EFFICIENCY THEORIES

3.4.1 Universalism Under Efficiency Theory

Efficiency theories applied to the employment relationship are inspired by economic theories about the functioning of labour markets. These economic theories can be divided into two camps: neo-classical economic theory and new institutional economic theory. The starting point for both theories is the liberal conviction that individual freedom is the highest social aim. Individuals (as rational, autonomous beings) should be given the greatest space possible to pursue their own autonomous ends. Thus, both theories are convinced by the value of freedom of contract. They suggest that (in the absence of market failure) freedom of contract between employers and employees provides the best and most efficient allocation of resources, because individuals are in the best position to decide what is in their own interests (and can act flexibly to manage those interests). Both kinds of economic theory also suggest that a well-functioning market not only provides the best individual allocation of economic resources, but is also beneficial to society as a whole. The wealth generated from economic processes will 'trickle-down' to those

---

[76] T Brodkorb, 'Employee Misconduct and UK Unfair Dismissal Law: Does the Range of Reasonable Responses Test Require Reform?' (2010) 52 (6) *International Journal of Law and Management* 429, 437

who need it most.[77] Therefore, efficiency theories are universalistic: they suggest that regulation which creates a well-functioning economy provides benefits to all parties within the industrial system, as well as to the wider society.

Efficiency theorists challenge both of the precepts of classical labour law theory: namely that there is an inequality of bargaining power between employers and employees which is in need of correction, and labour law should act to counteract the commodification processes of capitalism which serve to dehumanise workers. In neo-classical economic theory, commodification is not only inevitable in capitalist systems, it is also desirable.[78] It is the means by which individuals enter into the labour market and can be part of the wealth-generating processes of capitalism. Commodification is not of itself a 'problem' to be addressed by legal sanction. The labour market operates like other markets, in being determined by the market processes of supply and demand. Workers form the essential elements of the labour market and are themselves subject to all the normal economic processes. It is because workers are commodities and subject to all the normal economic processes that they can be part of the wealth-generating processes of capitalism, and are ultimately able to fulfil their desires through work. The commodification of labour is therefore desirable because workers can use their labour to satisfy their own individual preferences, and are not beholden to 'external' manipulation by other (political) forces which would disrupt their desires.

Furthermore, the commodification of labour is a useful theoretical tool. This is because the theoretical perspective is essentially an economic one, and economic theory operates by reducing real world phenomena (workers) to theoretical elements (labour), in order to build theoretical models which will predict the most efficient outcome for markets and ultimately for workers.[79] The idea that labour will act as a 'commodity' in a predictable and rational way is essential to these models, because it is only in this way that both labour market and economic outcomes can be forecast. Therefore, on this view, it is difficult to see commodification as a problem in itself. To view commodification itself as a problem would imply not only a rejection of capitalist processes of production, but also

---

[77]   ACL Davies, *Perspectives on Labour Law* (Oxford University Press 2009) 27

[78]   R Epstein, 'In Defense of the Contract at Will' (1984) 51 *University of Chicago Law Review* 947

[79]   H Collins, 'Justifications and Techniques of Legal Regulation of the Employment Relation' in H Collins, P Davies and R Rideout (eds), *Legal Regulation of the Employment Relation* (Hart 2000)

the reliance on economic theory as a whole. Instead, the problems are presented as particular, and as an inability of certain individuals to realise the benefit of the advantages of the knowledge economy.[80]

Likewise, the notion of inequality of bargaining power is a 'form of economic nonsense' if intended to be a claim within neo-classical theory.[81] It simply is not possible to reconcile this notion with the notion of the existence of an employment contract between equal and autonomous parties. That said, lawyers inspired by the findings of new institutional economics are more sympathetic to the idea of inequalities of bargaining power. From the new institutionalist perspective, it is understood that the economic market does not always produce the most efficient results, and that it is dogged by certain 'market failures'. These market failures *include* inequality of bargaining power. The argument is that inequality of bargaining power can exist in the labour market, and where it does exist it creates inefficiencies because it tends to promote opportunistic behaviour on the part of employers to exploit this power. This is a problem for individual (vulnerable) workers because they do not have the opportunity to challenge this behaviour. It is also a problem for the economy as a whole as it means that employers tend to focus on short-term goals, rather than long-term investment in employees. For developed economies, which rely on the knowledge and skills base of their workers, this means that the economy as a whole would be less efficient. In this situation, there may be an argument for intervention in the market, for example, through labour laws which encourage training programmes and employment security.[82]

---

[80]   The example of 'atypical' or 'precarious' work is illustrative. Under the narrow view, 'atypical work' is not necessarily seen as a problem in itself. This kind of work presents certain distinct benefits to employees (as well as to employers). Firstly, the existence of atypical work means that employers have the opportunity to create more jobs, meaning that there are likely to be more jobs available for the workforce as a whole. Secondly, the existence of atypical work means that workers have more flexibility themselves in determining their work/life balance. Furthermore, many individuals have benefitted from the dissolution of traditional work forms (the 'knowledge' workers). Difficulties which arise are particular rather than systemic. For example, individual atypical work contracts may not allow the same access to training that 'typical' work contracts allow. For the individuals under these particular contracts, it will be difficult to take advantage of the benefits of the global knowledge economy.

[81]   B Langille, 'Labour Law's Theory of Justice' in G Davidov and B Langille (eds), *The Idea of Labour Law* (Oxford University Press 2011) 105

[82]   H Collins, 'Regulating the Employment Relation for Competitiveness' (2001) 30 *ILJ* 17, 29

The application of efficiency theories to labour law has, on the one hand created a deregulatory pressure. For example, many arguments for the dismantling of unfair dismissal law in Europe have been based around the inefficiency of this regulation and the unnecessary cost burden imposed on individuals through this regulation.[83] On the other hand, a number of suggestions have been made for re-regulation of the employment relationship in line with economic changes. A particular preoccupation has been how to deal with the decline in the 'standard employment relationship' and the increase in 'precarious work' (the economic context of precarious work is discussed in detail in the previous chapter). Traditionally, legal categorisations have been based on the notion of inequalities of bargaining power under standard employment contracts (full-time, permanent work with the same employer). However economic changes have dictated that the standard employment relationship and associated notions of subordination do not match economic reality. This is a problem for labour law as without an understanding of the economic landscape it will be impossible to determine where the market failures lie. The result will be a labour law which is both over-inclusive (it fails to recognise the increasing autonomy of labour law subjects) and under-inclusive (it focuses on 'core' workers at the expense of more peripheral, marginal or precarious elements of the workforce). The new institutionalist argument proceeds that legal categorisations need to be amended to more precisely fit economic reality.

3.4.2   Traditional Legal Categorisations and the Problem of Precarious Work

The reliance of traditional labour law on subordination under a standard employment relationship can be illustrated with a number of examples. One example is the use of the legal categorisation of subordination to justify those who are in need of protection (that is, dependent employees) and those who are not (that is, independent contractors).[84] The argument is that, for those in subordinate relationships, market failures will mean that they have to live with terms and conditions that society finds unacceptable. As a result, they are vulnerable and deserving of legal protection. By contrast, 'independent contractors' are capable of achieving contracts with employers which are socially acceptable as a result of

---

[83]   Davidov (n 73) 117

[84]   G Davidov, 'The Three Axes of the Employment Relationship: A Characterization of Workers in Need of Protection' (2002) 52 *University of Toronto Law Journal* 357, 357

their increased market power. They therefore do not require the protection of the legal system as they can 'take care of themselves'.[85] In this
context, precarious workers face the risk of falling outside the boundaries
of legal protection. The law fails to recognise their subordination because
their contracts do not comply with the standard contract of employment.
This means that they are judged to be independent contractors and
therefore fall outside the law.

In British labour law, 'subordination' is judged according to two
elements:

(1) the level of 'control' of an employer over an employee, and/or
(2) the level of economic dependence exhibited by an employee (in
     terms of economic risks undertaken by the employee).

These elements are assessed on a case-by-case basis according to a
number of (factual) indicia, including the ownership of plant and
materials,[86] arrangements for the payment of tax and national insurance,[87] arrangements for holiday and sick pay,[88] and the label given to
the relationship by the parties.[89] However, there are considerable problems associated with these elements of 'subordination' and their application in practice. The notion of 'control' is extremely vague and difficult
to determine, especially with the increase in the diversity of production
models (out-sourcing, piece-working, and so on).[90] For instance, a
worker may agree to a general power of direction, but maintain considerable autonomy in the nature of their work. Such a worker may, as a
result, consider themselves an independent contractor *in fact*, but actually
come closer to the definition of a dependent worker in legal terms. There
are also considerable problems with the notion of economic dependence,
which attempts to measure how far a worker bears the risk of profit or
loss involved in a particular venture. The idea is that 'independent
contractors' can be identified as those persons who take on these risks,
whereas 'employees' are protected from these risks by their employers,

---

[85] Ibid 359
[86] *Ready Mixed Concrete v Minister for Pensions and National Insurance*
[1968] 2 QB 497 (QB)
[87] *Lane v Shire Roofing Co Ltd* [1995] IRLR 493 (CA)
[88] *O'Kelly v Trusthouse Forte Ltd* [1983] ICR 728
[89] *Massey v Crown Life Insurance Company* [1978] ICR 590 (CA)
[90] H Collins, 'Independent Contractors and the Challenge of Vertical Disintegration to Employment Protection Laws' (1990) 10 (3) *Oxford Journal of Legal
Studies* 353, 353

or are compensated for the risks by payment of a wage.[91] However, in actual fact, 'employees' often bear significant economic risks. One of the most obvious is the risk of job loss,[92] but many employees also take on the risk of reduced income from poor performance, or stand to benefit from increased effort through profit-related pay schemes.[93] Furthermore, employees are often not compensated for these risks: employees with less job security are often those with lower wages and, even where there is some compensation for risk, this is 'far from being a full and realistic compensation'.[94]

Labour law that is sympathetic to new institutional economics is particularly concerned that the definitions and tests currently used to differentiate employees from independent contractors are unable to identify employees in 'atypical' relationships. Such workers are often deemed to be 'independent contractors' as they bear many of the risks of economic dependence (such as the unavailability of work) and may not be subject to the 'controls' associated with employment status.[95] They therefore fall outside the scope of labour law protection, which may be a problem for those vulnerable to both oppressive employment terms and the vagaries of the market.[96] This situation is compounded by the contractual nature of employment rights, even those laid down in statute.[97] Those with atypical contracts therefore find themselves unable to rely on the terms of their contract to guarantee protection (as these contracts are temporary, poorly constructed or exclude protection), as well as struggling to fulfil statutory criteria regarding the nature of their employment relation. The lack of legal protection for these marginal workers, it is argued, has created an incentive to firms to accelerate the vertical disintegration of production in order to avoid the costs associated with labour law, which in turn has led to greater worker insecurity and vulnerability.[98]

However, it is important at this juncture to note that 'atypical work' is not necessarily seen as a problem in itself by efficiency theorists. Indeed,

---

[91]   Ibid 370
[92]   Davidov (n 84) 390
[93]   Collins (n 90) 353
[94]   Davidov (n 84) 390
[95]   S Fredman 'Women at Work: The Broken Promise of Flexicurity' (2004) 33 (4) *ILJ* 299, 300
[96]   Collins (n 90) 372
[97]   B Hepple, 'Restructuring Employment Rights' (1986) 15 (1) *ILJ* 69, 69–70
[98]   Collins (n 90) 374

efficiency theorists have identified a number of distinct benefits attaching to this kind of work. The existence of atypical work means that:

(1) employers have the opportunity to create more jobs, meaning that there are likely to be more jobs available for the workforce as a whole; and

(2) workers have more flexibility themselves in determining their work/life balance.[99]

Furthermore, many individuals have benefitted from the dissolution of traditional work forms (the 'knowledge' workers). Difficulties which arise are particular rather than systemic. It is these particular difficulties which need to be regulated under labour law. For example, individual atypical work contracts may not allow the same access to training that 'typical' work contracts allow. For the individuals under these particular contracts, it will be difficult to take advantage of the benefits of the global knowledge economy. This issue should be addressed to increase both individual worker competitiveness and also the competitiveness of the business in the global economy.

3.4.3 Universalism in Practice: Matching Economic Reality and Employment Regulation

A number of strategies have been suggested to ensure that labour law better covers those in need of protection. One approach has been to suggest targeted measures to ensure that atypical workers attain the core rights and benefits of employment law. For example, it has been suggested that informal (domestic) work would best be regulated through a 'Framed Flexibility Model'. The aim of this model is to ensure that working time (maximum daily and weekly hours, minimum rest periods) is properly protected for this group, while at the same time leaving space for employers and workers to meet their need for flexibility. The Model is comprised of three sets of standards:

(1) A framework of limitation on hours and the instigation of rest periods (in line with working time legislation in existence within the formal regulatory system).

(2) 'Flexibility norms' for workers and employers to allow employers to meet the need for workers to be at home in urgent circumstances,

---

[99] ACL Davies (n 77) 82

and for workers to meet unforeseen responsibilities arising in their family lives or other personal commitments.

(3) Procedural standards (the Effective Regulation Standards) which are 'tailored towards ensuring that the substantive standards exercise a decisive influence on the actual practices of working life'.[100]

Another approach has been to expand the personal scope of labour law generally to ensure that more 'atypical' workers fall within its scope. In the UK, there has been an attempt to extend this personal scope through the introduction of the category of the 'worker' into employment legislation. This category was a feature of much legislation introduced by the Labour government in Britain (1997–2010), and appeared, for example, in the Working Time Regulations 1998 (SI 1998/1833) and the National Minimum Wage Act 1998. The term 'worker' includes all employees, plus those who agree to perform work personally, provided that they are not in business on their own account.[101] Its aim is to capture those persons who do not qualify for employee status, as they do not meet sufficient of the indicia necessary (in terms of control, risk, and so on), but who are nevertheless in a position of dependency vis-a-vis their employer.[102] In some cases, the worker test has been successful and allowed the courts to push the boundary of protection in the worker's favour.[103] On other occasions, dependent status has been denied, despite evidence of personal service and the inability on the part of the claimants to spread economic risk.[104]

The problems associated with the application of the worker test have been blamed on a number of features. The first is that the worker test relies on many of the same indicia as the test for employee status, although the dividing line is supposedly more in the worker's favour.[105] Thus, the worker test suffers from the same inconsistencies associated with the application of indicia to reality as the employee test. Furthermore, the use of the same criteria introduces rigidities into the worker

---

[100] D McCann and J Murray, 'Promoting Formalisation through Labour Market Regulation: A "Framed Flexibility" Model for Domestic Work' (2014) 43 (3) *Industrial Law Journal* 319, 337

[101] G Davidov, 'Who is a Worker?' (2005) 34 *ILJ* 57, 59

[102] *Byrne Brothers (Formwork) Limited v Baird* [2002] IRLR 96 (EAT), para 2(5)

[103] *Redrow Homes (Yorkshire) limited v Wright* [2004] 3 All ER 98

[104] *Firthglow Limited (t/a Protectacoat) v Descombes and Another* [2004] All ER (D) 415

[105] Davidov (n 101) 59

test which may not have been intended in the drafting of the definition. An example is the continued use of the concept of 'mutuality of obligation' (one of the main tests to determine employee status) to determine worker status in situations where there is more than a single wage-work bargain.[106] The result is the exclusion of many contracts which may otherwise have been included in the definition. The second problem with the worker test is the lack of explanation in legislation of what constitutes a 'business' for the purposes of the test.[107] This lack of definition can make the use of the worker concept meaningless: a work relationship characterised by significant dependency on a single employer might also involve a business conducted by a worker. The existence of such a 'business' might therefore mean that the worker does not qualify for employment rights, despite other conditions of dependency.[108] Thirdly, there are problems regarding the requirement in the worker test for 'personal service'. This is because there have been cases of employers successfully avoiding a finding of worker status by the use of a 'substitution clause', despite personal service existing in practice. An example is provided by the case of *Tanton*.[109] In this case, the claimant worked under an 'agreement for services' which required him to arrange a substitute should he be unable or unwilling to work. The Court of Appeal held that the claimant was not a worker as he was allowed to arrange for another person to carry out his work and could therefore not fulfil the criteria for 'personal service' in the worker definition. This decision stood despite the fact that no substitutes were actually used in practice.[110]

The problems with the worker category have led some authors to suggest alternative (and possibly more wide-ranging) solutions. Freedland suggested the introduction of a new conceptual category of the 'personal employment contract' to capture all those in need of protection.[111] Under his scheme, the labels of 'employee', 'worker' and 'independent contractor' were rejected. Rather, eligibility for protection

---

[106] ACL Davies, 'The Contract for Intermittent Employment' (2007) 36 (1) *ILJ* 102, 105

[107] D Brodie, 'Employees, Workers and the Self-employed' (2005) 34 (3) *ILJ* 253, 254

[108] Ibid 254

[109] *Express and Echo Publications Limited v Tanton* [1999] ICR 693 (CA)

[110] S Deakin, 'Does the Personal Employment Contract Provide a Basis for the Reunification of Employment Law? (2007) 36 (1) *ILJ* 68, 78

[111] M Freedland, *The Personal Employment Contract* (Oxford University Press 2003) 13

was to be decided at the boundary between work carried out in person as opposed to work 'in the conduct of an independent business or professional practice'. The intention was to narrow the concept of 'business' (such as in the worker definition) so that fewer 'independent contractors' were excluded from employment protection.[112] The 'personal employment contract' could also be used as a vehicle to include a greater number of 'casual' or 'marginal' workers within the scope of employment protection. This is because, under Freedland's scheme, an employment contract could exist even where the relationship was not continuous, for example, as a 'contract for intermittent employment' or a 'contract for occasional employment'.[113] This continuity is currently denied on the basis of 'mutuality of obligation' arguments, and the lack of recognition by the courts that a contract of employment might contain a broad power of suspension.[114]

Freedland's analysis is a good example of an attempt to ensure that labour law is more responsive to the reality of current employment contracts in the global knowledge economy.[115] It reflects the central idea of efficiency theory that the legal system can *create* vulnerability where it fails to respond to the realities of the economic system, and that this can fall hardest on those marginal to the functioning of the economy. However, like Davidov's analysis before it, it also demonstrates the difficulties and limitations of this kind of analysis (for vulnerable workers). Decisions about employment status remain contractual, and there remains a dividing line between those that have sufficient contractual status to be determined an employee/worker, and those that do not. Those workers who are unable to show this contractual status may be able to take the economic risks associated with independent contractor status, but there will also be marginal or precarious workers who continue to fall within this category. If those workers are to take the

---

[112]   Ibid 25
[113]   Ibid 109–111
[114]   Davies (n 106) 107–108
[115]   It is also worth noting the development of these ideas in M Freedland and N Countouris, *The Legal Construction of Personal Work Relations* (Oxford University Press 2011). Here the authors present the idea that employment should be viewed as a set of personal work relations. They assert that the idea of a personal work relation should form a new basis for the whole range of ways in which employment contracts are governed. This governance should be through a set of values: dignity, capability and stability which will enable greater fairness and create a more sustainable labour law.

benefit of employment status, they depend on a purposive approach to employment contracts in the courts.

The purposive approach to the interpretation of worker rights means that the courts have been (increasingly) willing to look beyond the contractual agreement to determine what actually happens on a day-to-day basis between the parties. It could be argued that this is particularly important in the context of modern 'flexible' contracts where standard form contracts entered into by the parties at the beginning of the employment relationship are not adequately representative of the 'bureaucratic' power exercised by the employer in the determination of the activities of the employee.[116] However, there remains great inconsistency in court decisions in this area.[117] The main problem is the conflict between the notion of bureaucratic power and the idea of freedom of contract, and certainly this conflict is difficult to reconcile with efficiency theory.[118] There is also the problem that, of necessity, a purposive approach is no guarantee of a particular outcome, as the approach is completely dependent on the facts of the case. The result is that rights for

---

[116] H Collins, 'Market Power, Bureaucratic Power and the Contract of Employment' (1986) 15 *ILJ* 1, 1

[117] A comparison can be made here between the decision in *Massey v Crown Life Insurance Company* [1978] ICR 590 (CA) and *Ferguson v John Dawson & Partners (Contractors) Limited* [1976] IRLR 346 (CA). In both cases the parties agreed to self-employment status (and took advantage of this status in terms of the payment of tax), but whereas this was deemed to reflect the reality of the situation in the former case, this was not so in the latter case.

[118] A good example of this conflict is *Consistent Group v Kalwak* [2008] IRLR 505 in which the Court held that: 'It is not the function of the Court or an employment tribunal to recast the parties' bargain. If a term solely agreed in writing is to be rejected in favour of a different one, it can only be done by a clear finding that the real agreement was to that different effect and that the term was included by [the parties] so as to present a misleadingly different impression. In that regard, a finding that the contract is in part a sham require[s] a finding that both parties intended it to paint in that respect a false picture as to the true nature of their respective obligations.' However, this is a slightly different position to the more recent decision in *Protectacoat Firthglow Limited v Szilagyi* [2009] IRLR 365. Here, the Court stated that a tribunal should look to the contract first as this is 'ordinarily where the answer is to be found' as to the nature of the employment relationship. However, if the terms of the contract are brought into question by either party, then it is up to the Court to decide the true nature of the relationship (paras 55–56). This position has been followed in the latest decisions, including *Autoclenz Ltd v Belcher & Ors* [2009] EWCA 1046 and *Pulse Healthcare v Carewatch Care Services Limited* [2012] All ER (D) 113 (Aug).

workers can be eroded, just as easily as they can be constructed.[119] These practical effects will be discussed in more detail in Chapter 5 (the case study on agency work).

3.4.4 Precarious Work and Human Rights

On efficiency theory (and this might include both neo-classical and institutional approaches), it is possible to argue that precarious workers should be dealt with outside the labour law system completely, because the concerns in relation to these individuals do not match the average labour market participant (and therefore they should not be regulated in the same way). At the extreme end, marginalised workers suffer abuses of 'humanity' and so are best dealt with by the system of human rights rather than by labour law.[120] These human rights protections can act to prevent extreme abuse in the labour market without unduly interfering in economic functioning. In relation to 'first generation' civil and political rights (such as freedom from torture and freedom from slavery), these rights also fit with the liberal underpinnings of efficiency theory. These rights are individual and universal. They apply equally to everyone regardless of status. They also promote 'negative' freedoms and so do not demand excessive interference from the state. The problem is, of course, that the protections under the civil and political rights sections of human rights instruments are difficult to claim for labour subjects (because of the complexity of the public court system and the stringent nature of legal criteria to claim), and they also do not reflect the majority of labour's concerns. Indeed, it has been suggested that, in order for civil and political rights to bring real benefits, these must be 'integrated' with social rights protections (such as the right to work and the right to health).[121]

---

[119]   An example is the case of *Jivraj v Hashwani* [2012] IRLR 827. In this case, it was decided that the arbitrator was an independent provider of services in order that the arbitration clause in the commercial agreement would not be void. However, the effect of this decision may be that it is harder for Claimants to fall within the definition of employment under the Equality Act 2010.

[120]   A good example is in the case of the protection of domestic workers which will be discussed in more detail in Chapter 6.

[121]   V Mantouvalou, 'Labour Rights in the European Convention on Human Rights: An Intellectual Justification for an Integrated Approach to Interpretation' (2013) *Human Rights Law Review* 529; V Mantouvalou, 'Work and Private Life: Sidabras and Dziautas v Lithuania' (2005) 30 (4) *European Law Review* 573

However, 'social rights' protections traditionally fit less well with efficiency theory.[122] They reach into spheres which might be considered 'private' under economic theory and are therefore outside the proper scope of government intervention. They also often require some level of market interference and active redistribution of economic resources through positive government action. This suggests that the instigation of social rights could be a drain on economic functioning and economic freedoms (such as the freedom of contract). There is also the question about the justiciability of social rights. These kinds of rights can be viewed as creating obligations which are too vague or too complex to be directly enforceable in the courts. These rights are progressive in nature and are best dealt with by political direction rather than judicial enforcement. Indeed, it has been argued that the courts lack the institutional capability to assess the detail of budgetary allocation or to evaluate whether that allocation meets the requirement of 'justice'.[123] Efficiency theorists are therefore likely to view social rights negatively: they not only require excessive interference in market processes, they also result in inefficient outcomes in terms of economic growth.

That said, there has recently been the suggestion that labour rights as 'social rights' should not be rejected on the basis that they are a drain on economic functioning. Under the 'capabilities approach' first suggested by Deakin and Wilkinson,[124] it is argued that workers are vulnerable because they do not achieve their economic potential, which results from a lack of 'capabilities'. This is both a personal problem for workers, and also an economic problem, because it highlights the absence of (economic) institutions which can further individual and economic progress. This is particularly the case in the knowledge economy, where the effective functioning of individuals, and the development of their skills, is essential to economic competitiveness.[125] This kind of capabilities argument has been used to suggest particular developments in the way

---

[122]   H Collins, 'Theories of Rights as Justifications for Labour Law' in B Langille and G Davidov (eds), *The Idea of Labour Law* (Oxford University Press 2011)

[123]   J Fudge, 'The New Discourse of Labour Rights: From Social to Fundamental Rights' (2007–8) 29 *Comparative Labor Law and Policy Journal* 29, 45

[124]   S Deakin and F Wilkinson, *The Law of the Labour Market: Industrialization, Employment and Legal Evolution* (Oxford University Press 2005)

[125]   C Barnard, S Deakin and R Hobbs, 'Capabilities and Rights: An Emerging Agenda for Social Policy' (2000) 32 (5) *Industrial Relations Journal* 464, 466

that labour law should be constructed.[126] This includes expanding the ambit of discrimination law so that it guarantees both a level of substantive and formal freedom, where market circumstances allow.[127] However, although such a capabilities approach may allow a more positive development of economic efficiency theory in relation to the regulation of precarious work, it is important to recognise its limitations. This capabilities theory starts from the position that regulation must fit with economic functioning, and individual 'resources' are measured according to that functioning. This is a rather reductionist view, and one which limits thinking about the nature of the labour subject and the relationship of the labour subject to law.

The next sections discuss approaches which attempt to engage in detail with the complexity of the vulnerability of the labour subject, which is acted on not only by 'external' elements but is also affected by the ever-changing relationship between internal or personal vulnerability and those external pressures on individual subjects. Section 3.5 will concentrate on the theory of the sociology of law as applied to labour: social law. This section will look at how the particular goals of labour law are linked to the personal and group vulnerability of individual labour subjects. Section 3.6 will investigate the theory of the vulnerable subject and the added value that this theory could bring to the theorisation of solutions to vulnerability and (therefore) precarious work.

3.5   GOALS OF SOCIAL LAW AND VULNERABILITY THEORY

3.5.1   The Centrality of Mid-spectrum Goals for Labour

It appears that there are real problems with traditional labour law theories and efficiency theories in terms of meeting the needs of workers generally and precarious workers specifically. Traditional labour law has become too selective and, therefore, very inflexible in the face of various social and economic changes. For example, the reliance on trade union action harks back to a particular social era when trade union density was higher and there was a social compromise which allowed trade unions a central place in social organisation. With the decline in the homogeneity of the workforce, and other wider social pressures, autonomous trade

---

[126]   Ibid 466

[127]   S Deakin, 'Contracts and Capabilities: An Evolutionary Perspective on the Autonomy-Paternalism Debate' (2010) 3 (2) *Erasmus Law Review* 141, 152

union action no longer appears to be a panacea for the operation of industrial systems. Likewise, the use of law as a means of worker protection provides difficulties when definitions of 'worker' or 'employee' exclude those most in need of protection. This ignores wider social or mid-spectrum goals and decreases the legitimacy of labour law. In relation to efficiency theories, the translation of universalistic to selective goals is problematic. These universalistic goals favour the maximisation of economic production and therefore tend towards the maintenance of the status quo except in the most extreme cases of labour market abuse. Any selective approaches therefore have at best only marginal impact.

The difficulty that presents itself is how to create labour law which is selective, but also flexible and able to achieve wider (mid-spectrum) ends. Two (related) approaches will be discussed in this section which aim to do just that. The first approach will be that suggested by 'social law' and the second will be the 'vulnerable subject' approach. On these approaches, it is not possible to see the labour subject as separate from the society in which that subject acts. Individuals are seen as multi-dimensional agents who must be treated according to their relationship with other individuals and with society as a whole. Only regulation which allows individuals agency and resilience under constantly changing social conditions will be accepted, as it is only this kind of regulation which will allow individuals to find their place in society and therefore society to function properly.

3.5.2 Mid-spectrum Goals Under Social Law

Theorists in this social law tradition reject the tenets upon which classical labour law and economic efficiency views of labour law are based. First, they reject the universalism and individualism of liberal theory espoused under economic efficiency views. They argue that law based on liberal ideals not only fails to accurately reflect social and individual processes, but it is also damaging to the labour subject. It is damaging because it is based on the separation of a public realm of law represented by universal values from a private realm of arbitrary desires which is excluded from the law. Where private law does intervene, it is ultimately state directed rather than directed by society itself. Law is not only externally imposed, it also reflects external rather than internal vulnerabilities, or fails to reflect any actual vulnerabilities at all. Under the social law approach, law gains its legitimacy from society itself. As a result, the more (social) law that there is, the more sophisticated society is and the greater social progress. Secondly, social lawyers reject the idea that inequalities in society are fixed as might be espoused under classical labour law. They view the (Marxist) idea that society is divided into classes which are economically determined as reductionist and out of step with social reality. On this social law view, groups are formed on all sorts of different lines, and associations may have more or less economic value. The status of these groups is not predetermined and is subject to change depending on a variety of (social) factors.

The social law scheme is founded on the idea of the individual as a social being. Individual welfare determines the proper operation of society, and the proper operation of society determines individual welfare. It follows that regulation under this scheme cannot be overly selective, because this ignores the wider position of the individual in society. It can also not be universalistic, as these propositions tend to maintain invalid inequalities imposed on society through external (market) forces. Rather, goals under the social law scheme (and indeed under the vulnerable subject approach discussed below) tend to be on the mid-spectrum: they aim to create benefits for individuals as well as society as a whole. Of course, mid-spectrum goals are extremely broad concepts and social law inevitably puts forward a particular view of the operation of those concepts to aid labour. For example, in relation to social inclusion, the idea is more aspirational than some social inclusion programmes. The idea of social inclusion policy for social law is not to tackle absolute disadvantage for certain groups (indeed, it is possible to argue that those in employment have already achieved a level of advantage over other groups).[128] Rather it aims to achieve the participation of all workers in social life through both state and collective action in the labour field.

The first element of social law is the belief that the law itself is a social function and it can be co-opted to serve social ends. According to Durkheim's scheme of organic solidarity, law emerges 'automatically' from the division of labour.[129] As workers increasingly interact with each other through exchange, the modes of interaction become cemented into rules of conduct. These rules of conduct allocate rights and duties and are systematically transformed into legal rules upon which society relies

---

[128]   H Collins, 'Discrimination, Equality and Social Inclusion' (2003) 66 (1) *Modern Law Review* 16, 22
[129]   Durkheim, *The Division of Labour in Society* (Macmillan Press Limited 1984 [1893]) 302

(through group mediation).[130] Ultimately, law becomes the external index of social solidarity and serves to reinforce the preferred social arrangement to the benefit of all.[131]

Furthermore, under the social law scheme, if solidarity is to be maintained, then the role of the state must increase beyond that envisaged by either efficiency or classical labour law theory.[132] The state is charged with maintaining the more considerable legal code which accompanies the division of labour and it is also increasingly charged with the reinforcement of solidarity itself.[133] This expansion of the role of the state and law under the social law scheme has been termed the *socialisation* of the law. This means that the functions of the law expand, as the 'true and only voice' of democracy; and the state becomes involved in a myriad of previously excluded activities.[134] Law can thus interfere in areas which were previously excluded by the traditions of classical private law, in particular labour law, which has been deemed one of the 'privileged legal fields' of this type of law.[135] It can also directly intervene in the market, which is strictly limited under a liberal conceptualisation of the role of law. Under liberal ideals, it is stipulated that the market is the best mechanism for the creation of wealth, and that regulation is essentially second best to market allocation.[136] Under the social law scheme, regulatory legitimacy stems not from the market, but through the interactions of society, and equilibrium is not based on economic but on societal factors. Indeed, the aim of social law is not the

---

[130]   A Rawls, 'Conflict as Foundation for Consensus: Contradictions of Industrial Capitalism in Book III of Durkheim's *Division of Labour* (2003) 29 *Critical Sociology* 295, 298

[131]   Durkheim (n 129) 24

[132]   Ehrlich states as follows: 'As the conviction grows stronger that everything that is in society concerns society, the idea appears that it would be a great advantage if the state should prescribe a unitary legal basis for each and every independent association in society.' E Ehrlich, *Fundamental Principles of the Sociology of Law* (Harvard University Press 1936 [1913]) 155–156

[133]   Durkheim states that: 'Life in general cannot enlarge in scope without legal activity similarly increasing in a corresponding fashion.' Durkheim (n 129) 25

[134]   M Zambioni, 'The Social in Social Law: An Analysis of a Concept in Disguise' (2008) 9 *Journal of Law and Society* 63, 80

[135]   D Kennedy, 'Three Globalizations of Law and Legal Thought: 1850–2000' in DM Trubek and A Santos (eds), *The New Law and Economic Development: A Critical Appraisal* (Cambridge University Press 2006) 21

[136]   T Prosser, 'Regulation and Social Solidarity' (2006) 33 (3) *Journal of Law and Society* 364, 378

establishment of economic equilibrium, but a stable social order. This allows intervention in the market on a number of bases (equality and equity) other than the maximisation of wealth, and means that the state can take charge of decisions about which areas of human interaction will be subject to the market and which de-marketised.[137]

Under the social law scheme then, there is an awareness of the dangers of the unhindered operation of market forces for individuals and for society as a whole. At an individual level, there is a recognition that workers are vulnerable in the capitalist system where they have no control over their work and do not work according to their capability, but purely according to the demands of 'external forces'. Under these conditions a worker becomes merely a 'lifeless cog' who will achieve no personal satisfaction from work.[138] Therefore, it is essential that workers are given the freedom to work according to their capabilities, because this in itself allows the worst excesses of commodification to be avoided. Furthermore, the freedom to work according to capability is important because it allows workers to find their position in society. As the economic position of workers is socially defined, the solutions must also be 'social' or recognise the social connection. Under the social law scheme, group membership becomes *the* category upon which juridical treatment depends.[139] Indeed, as the task of the law under the social law scheme is to recognise socially legitimate interests and give them the means to fulfil their social function, group membership becomes necessary for all.[140] It is the means by which 'rights' are recognised for different group members.

Durkheim devoted a whole new preface in the second edition of the *Division of Labour* to the position of 'secondary groupings' in both society and law. Durkheim argued that if the system of organic solidarity were to function correctly, then it could not be maintained by an all-controlling state. The state is too far removed from individuals and its powers are far too superficial to be able to create the necessary moral consensus.[141] Rather, society could only be sustained by the establishment of secondary groups which mediate between the individual and the state. Durkheim suggested that 'professional' groupings are most fitting

---

[137]   C Courtis, 'Social Rights as Rights' (date unknown) 37 <http://islandia. law.yale.edu.sela.ecourtis.pdf> accessed 7 December 2014
[138]   Durkheim (n 129) 306
[139]   Ibid 38
[140]   F Ewald, 'A Concept of Social Law' in G Teubner (ed), *Dilemmas of Law in the Welfare State* (Walter de Gruyter 1986) 58
[141]   Durkheim (n 129) liv

to serve this function. These professional groupings are an inevitable outcome of the increased contact between (working) individuals under the division of labour. They are also desirable in that they counteract many different kinds of vulnerability. For the individuals in the division of labour, they represent a 'source of satisfaction' and have a function in the prevention of both individual and group conflict.[142] These professional groupings also further social inclusion because they bring individuals closer to society and are directly involved in a number of educational and recreational activities.[143] Finally, they play a direct role in the political system and maintain the stability and accountability of democratic state function.[144]

3.5.3 Expanding the Boundaries of the 'Collective'

The theory of social law can be seen as generally sympathetic to trade unionism and collective bargaining practices. Indeed, collective bargaining and agreements in the field of labour law have been seen as 'a major practice of social law'[145] and the collective contract and its enforcement are a good example of the 'subject of the new Social Law'.[146] However, in practice, trade unions have largely failed to fulfil the functions envisaged on the social law scheme.[147] Although trade union strategies are now changing, trade unions have, in the past, failed to incorporate adequately different labour market interests. This has meant a steady decline in trade union membership and recurrent questions over the legitimacy of the trade union movement. Two reasons for this emerge:

(1) The inequality of access to collective bargaining, and the exclusion of workers from groups traditionally disadvantaged in the labour market.
(2) The traditional concerns and preoccupations of collective bargaining which have shied away from matters of equality and the protection of vulnerable groups, and have even sometimes endorsed

---

[142] Ibid xlii
[143] Ibid 24–27
[144] A Giddens, *Capitalism and Modern Social Theory: An Analysis of Marx, Durkheim and Weber* (Cambridge University Press 1971) 104
[145] Ewald (n 140) 55
[146] O Boulanger, 'Notes on Social Law' (1920) 40 *Canadian Law Times* 399, 400
[147] A Blackett and C Sheppard, 'Collective Bargaining and Equality' (2003) 142 (4) *International Labour Review* 419, 420

racist and exclusionary anti-immigration policies where these were seen as a threat to the dominant workers in a particular industry.[148]

The inequality of access to collective bargaining stemmed from the original design and application of collective bargaining machinery, which overlooked or excluded certain categories of workers because they were not part of the dominant paradigm.[149] This dominant paradigm followed the post-war social consensus which viewed the labour force as unfragmented and composed of full-time male workers in regular employment.[150] It was, therefore, not seen as problematic to exclude women, for example, from involvement in collective bargaining, because either they were involved in non-productive work in the home or their involvement in the labour market was temporary and contingent, and simply a supplement to the work of the male breadwinner.[151] Traditional liberal/ Fordist accounts also presumed homogeneity in society, and failed to acknowledge labour market segmentation on racial, ethnic or other grounds.[152] Furthermore, trade unions have, in the past, argued that 'identity politics' undermine class-based interests and worker solidarity.[153] The interest of vulnerable groups in 'equality' has been problematic. This interest has resulted in the association of these claims with the pursuit of individualistic human rights goals rather than the collective or social goals of collective bargaining.[154] Finally, trade unions have traditionally operated at workplace level and reflected the needs of the workers of a particular industry. It has been argued that this is difficult to reconcile with wider issues of inequality (of under-represented groups), which are often systemic in nature.[155] The result is that trade unions have not traditionally been effective in promoting the interests of vulnerable groups.[156]

---

[148]   Ibid 433

[149]   Ibid 422

[150]   J Fudge, 'Reconceiving Employment Standards Legislation: Labour Law's Little Sister and the Feminization of Labor' (1991) 7 *Journal of Law and Social Policy* 73, 77

[151]   Ibid 77

[152]   Blackett and Sheppard (n 147) 425

[153]   Ibid 435

[154]   Ibid 434

[155]   Ibid 433

[156]   C Bonner, 'Domestic Workers around the World: Organising for Empowerment' (30 April 2010) 9 <http://www.dwrp.org.za/images/stories/DWRP_Research/chris_bonner.pdf> accessed 20 January 2014

Of course, a trade union strategy which shies away from the representation of particular group interests can never be successful on the social law scheme, as failure to represent particular interests suggests that the particular group (the trade union) has insufficient flexibility to change in line with labour market conditions. It also suggests that the group does not understand the way in which arguments on the basis of equality (not solely represented by individualistic notions of formal equality) are essential to all kinds of status in society. More recently, trade unions have started to recognise these arguments, and the importance of the representation of group interest for its own legitimacy. Trade unions have now been involved in advocating for minority rights; for instance, they were central in lobbying for legislation determining equal rights for agency workers in the UK. They have also increasingly attempted to encourage membership among previously excluded groups.[157] This is true in terms of agency workers in the UK, but it is also true on a much wider, global scale. A good example is provided by the increasing willingness of trade unions to countenance membership by domestic workers, a group previously unrecognised. More information will be provided on these new trade unions in Chapter 6, but suffice to say that domestic worker unions now exist in South Africa (the South Africa Domestic Service and Allied Workers Union) and in Hong Kong (the Hong Kong Domestic Workers General Union).[158] Domestic workers have also been able to join unions with a wider focus in Kenya (the Kenya Union of Domestic, Hotels, Educational Institutions, Hospitals and Allied Workers) and India (the Self Employed Women's Association).

However, one of the benefits of the social law scheme over other 'group' schemes is precisely that it does not dictate the form of group interests or the form of representation of those interests. This leaves room for workers to organise outside the trade union movement, and to improve or expand the functions of such groups. There have been a number of instances where that organisation has been successful. For example, in Chapter 6, the strategies of organisation among domestic workers will be discussed. These strategies reveal that domestic workers have been successful at organising within member-based organisations

---

[157] Indeed, it is worth noting that female membership has overtaken male trade union membership in the UK. In 2012, 28 per cent of female employees were trade union members, as opposed to 22 per cent of male employees. BIS, 'Trade Union Membership 2014' (June 2015) 5 <https://www.gov.uk/government/uploads/system/uploads/attachment_data/file/431564/Trade_Union_Membership_Statistics_2014.pdf> accessed 19 August 2015

[158] Bonner (n 156) 9

outside the confines of the trade union movement.[159] They have also set up worker co-operatives which extend the functions normally associated with trade unions. These worker co-operatives not only act to market domestic workers' services and provide training sessions for workers,[160] they also have a social and political agenda that seeks to improve working conditions for all domestic workers. Arguably, these worker cooperatives operate in just the way groups should work on the social law scheme. They represent a set of professionals who have a particular set of interests which include improving working conditions, but which extend beyond the workplace. This kind of organisation therefore represents a real opportunity for these workers to improve not only employment status but also social status, and achieve full integration into social life.

3.5.4   Legislating for Equality and Mid-spectrum Goals

There is a further implication of the social law scheme for the consideration of solutions to vulnerability under this section. This is the place and function of regulation based on equality. Under the social law scheme, the state has a much greater role in the consideration of the function and effect of inequalities in society; with the rejection of liberal conceptualisations of universality both material inequalities and legal inequalities can be considered. Equality law becomes central to the function of the state on the social law scheme. This kind of law is seen as particularly useful because it allows a consideration of group relationships; it is more concerned with rights *between* groups than (absolute) rights for individuals. Furthermore, equality law has the potential to correct settlements and balances between groups which are artificially created (for example, through inherited wealth). On the social law scheme, the state is given the space to intervene to equalise or compensate for social inequalities which are considered undesirable, and which might have been historically generated, and to intervene in diverse areas of social life, not limited by the liberal public/private distinction.[161] Judicial regulation on the basis of social law uses state power to equalise disparate situations, through better opportunities for passed-over social groups, or to make up for the

---

[159]   Ibid 6

[160]   An example here is the Choices Cooperative in Calfornia's San Fransisco Bay Area. See P Smith, 'Organizing the Unorganizable: Private Paid Household Workers and Approaches to Employee Representation' (2000) 79 *North Carolina Law Review* 45, 87

[161]   Courtis (n 137) 38

differences in power between groups.[162] This correction is important to the social law scheme, because it implies that all persons have the opportunity to participate properly in social life, and contributes to the overall (mid-spectrum) aim of the elimination of social exclusion.

Although it is possible to see some elements of 'social law' in modern equality (anti-discrimination) law, it is important to point out that modern equality (anti-discrimination) law reflects a whole range of different aims which may or may not achieve the aims of this scheme. For example, the principle of formal equality which underpins much modern anti-discrimination law represents liberal ideals and only weakly responds to any aspirations under social law. At the level of employer and employee, the notion that likes should be treated alike is no more than a relative principle and does not distinguish between treating people equally badly and treating them equally well.[163] It does not guarantee any substantive outcome for different labour market groups. Formal equality is also based on individual notions of justice. The individualised nature of this kind of justice means that such laws have little moral force on the social law scheme, and they introduce a number of practical problems due to the abstract nature of their operation and the cost (social and economic) of their enforcement.[164] On the other hand, there are some ways in which a system of formal equality could meet social law aspirations. If the principle of formal equality is applied at the point of recruitment, for example, this would mean that no considerations based on prejudice would be allowed to interfere in the assessment of a person's ability to do a particular job. All people would therefore have the opportunity to work according to their capabilities. This would contribute to the establishment of a procedure for achieving equality of opportunity for all.

However, equality of opportunity in the social law scheme generally accords much better with group-based models of justice rather than liberal models such as 'formal equality'. These group-based models have been incorporated into modern discrimination law to a greater or lesser extent to counteract the harshness of the formal equality rule and the problems associated with its enforcement.[165] They aim towards social inclusion rather than equal treatment, suggesting that 'equality' requires not just a fair process (through formal equality), but must also have a

---

[162]   Ibid 40–41

[163]   S Fredman, 'Equality: A New Generation?' (2001) 30 (2) *ILJ* 145, 155

[164]   M Bell and L Waddington, 'Reflecting on Inequalities in European Equality Law' (2003) 28 (3) *European Law Review* 349, 351

[165]   McHarg A and Nicolson D, 'Justifying Affirmative Action: Perceptions and Reality' (2006) 33 (1) *Journal of Law and Society* 1

substantive or redistributive goal in order to achieve an improvement in the relative position of vulnerable groups.[166] This aim of social inclusion appears to be in line with the aim of social law towards a particular social (rather than just individual) outcome. In terms of the equality of opportunity required under the social law scheme, there is the recognition that a certain level of redistribution is required for its achievement, as 'equality' can be influenced by different starting points between different groups. This can be illustrated by Durkheim's criticism of the institution of inherited wealth. For Durkheim, this institution presents a real barrier to equality of opportunity and the achievement of social order. Such an institution obscures the social value of exchange because those with fewer resources have a lower bargaining power and are therefore obliged to accept conditions which are unfavourable. That in turn means that the individual is not working at his level of capability and feels constrained. That constraint is terminal to solidarity: 'In the final analysis what constitutes liberty is the subordination of external to social forces, for it is only in this condition that the latter can develop freely.'[167]

The problem is that when equality of opportunity is used alongside liberal notions of equality, it has not always been able to achieve any of its redistributive goals. Firstly, there is a continual tension between goals of formal equality and more substantive notions of equality. Courts are therefore involved in a balancing act between the two ideals, and will most likely try to avoid the 'dangerous sacrifice' of the principle of equal treatment.[168] Secondly, liberal notions persist in the requirement that an action is pursued by an individual complainant regardless of whether the aim of the legislation is equal treatment or equality of opportunity. For example, the notion of 'indirect discrimination' in UK discrimination law seeks to reduce institutional barriers to discrimination and thereby achieve greater equality opportunity for disadvantaged groups. However, the legislation requires an *individual* to show that the rule or practice disproportionately affects one of the protected groups and does not permit class action. This presents a limitation of the transformative power of such a rule to challenge institutional discrimination, particularly given the difficulties for individuals to access the justice system.[169] Thirdly, liberal or neo-liberal governments have used the rhetoric of substantive

---

[166]   C McCrudden, *Buying Social Justice: Equality, Government Procurement and Legal Change* (Oxford University Press 2007) 70

[167]   Durkheim (n 129) 321

[168]   H Collins, 'Discrimination, Equality and Social Inclusion' (2003) 66 *MLR* 16, 18

[169]   Bell and Waddington (n 164) 254

equality while continuing with an individualist agenda, which has further reduced the impact of these notions for improving the position of vulnerable groups. This equality of opportunity approach is based on an *individualistic* notion of equality. It seeks to ensure individual autonomy; that all individuals (regardless of gender, ethnicity, sexual orientation and age) should be free to determine their labour market outcomes.[170] It is also based on the ideal that markets produce a fair distribution of wealth for most people, provided that everyone has a fair opportunity to participate.[171] Although the equal opportunity approach seeks to remove formal barriers to progress, this is largely pursued as a procedural notion and does not guarantee any substantive fairness of outcome.[172] Where a substantive outcome is pursued, this is justified on the basis of 'merit'. However, this criterion of 'merit' is very problematic. For vulnerable groups who have suffered disadvantage in the past, they may not have had the opportunity to acquire 'merit' and therefore remain in a preju-diced position. As a result, the substantive potential of equality of opportunities, that is, to ensure that all persons from all sections of society have a genuinely equal chance of satisfying the criteria for access to a particular social good, cannot be attained.[173]

3.5.5 The Promise of Vulnerability Theory

Vulnerability theory shares a great deal with the social law approach. The starting point for this theory is that liberal models of justice fail, a view shared under the social law approach. However, vulnerability theory places particular emphasis on the failure of liberal theory as a result of its foundation in the myth of the autonomous, independent (and invulner-able) subject.[174] The example of anti-discrimination law is used to

---

[170]   A Coffey, *Reconceptualising Social Policy: Sociological Perspectives on Contemporary Social Policy* (Open University Press 2004) 63

[171]   H Collins, 'Is There a Third Way in Labour Law?' in J Conaghan, RM Fischel and K Klare (eds), *Labour Law in an Era of Globalization: Transformative Practices and Possibilities* (Oxford University Press 2004) 452

[172]   S Fredman, *Discrimination Law* (Oxford University Press 2002) 15

[173]   B Hepple, 'Discrimination and Equality of Opportunity – Northern Irish Lessons' (1990) 10 *Oxford Journal of Legal Studies* 408, 411

[174]   C Mackenzie, W Rogers and S Dodds, 'Introduction: What is Vulnerability and Why Does It Matter for Moral Theory' in C Mackenzie, W Rogers and S Dodds (eds), *Vulnerability: New Essays in Ethics and Feminist Philosophy* (Oxford University Press 2014) 5

illustrate this point. The argument is that the foundation of anti-discrimination on the liberal subject means that it is far too individualistic. It does not challenge systemic problems of inequality effectively. It is also limited in that it fails to address the multi-dimensional nature of vulnerability and, as it is tethered to historically defined and context-specific categories, tends to be divisive rather than constructive. According to vulnerability theory, social inequalities should not be viewed as inevitable and beyond challenge. Rather they should be viewed as 'produced and reproduced by society and its institutions'.[175] Equality law should be more active in addressing inequality and building institutional arrangements which serve to reinforce resilience.[176] The vulnerable subject approach also reflects the preoccupations of social law with relationships beyond the individual and towards the group. Within vulnerability theory there is a recognition of the embedded nature of the vulnerable subject in society. As a result of this recognition, vulnerability theory points to the need to capture the potential of social arrangements to build resilience and mediate vulnerability. This requires a recognition of the complexity of institutional and group arrangements, and also that, while society and other institutions cannot eradicate vulnerability, they do 'mediate, compensate and lessen our vulnerability'.

However, it is argued that the vulnerable subject approach actually takes the social law approach presented above further in a number of ways. First, there are a number of layers of vulnerability presented by the vulnerable subject approach which do not feature under the approach of social law as conceived in the above section.[177] For example, the vulnerable subject approach is particularly concerned with vulnerability over a person's lifecycle. This vulnerability is personal (affected by both old age and childhood), but it is also institutional (how institutions deal with those groups affects their resilience over time). Work 'quality' or work 'satisfaction' can be developed and supported through the lifecycle of the worker. Second, there is a concern with the implication of the state and its institutions in the *creation* of vulnerability. On the social law

---

[175]   M Fineman, 'The Vulnerable Subject: Anchoring Equality in the Human Condition' (2008) 20 (1) *Yale Journal of Law and Feminism* 2, 5

[176]   Ibid 21

[177]   It is worth noting that there are many definitions of 'social law'. In this book, the normative vision of social law is adopted, and relies on Durkheim's and Ehrlich's approach which was subsequently adopted by authors such as Ewald. It is also possible to present social law as the entirety of a country's labour and social security laws. This notion is broader but does not of itself have normative content.

scheme, law is dependent on the negotiations of the different (group) interests in society, and the recognition by the state of certain of those interests as being in need of protection. The difficulty is that this reliance on the state's recognition of legitimate interests has the potential to undermine the aspirations of this theory. As weaker social groups have no independent 'higher' principle of law on which to base their negotiations (these being liberal absolutist concepts rejected on the scheme of social law), and the creation of law is dependent on those negotiations, it would appear to favour the stronger groups in co-opting the law for themselves. At best, this fails to deal with inequalities in a socially useful way. At worst, it actually increases social vulnerability. By contrast, on the vulnerable subject approach, there is place for pre-determined and pre-defined rights in the regulation of labour law, as long as these also respond to both individual and social experience.

3.5.6 Vulnerability and the Lifecycle Approach

One of the basic concerns of the social law approach is that workers should achieve satisfaction through work, and that this is necessary for social solidarity. This implies a level of job quality. However, neither of the solutions suggested so far (collective negotiation and reliance on equality law) address this requirement specifically. Furthermore, on the social law scheme above, the development of a worker's career and job satisfaction is viewed in a linear way. Each person is seen as imbued with certain 'capabilities' which form the basis for the correct job match. Once a person finds a job which meets those capabilities then job satisfaction is (permanently) guaranteed. Of course, this kind of approach does not recognise the insight provided by vulnerability theory that there is in fact a 'wide range of differing and interdependent abilities over the span of a lifetime'.[178] According to vulnerability theory, a person's capability is not fixed or permanent and the development of capabilities is dependent on a number of factors (for example, institutional support for capability or changes in a person's lifecycle which affect capabilities). Indeed, according to this vulnerability theory, the suggestion that capability is a fixed and immovable element illustrates a 'belief that our rationality as thinking beings is somehow independent of our animality'.[179] This belief is the reason why current moral theory is flawed, and the reason why there is a need for a new approach to contemporary moral and political

---

[178] M Fineman (n 175) 12
[179] A MacIntyre, *Dependent Rational Animals: Why Human Beings Need the Virtues* (Open Court Chicago 1999) 5

theory which understands the vulnerability and dependency of all subjects through their lifecycle.

The question is, then, how to translate this approach to vulnerability
and dependency into labour law.[180] One approach which addresses some
of these concerns is that suggested by Alain Supiot in his book *Beyond
Employment*.[181] The starting point of this work is the argument (from
efficiency theory) that developments in the labour market have increased
the level of flexibility demanded from labour market participants. In a
post-Fordist world, there is a great deal more internal flexibility (different
jobs within the same employment entity) and external flexibility (for
example, in the casualisation of work). Individuals are expected to avail
themselves of the opportunities that this flexibility presents (for example,
by undergoing training between assignments), but are not given any
security guarantees to allow them to do so.[182] The result is that the
capabilities of individuals are compromised. Supiot suggests that labour
law should be redesigned to reflect this vulnerability and allow individuals security between transitions in the labour market. The solutions
suggested are far-reaching and ambitious and go far beyond what would
be suggested by efficiency solutions to precarious work.

Supiot suggests that the idea of labour market status should not be tied
to a particular job, but should be based on the entire career of an
individual. He suggests that new legal instruments should be designed to
ensure that labour market status continues between periods of 'work' and
'non-work'. The value of 'non-work' elements should be recognised by
the state. It is also recognised in Supiot's work that there needs to be
public support for collective bargaining mechanisms which help individuals in the face of increasing flexibilisation of the labour market.
Finally, there is the conviction that the state should provide overall
support for the increased vulnerability of individuals through a set of
social rights. It is envisaged that these social rights would be the subject
of continual negotiation between individuals and the state, and that this
negotiation would be facilitated through intermediate agencies. These
social rights would provide substantive guarantees to all individuals,

---

[180]   The relationship between vulnerability theory and employment law has
also been explored (in the American context) in J Fineman, 'The Vulnerable
Subject at Work: A New Perspective on the Employment-at-Will Debate' (2013)
43 *Saskatchewan Law Review* 275
[181]   A Supiot, *Beyond Employment: Changes in Work and the Future of
Labour Law in Europe* (Oxford University Press 2001)
[182]   Ibid 221

based on the basic principles in the EU Charter of the Fundamental Social Rights of Workers.

This approach is particularly interesting in the context of this book. It appears to address some of the concerns of vulnerability theory, while recognising the specific labour market situation in which workers currently find themselves. It therefore appears to suggest a way forward in the intersection between labour law, vulnerability and precarious work. The state is tasked with responding to the particular vulnerabilities arising from labour market changes. The involvement of the state is multi-functional and involves elements which would be disregarded on an efficiency-based approach. For example, the state is tasked with the recognition of activity which might be considered 'non-work', and therefore not be recognised under a more liberal efficiency-based approach. The recognition of this 'non-work' is based not on its contribution to economic profit in the short term, but in terms of its long-term social and economic benefits. Furthermore, the state is tasked with helping associations of workers to flourish. On an efficiency based approach, these associations would at best be viewed with scepticism, and at worst would be viewed as damaging to economic efficiency and therefore undesirable. Finally, there is the suggestion that the instigation of social rights is fundamental to the development of any new labour status. These social rights ensure a basic level of protection for all, but are also viewed with scepticism on a more efficiency-based approach. A more detailed examination of the promise of social rights for achieving the aims of vulnerability theory in the context of the labour market will be discussed further in the next section.

3.5.7   A More Integrated Approach: The Vulnerable Subject and Social Rights

Under the efficiency paradigm, solutions to precarious work might consider the protection of workers' human rights but would not advocate the protection of their social rights. On the one hand, the idea of human rights fits with the liberal paradigm from which efficiency theories emanate. Human rights are individual rights which are universal and immutable. The aim of human rights is the protection of negative freedom and therefore they do not require government intervention which would be seen as damaging on the liberal view. On the other hand, social rights advance different ideals and require different kinds of action by the state. Social rights (the right to work, the right to health) advance the ideal of positive freedom, or, in other words, equipping individuals with the resources to allow them to pursue their life plans. In contrast to human rights, social rights can require distributive action by the state, and in that sense can be resource-demanding. It is argued that these social rights are damaging to economic functioning, and may not qualify as 'rights' at all.[183] By contrast, advocates of vulnerability theory are much more likely to recognise the value of social rights. The vulnerable subject is recognised as one who builds capabilities and resources through a lifetime. The greater the access to resources, the greater resilience that an individual will have. The instigation of social rights might allow individuals to build resilience, and is justified on that basis.

In this sense, although the vulnerable subject approach might use the language of 'capability', it differs from the capabilities approach as traditionally applied to labour law (under the efficiency paradigm). On the vulnerable subject scheme, the end of the development of capabilities is not more efficient economic functioning (although that may be a by-product). The aim of the building of capabilities is an increase in autonomy and dignity of the labour subject. This increase in autonomy allows individuals to find greater internal resilience in the face of institutional, personal and economic change. It reduces the precarity of labour in a more sustainable way than that suggested under the traditional capabilities approach. Furthermore, under the vulnerable subject approach, the state plays an active role in the development of capabilities, and that role is not determined solely by economic motivations. As the labour subject is not the atomised, autonomous being of liberal theory, resilience can only be built by the interaction of personal, relational and institutional elements, and the institutional recognition of the value of building capability of workers in the widest sense.

The vulnerable subject approach also contrasts with the social law approach on the question of rights. According to the social law approach, rights are not absolute but are benefits to be bargained for during negotiation processes. The idea is that there is a move away from rarefied liberal rights towards rights which have meaning for individuals and groups. However, the downside of this approach is that the bargaining power of weaker groups in society can become compromised. If those weaker groups do not have a minimum standard against which to measure and contest for their position, their claims might be lost. This actually increases rather than decreases their vulnerability, as it denies them the means through which they might improve their resilience. Under vulnerability theory, the instigation of strong rights can provide assets to individuals which can, in turn, increase their capability set.

---

[183]   C Gearty and V Mantouvalou, *Debating Social Rights* (Hart 2011) 87

There is, therefore, no foundational or fundamental distinction between the value of civil and political as opposed to social rights (both can build resilience). The important element is that the access to these rights is as broad as possible, because only then will mid-spectrum goals (such as social inclusion and democracy) be achieved. Indeed, rights themselves become mid-spectrum goals because they build individual capability as well as social capability and resilience.

Under vulnerability theory, law must be expanded to be socially useful and effective at tackling vulnerability. This implies that it must be expanded to achieve the maximum mid-spectrum goals (that is, goals that recognise simultaneous benefits to labour and to society as a whole). This allows law to have a social conscience while meeting individuals' vulnerabilities. It also combines a number of components of the different theories stated in this chapter. It allows an opportunity for the development of (industrial) democracy as advocated on the classical view, without abandoning the space for law to also aim towards social inclusion (the setting of minimum standards through labour law). It can provide recognition for particular social vulnerabilities as they develop and change over time, and is therefore able to take the insights of efficiency theory without being constrained by its liberal foundations. It provides a tool for examining all the possible connotations of 'precarious work', recognising that such precarity can be a systemic rather than isolated problem (and can attach to all levels of work). Finally, vulnerability theory is able to take advantage of the insights of social law, recognising the positive elements of work and the need for individuals in the labour system to build resilience for themselves. However, contrary to the assertions of social law, vulnerability theory recognises the danger as well as the value of the creation of 'rights as swords'. According to vulnerability theory, rights must be used in the best way to maximise the avoidance of all vulnerability, and that instigation of resilience is ultimately in the public interest.

In the chapters that follow, there will be an examination of how far current attempts to regulate for vulnerability or precarious work meet the precepts of vulnerability theory. In Chapter 4, this examination will consider the law at each geographical level: (1) national level (focussing on the UK); (2) supra-national level (focussing on the EU); and (3) international level (focussing on the ILO). These elements will then be taken forward to consider vulnerability in the context of two case studies. The first case study will look at the position of temporary agency workers, and the second will investigate the position of domestic workers. Both of these groups have variously been labelled as precarious or vulnerable in the literature. There will be a focus here on how far the law builds resilience for these workers, and aims towards the achievement of the mid-spectrum goals of social inclusion, democracy and rights.

3.6 CONCLUSIONS

This chapter exposed the relationship between the theorisations of labour subject vulnerability introduced in Chapter 2 and the construction of solutions to that vulnerability. In Chapter 2 it was argued that classical labour law theory and efficiency theory are underpinned by the idea of the existence of a (liberal) autonomous subject. Under classical labour law that autonomy is threatened by the operation of the exploitative and commodifying processes of capitalism. Two mechanisms for the protection of autonomy in particular are suggested: the development of collective bargaining and labour law, which counteracts the worst pressures of capitalism for workers. Under efficiency theory, there is a similar belief in the inherent and sui generis nature of worker autonomy. However, under efficiency theory, this identification of worker autonomy suggests different results. Under this theory, the autonomy of labour subjects means that they should largely be left to their own devices, except where elements of labour market 'abuse' can be detected (even then regulation may not be through a system of labour law but may rely on the human rights regime). It is only when labour subjects are free from state interference in employment relationships that they can properly develop their autonomy and benefit from all that the market systems have to offer. The approach to autonomy under vulnerability theory (as introduced in Chapter 2) is different. Under vulnerability theory (and, to a certain extent, social law), all individuals are inherently vulnerable. They rely on individual, social and institutional factors to build their resilience and autonomy. This implies that solutions must enable the development of resilience in all of these (individual, social and institutional) dimensions. As a result, the solutions to vulnerability tend to be directed not just to individuals in narrowly defined work situations, but also towards broader mid-spectrum goals (democracy, social inclusion and rights).

It is suggested that the approach to labour law put forward under vulnerability theory has considerable advantages to approaches under either classical labour law theory or efficiency theories. The view of labour law solutions under the classical view suffers from a rather narrow frame: solutions are selective and based on serving specific worker interests. The problem with this approach is that this selectivity creates law and social institutions which are inflexible and unable to move with institutional or social changes. This is exposed, for example, by the reliance on a view of the importance of collective bargaining through trade unions. In the wake of a decline in trade union membership, questions are raised about the ability of trade unions to meet the needs faced by vulnerable/precarious workers. The opposite problems appear in relation to efficiency theory. Here, there is too much flexibility in terms of bending worker needs to market considerations. The result is a tendency towards deregulation or even solutions which favour employer prerogative on the basis of enhancing competitiveness. Real worker problems remain unaddressed. It is argued in this chapter that the best solution for labour problems lies in developing the tenets of social law through vulnerability theory. This enables solutions which correspond to the multi-dimensional nature of the labour subject and their social embeddedness. These solutions are better placed to allow sustainable worker progress. By promoting mid-spectrum goals (democracy, social inclusion and rights), there develops a more sustainable and flexible mechanism for ensuring the development of worker capabilities and social progress as a whole.

4. Vulnerability and precarious work in the law

4.1 INTRODUCTION

The aim of this chapter is to investigate the law and policy relating to precarious work and vulnerable workers at international, supranational and national levels. This law and policy will be positioned in relation to the possible theoretical perspectives on vulnerability introduced in the previous chapters of this book. In particular, there will be a comparison between the different geographical levels in terms of how far the law and policy aims towards selective, universalistic or mid-spectrum goals, and how far the law and policy suggest top-down or 'bottom-up' approaches to regulation. There will be a particular focus on the 'fit' of the law in these different jurisdictions with the vulnerability theory introduced in the previous chapters. It will be suggested that, at each geographical level, approaches which correspond to some degree with the vulnerable subject approach can be identified, but that a more comprehensive and systematic approach needs to be adopted if the precepts of vulnerability theory are to be properly realised.

Of course, this analysis is complicated by a number of factors. First, the law and policy of the different institutions responsible for regulation (and particularly the regulation of precarious work) at different geographical levels has changed over time. These changes reflect different social and economic developments, but also represent the development of a changing theoretical focus within the institutions concerned. For example, the Preamble of the ILO Constitution reflected an approach aligned with the classical view of labour law, namely the need to protect all workers disadvantaged by integration into a capitalist system of production. This focus changed with the development of Conventions specifically dealing with precarious work, and has since changed again with the move away from standard setting towards setting more general principles (for example, 'decent work'). Second, the separation of the different geographical levels is rather artificial. The law and policy adopted at each geographical level is extremely fluid, in the sense that one approach adopted at one geographical level influences the position at other geographical levels. For example, the existence of the Private Employment Agencies Convention at ILO level influenced the instigation and design of the Temporary Agency Workers Directive at EU level. Furthermore, ILO standards are increasingly being referred to in EU external relations, and are referred to consistently in EU jurisprudence. This chapter starts with an analysis of the ILO's approach to precarious work. This approach is considered first because it shows most clearly the development from the classical law position towards a concern for the regulation of precarious work. It also presents an interesting point of departure for thinking about the vulnerable subject approach, as recently law and policy emanating from this institution has moved away from a focus on standard setting towards an interest in job creation and social inclusion. The chapter then considers the position of the EU. The EU embraced the notion of the regulation of precarious work as part of the 'flexicurity' agenda (flexibility in the labour market combined with security for workers). However, despite the potential of that agenda for corresponding with the vulnerable subject approach, the reality has been to encourage flexibility over security and to privilege efficiency over protection. Finally, the position of law in relation to precarious work at UK level will be considered. The EU position has dramatically influenced the regulation of precarious work in its member states. Although many states embraced the flexicurity agenda and the legislation on precarious work, recent pressure from the EU in the wake of the financial crisis has forced an (even more) deregulatory stance to be adopted. This has arguably hit the most vulnerable (or the most precarious) the hardest. The vulnerable subject approach, despite its potential, is hardly recognisable in the law and policy relating to precarious work in the UK.

4.2 THE ILO AND LAW AND POLICY CONCERNING PRECARIOUS WORK

The foundations of the ILO rest on the classical labour law view of vulnerability. The constitution is based implicitly on the 'paradigm of subordinate labour',[1] under which work is simultaneously the site of: (1) the greatest social oppression; (2) the greatest inequality of bargaining power; (3) the most revolting excesses of power, and (4) the greatest

---

[1]   A Hyde, 'What is Labour Law' in G Davidov and B Langille (eds), *Boundaries and Frontiers of Labour Law* (Hart Publishing 2006) 46

social conflict.[2] The preamble to the constitution refers to the existence of 'injustice, hardship and privation [for] large numbers of people' forced to work under poor conditions, and calls for an 'urgent improvement of those conditions'.[3] These poor labour conditions are stated to be a threat in two ways: (1) they represent a threat to 'justice and humanity' for workers, and (2) they represent a wider threat to 'the peace and harmony of the world' through the unrest among workers subject to these conditions.[4]

The 'fundamental principle' of the ILO that 'labour is not a commodity'[5] derives from these foundations. It recognises the Marxian notion that under capitalism, labour is commodified, and aims to tackle that through the promotion of the 'dignity of labour and the recognition of its value'.[6] Although it identifies the reality of the buying and selling of labour, it argues that market mechanisms should be subordinate to the 'higher goals' of personal wellbeing and social justice for all.[7] Like the classical labour law theorists discussed in Chapter 2, the importance of freedom of association and collective bargaining in the achievement of these 'higher goals' is recognised.[8] Indeed, it has been argued that the ILO Conventions on freedom of association and the right to collective bargaining (C87 and C98) have achieved a 'special constitutional status'[9] or a 'status akin to the rules of customary international law' as a result of their 'normative effects'.[10] A particularly pertinent example of this

---

[2]   Ibid 46

[3]   ILO, 'Preamble' of the Constitution of the International Labour Organization, 1919 <http://www.ilo.org/ilolex/english/iloconst.htm> accessed 19 September 2012

[4]   Ibid

[5]   Ibid I (a) Annex to the Constitution: Declaration Concerning the aims and purposes of the International Labour Organization (Declaration of Philadelphia)

[6]   G Rodgers, E Lee, L Swepston and J Van Daele, *The ILO and the Quest for Social Justice 1919–2009* (International Labour Office 2009) 7

[7]   Ibid 7

[8]   ILO (n 3) The Annex to the ILO constitution determines that 'freedom of expression and of association are essential to sustained progress' at I (b)

[9]   B Langille, 'Core Labour Rights – The True Story (A Reply to Alston)' (2005) 16 (3) *European Journal of International Law* 409, 424

[10]   B Creighton, 'Freedom of Association' in R Blanpain and C Engels (eds), *Comparative Labour Law and Industrial Relations in Industrialised Market Economies* (Kluwer Law International 2001) 259 quoted in G Biffl and J Isaac, 'Globalization and Core Labour Standards: Compliance Problems with ILO Conventions 87 and 98. Comparing Australia and other English-speaking Countries with EU member states' (2005) 21 (3) *International Journal of Comparative Labour Law and Industrial Relations* 405, 438

special constitutional status is provided in terms of the enforcement mechanisms available at ILO level. Once a state has ratified a Convention, then the ILO has a complaints procedure which enables governments, trade unions and employer organisations (in addition to the ILO's governing body) to initiate complaints for violation of a Convention. In the case of freedom of association violations however, there is a special Committee on the Freedom of Association which considers these complaints. As a result of the constitutional status of this right to freedom of association, this Committee hears complaints even where a relevant convention has not been ratified.[11]

The ILO's commitment to freedom of association and worker voice may also theoretically be demonstrated by the tripartite nature of the organisation. Within this tripartite structure, worker representatives participate in ILO decisions alongside employers' organisations and government representatives and therefore, supposedly, have the opportunity to further the interests of workers and to 'add the perspectives of ... workers' rights to governments' priorities'.[12] However, the tripartite structure has been criticised. It has been argued that the tripartite structure of the organisation has actually inhibited its ability to help those most in need (or the most vulnerable). This structure simply reinforces the global hegemony of capital(ism) through the support of organised labour for corporatism and limited social reform (as opposed to the transformation of industrial relations under capitalism).[13] Furthermore, the tripartite structure implies that the ILO needs to achieve legitimacy among government representatives. At all times, therefore, there is a balance between responding to (liberal) government pressures, while also driving labour standards forward.

4.2.1 ILO and Conventions Concerning Precarious Work

Since its inception, the ILO has produced a whole range of Conventions to attempt to protect worker rights and improve working conditions.[14] Of

---

[11] G MacNaughton and D Frey, 'Decent Work, Human Rights, and the Millennium Development Goals' (2010) 7 *Hastings Race and Poverty Law Journal* 303, 313

[12] G Rodgers, E Lee, L Swepston and J van Daele, *The ILO and the Quest for Social Justice 1919–2009* (International Labour Office 2009) 16

[13] L Vosko, 'Decent Work: The Shifting Role of the ILO and the Struggle for Global Social Justice' (2002) 2 (1) *Global Social Policy* 19

[14] Some examples are ILO Convention 3 'Maternity Protection Convention' (International Labour Office 1921), ILO Convention 47 'Forty-Hour Week

particular interest to this book, however, are the Conventions concerning marginal workers adopted over the course of the 1990s: (1) the Part-time Work Convention (PWC),[15] (2) the Private Employment Agencies Convention (PEAC)[16] and (3) the Home Work Convention (HWC).[17] On the face of it, the introduction of these Conventions signals a move away from classical labour law preoccupations. For example, the Convention preambles all correspond to the understanding within efficiency theory (as applied to labour law) that 'atypical' work can be economically beneficial and should be encouraged, but under certain circumstances can be subject to abuse. It is that abuse which should be regulated to allow workers to take advantage of developments in the labour market. In the Preamble to the PWC, 'the economic importance of part-time work' and its role in 'facilitating additional employment opportunities' is recognised. However, it is suggested within this Convention that there does need to be protection for part-time workers in the areas of access to employment, working conditions and social security. Likewise, the PEAC starts by stating that the ILO recognises the 'role which private employment agencies may play in a well-functioning labour market', but that in certain circumstances, this should be balanced with the 'need to protect workers against abuses'. Furthermore, efficiency theory is evident in the fact that the protection afforded to workers under these Conventions is limited and based on formal equality mechanisms. There is some suggestion that minimum standards should be instigated for these kinds of workers, but those minimum standards tend to be subject to wide derogations. For example, in the PWC, it is stated that all part-time workers should receive comparable protection in relation to 'discrimination in employment'.[18] It is also stated that ratifying states should ensure that part-time workers receive conditions equivalent to comparable full-time workers in relation to maternity protection, termination of employment, paid annual leave and sick leave. However, states are permitted to derogate from those latter protections where the 'hours of work or

---

Convention' (International Labour Office 1935) and ILO Convention 155 'Occupational Health and Safety Convention' (International Labour Office 1981)

[15]   ILO Convention 175 'Convention Concerning Part-time Work' (International Labour Office 1994)

[16]   ILO Convention 181 'Convention Concerning Private Employment Agencies' (International Labour Office 1997)

[17]   ILO Convention 177 'Convention Concerning Home Work' (International Labour Office 1996)

[18]   Article 4

earnings are below specified thresholds'.[19] The level of those thresholds is not set by the Convention. All that is stated in the Convention is that those thresholds should be low enough that they do not exclude a large percentage of part-time workers.

That said, there are elements of these Conventions which suggest that the classical view still holds sway. There remains a distinct focus on the importance of collective bargaining. In relation to the PWC, there is no derogation permitted for member states in relation to ensuring the 'right to organise, the right to bargain collectively and the right to act as workers' representatives'.[20] That position also holds true in the PEAC.[21] The problem, of course, with this position in relation to 'precarious workers' is the great difficulty that such workers have in accessing collective bargaining mechanisms in the first place. As explained in Chapter 3, trade unions are not necessarily the best way in which such precarious workers can achieve empowerment. Indeed, this very fact was recognised in the provisions of the HWC (although the status of this Convention was later downgraded as will be explained below). In terms of the HWC, there are specific measures calling for ratifying countries to consult with 'the most representative organisations of employers and workers, and where they exist, with organisations concerned with home-workers and those of employers of homeworkers'.[22] The aim of this provision is to give groups concerned with the interests of homeworkers without trade union status the opportunity to be consulted, and hopefully allow this marginal group some voice.[23]

Despite this concession, the Conventions on precarious work are far from meeting the precepts of vulnerability theory. First, the provisions are not defined by vulnerability: member states are permitted to derogate from the Convention protections in relation to the most vulnerable workers (those part-time workers employed for the fewest hours). Second, there is insufficient attention to the achievement of mid-spectrum goals. For example, despite the reference in the Preamble of the PWC to

---

[19]   Article 8 PWC
[20]   Article 4 PEAC
[21]   Article 2(4)(a) PEAC provides that member states can 'exclude, under specific circumstances, workers in certain branches of economic activity, or parts thereof, from the scope of the Convention or from certain of its provisions, provided that adequate protection is otherwise assured for the workers concerned'. However, that does not apply to Article 4 (the right to freedom of association) and Article 5 (protection from discrimination).
[22]   Article 2 HWC
[23]   Vosko (n 13) 33

the need to consider wide areas such as access to employment and the provision of social security benefits for part-time workers, these areas hardly feature in the Convention itself. Democracy is not mentioned and 'rights' are narrowly defined. Indeed, it might be argued that the narrow focus on collective bargaining through trade unions as the best way to achieve resilience shows a lack of understanding of the particular nature of the vulnerabilities of these groups of workers. Finally, there is a real problem with the enforcement of these Conventions. The ILO relies on a set of 'soft law' measures to encourage the implementation of the Convention provisions. States are required to produce national reports on the status of implementation, which are then scrutinised by the Committee of Experts. The Committee on the Application of Standards follows up the observations made by the Committee of Experts and can ask countries to respond to the criticisms raised. However, the lack of legal sanctions means that the requests made by the CAS are often ignored.[24]

4.2.2   The Move Away from Standard Setting

More recently, there has been a retraction at ILO level from a focus on the creation of binding Conventions. Arguably, this change has been driven by a change in the traditional (political and economic) environment in which the ILO originally operated. With 'globalisation' and economic liberalisation (evidenced by privatisation, labour market deregulation and the decline of the welfare state), there has been a lack of appetite among the member states of the ILO for intervention through the creation of binding legal rights.[25] The results have been two-fold. On the

---

[24]   For example, in 2011, the CE expressed its concern that measures concerning the privatization of prison labour in the UK could threaten the UK's compliance with the Convention on Forced Labour. It requested that the UK take measures to ensure that: 'Formal, freely given and informed consent is required for the work of prisoners in privately operated prisons, as well as for all work of prisoners for private companies, both inside and outside prison premises, such consent being authenticated by the conditions of work approximating those of a free labour relationship, as regards wage levels (leaving room for deductions and attachments), social security and occupational safety and health.' The CE was forced to repeat this request in 2013 following a lack of satisfactory response from the UK. Cf CEACR: Individual Observation on the Forced Labour Convention 1930 (n 29) United Kingdom (ratification 1931) Submitted: 2011; CEACR: Individual Observation on the Forced Labour Convention 1930 (n 29) United Kingdom (ratification 1931) Submitted: 2013

[25]   MacNaughton and Frey (n 11) 314

one hand, there has been an increase in the use of non-binding Recommendations to deal with worker rights. On the other hand, there has been an attempt to move away from standard setting completely towards a broader framework for action. This broader framework for action is represented by the Decent Work agenda[26] and the Declaration of Fundamental Principles and Rights at Work (the Declaration).[27] These elements will be discussed in the next section.

The preference for the use of Recommendations to cover standard setting is illustrated by the decision to downgrade much of the detail of the HWC to a non-binding Recommendation.[28] A further example is provided by the attempts to regulate for 'concealed' or 'disguised' employment. At the 1998 International Labour Conference, there were calls for measures to bring concealed or disguised employment within the scope of employment legislation. However, at this conference, the calls to implement such legislation were rejected, driven by the assertion by Employers Groups that the problem of disguised employment was not a suitable subject for standard-setting activity.[29] A Report in 2003 suggested the 'collection and exchange of information and promotion of good practice' in the two areas of disguised employment relationships and triangular employment relationships to try to address the perceived legislative lacuna in this area.[30] This Report suggested that Conventions

---

[26] ILO, Decent Work Report of the Director General, International Labour Conference, (87th session, Geneva 1999) 6 <http://www.ilo.org/public/english/standards/relm/ilc/ilc87/rep-i.htm> accessed 23 February 2010

[27] ILO, *ILO Declaration on Fundamental Principles and Rights at Work and its Follow-up* (International Labour Office, Geneva 1998)

[28] ILO Recommendation 184, 'Recommendation Concerning Home Work' (International Labour Office, Geneva, 1996)

[29] ILO, 'Meeting of Experts on Workers in Situations Needing Protection (The Employment Relationship: Scope)' *Basic Technical Document* (International Labour Office, Geneva 2000) paras 69–70. Employers groups argued that regulation in this area would constitute an unwanted interference in commercial contracts and a threat to 'economic activity and job creation'. In addition, along with some government representatives, they stated that a Convention in this area would create a 'third category' of workers, who would have a lower level of protection than dependent workers. This would result not only in lower conditions for these workers, it would also mean that current 'dependent' workers would fall into this new third category, to the detriment of their rights.

[30] International Labour Conference (91st session), *Report V – The Scope of the Employment Relationship – Fifth Item on the Agenda* (Geneva 2003) 75

or Recommendations could be adopted in this area, but when a question-naire was circulated on this issue,[31] the majority of governments would only contemplate a Recommendation and not a binding Convention.[32] The outcome was the Recommendation concerning the employment relationship,[33] which suggested that national policy should include meas-ures to clarify employment status and combat disguised employment,[34] as well as ensure that mechanisms are in place to allow workers in 'all contractual arrangements, including those involving multiple parties ... the protection they are due'.[35]

4.2.3 Decent Work and the Declaration of Fundamental Principles and Rights at Work

As a result of the lack of appetite for standard-setting at ILO level, the ILO sought alternative means by which to re-emphasise its message and to improve its waning visibility and voice. To that end, the ILO designed the 'Decent Work' agenda based around 'opportunities for women and men to obtain decent and productive work, in conditions of freedom, equity, security and human dignity'.[36] This Decent Work agenda was built around four strategic objectives or pillars: (1) fundamental prin-ciples and rights at work; (2) employment; (3) social protection and (4) social dialogue.[37] Within the first pillar, the ILO pledged to promote the Declaration. This Declaration would set up a system of core labour standards which would focus and improve upon the legalistic standard setting of Conventions (and Recommendations). In terms of the central themes of this book, the Declaration is worthy of some consideration. This Declaration compelled nations signed up to the ILO constitution to comply with a set of core labour standards in the following areas: (1) freedom of association and the effective recognition of the right to collective bargaining; (2) the elimination of all forms of forced or compulsory labour; (3) the effective abolition of child labour; and (4) the

---

[31]   ILO, *Report V (I) – The Employment Relationship – Fifth Item on the Agenda* (Geneva 2005) 57

[32]   ILO, *Report V (2A) – The Employment Relationship – Fifth Item on the Agenda* (Geneva 2006) 6

[33]   ILO Recommendation R 198, 'Recommendation Concerning the Employ-ment Relationship' (95th Conference, Geneva 2006)

[34]   Ibid Article 4 (a) and 4 (b)

[35]   Ibid Article 4 (c)

[36]   ILO (n 26) 1

[37]   Ibid 1

elimination of discrimination in respect of employment and occupation. The privileging of these 'procedural rights' responded to practical concerns about the 'unwieldy hotchpotch of complex and overly detailed international labour standards promulgated by the ILO'.[38] It set to streamline the ILO's message in order to increase its legitimacy on the world stage. To a certain extent, the Declaration has helped to increase that legitimacy. The narrow focus of the standards under the Declaration has meant that the Declaration has been viewed as compatible with the human rights agenda. The association of the Declaration with the human rights message has been useful because, within the international community, those rights have achieved a certain hegemonic status. The result has been that the Declaration has allowed some capture of that hegemonic status to promote labour standards. For example, the EU has required compliance with the core labour standards as part of its external investment activity and trading partnerships.[39] In the recent EU-CARIFORM economic partnership agreement (between the EU and states within the Caribbean Community), the EU has demanded that, as part of this partnership, there should be the promotion and effective application of core labour standards.[40] Under Article 72 of this agreement, it is stated that investors should act in accordance with these standards. This is reinforced by Article 73, which seeks to ensure that lowering of labour standards is not be considered as part of a legitimate investment strategy by participating states. Under the EU-CARIFORM agreement, the ILO has a role in monitoring compliance with the core labour standards, although ultimately enforcement is left to the states themselves.

It has also been argued that the privileging of the core labour standards increases the legitimacy of the ILO because it reinforces the ILO's original commitment to traditional understandings of labour law. Langille

---

[38] P Alston, 'Core Labour Standards and the Transformation of the International Labour Rights Regime' (2004) 15 (3) *European Journal of International Law* 457, 460

[39] This has been given particular impetus by the new provisions of the Lisbon Treaty (205 TFEU) which require that external relations comply with Article 21 TEU. This states that the founding principles of EU action are 'democracy, the rule of law, the universality and indivisibility of human rights and fundamental freedoms, respect for human dignity, the principles of equality and solidarity, and respect for the principles of the United Nations Charter and international law'.

[40] See also the commentary in A Perulli, 'Fundamental Social Rights, Market Regulation and EU External Action' (2014) 30 (1) *International Journal of Comparative Labour Law and Industrial Relations* 27, 41

argues that the core labour standards bring a 'deeper and better account of international labour law, and the ILO, into view'.[41] The core labour standards are theoretically coherent, because they ultimately rest on the ILO's fundamental commitment to social justice. This commitment denotes not the 'legal' enforcement of a range of substantive rights also reflected in the international human rights regime, but rather a commitment to procedural rights, most obviously by privileging freedom of association as a core labour standard and extending this to all of the four core rights.[42] Langille's argument proceeds that the protection of procedural rights is much more effective than substantive rights because this 'turn[s] up the bargaining power on the workers' side and addresses their lack of social power'.[43] These procedural rights are a necessary precondition for the achievement of a suitable substantive bargain between workers and employers (although they do not guarantee completely equitable bargains).[44] Further, Langille argues that the focus of the Declaration on a range of market 'unfreedoms' (other than a lack of collective bargaining power) is a *development* of the traditional concerns of labour law in the protection of procedural rights. In the classical theory, effective collective bargaining is sufficient for workers to create fair workplace norms and processes. However, the ILO's position is that there are other aspects of labour market 'unfreedom', other 'barriers to a bargaining process in which both parties are actors rather than objects'.[45] These other 'unfreedoms' (child labour, discrimination and forced labour) exclude workers or force them onto the labour market. In order to achieve the social justice espoused by the classical labour law theorists therefore (and at the core of the ILO vision), these other unfreedoms need to be removed so that the 'deep ontological Kantian notions of equal humanity' can be achieved.[46]

On the other hand, Alston argues that the privileging of a set of core labour standards in this manner detracts from labour rights protection for a number of reasons. First, it creates a hierarchy of standards which did

---

[41]   Langille, 'Core Labour Rights: The True Story (A Reply to Alston)' (2005) 16 (3) *European Journal of International Law* 409, 419

[42]   Ibid 426

[43]   Ibid 429

[44]   Ibid 431. According to Langille, this guarantee cannot be present because procedural rights cannot cater for all the possible unfreedoms that potentially exist in the human condition which might affect their bargaining power (hunger and lack of bargaining expertise).

[45]   Ibid 430

[46]   Ibid 431

not previously exist, so that rights which are not at the 'core' are relegated to secondary status.[47] Second, there is no theoretical consistency in the selection of these core rights. The selection does not stand up to philosophical, economic or legal argument.[48] Third, the focus on 'standards' rather than rights is problematic. In international law, using the terminology of 'principle' or 'standard' denotes a norm of lesser status than a right. The impact is wide-ranging. It means that the core labour standards attain only a low priority in international law. As a consequence, all of the other 'rights' previously established by the ILO (in the form of Conventions, for example) are downgraded. This downgrading is reinforced by the involvement of actors other than the ILO in the use and the enforcement of the ILO core standards (international financial institutions, corporations and NGOs).[49] Even though the core labour standards pay lip service to the human rights agenda (and also to the traditional agenda of the ILO), in practice these standards are unable to meet the aims of either of these elements. So far, there has been reference only to the first pillar of the Decent Work agenda. It appears that this pillar does not meet the demands of vulnerability theory as applied to the labour market (although it might be a good starting point). The Declaration starts from a liberal view of the subject of labour. Individuals are viewed as inherently free and autonomous within the economic system. The Declaration simply allows individuals to uphold that freedom: to 'claim freely and on the basis of equality of opportunity'.[50] Furthermore, the Declaration is premised on the 'link between social progress and economic growth'. The role of the Declaration is to maintain that link and ensure that individuals receive their 'fair share of the wealth which they have helped to generate'. Moreover, the Declaration (as with any other human rights instrument) is a top-down prescription of rights or standards and even though it may be viewed as promoting 'procedural' rights, those rights are too narrowly focused to allow vulnerable individuals to build resilience (there is a focus on collective bargaining). Vulnerability theory would advocate that substantive rights are also important in building resilience. These substantive rights (which might also be considered social rights) are fundamental creators of a level of positive freedom for individuals. Those substantive rights might include basic minimum standards of pay and conditions, but

---

[47]   Alston (n 38) 488

[48]   Ibid 485

[49]   Ibid 488

[50]   Preamble, *Declaration on Fundamental Principles and Rights at Work* (n 27)

would also include rights which really aid in building work quality (for example, access to opportunities such as training). The second, third and fourth pillars of the decent work agenda can be viewed as closer to these central concerns of vulnerability theory. The second pillar of the Decent Work Agenda was concerned with the creation of 'productive' employment opportunities for all through mainstreaming employment objectives into national policies.[51] These employment opportunities were based on an understanding of the mutually reinforcing benefits of work quality and economic productivity, and aimed towards guaranteeing personal development and the fulfilment of workers' expectations.[52] The third social protection pillar recognised the challenges to national social protection systems of increasingly flexible and unstable employment, arguing that this required 'more and better social protection, not less'.[53] The focus was on the developing world particularly: 'Social protection has proved its value in industrial countries. The ILO's task is to develop this economic and social strength in the world as a whole.'[54] Finally, the ILO maintained its commitment to social dialogue in the fourth pillar through: (1) serving as an effective advocate of social dialogue; (2) strengthening the social partners; (3) forging alliances with groups in civil society; and (4) showcasing examples of sound industrial relations practices.[55]

The difficulty has been the translation of these elements into either concrete international policy, or implementation at national level. This is particularly the case with social protection which has traditionally been viewed as the preserve of national governments and not an international matter.[56] That said, there may be a number of reasons to suggest that this position may be subject to change. First, in the ILO's *Declaration on Social Justice for a Fair Globalization*,[57] the ILO recognised that insufficient focus was being given to the substantive rights of workers.

---

[51]   Ibid 25

[52]   C Massimiani, 'Flexicurity and Decent Work in Europe: Can They Co-exist?' (2008) Working Paper of the Centro studi di Diritto Lavoro Europeo 'Massimo D'Antona' Universita degli Studi di Catania No 65/2008 <http://www.lex.unict.it/eurolabor/ricerca/wp/int/massimiani_n65-2008int.pdf> accessed 10 March 2014

[53]   ILO (n 26) 36

[54]   Ibid 36

[55]   Ibid 48

[56]   Certainly, the UK has ratified only part of Article 12 of the European Social Charter dealing with social protection.

[57]   ILO, *Declaration on Social Justice for a Fair Globalization* (August 2008) <http://www.ilo.org/wcmsp5/groups/public/@dgreports/@cabinet/documents/publication/wcms_099766.pdf> accessed 10 July 2012

Through the Declaration on Social Justice, the ILO agreed to apply a mechanism of cyclical review to those rights outside the core labour standards. This was to assure the international community of the ILO's continued commitment to non-core rights.[58] Second, the most recent Convention concerning 'precarious' work, the Domestic Workers Convention, demonstrates a concern to consider context and to instigate substantive rights more in line with the decent work agenda (and vulnerability theory). This Convention will be discussed in depth in Chapter 6, the case study on domestic work. Finally, at EU level, the introduction of the Lisbon treaty suggests that there may be renewed commitment to a more social agenda (which may include elements of the promotion of decent work). Under Article 9 of the Lisbon Treaty there is a 'horizontal social clause'. This stipulates that in defining and implementing its external policies and actions, the EU 'shall take into account requirements linked to the promotion of a high level of employment, the guarantee of adequate social protection, the fight against social exclusion, and a high level of education, training and protection of health'. The Commission has stated the 'fundamental' nature of this clause, and it has been referred to in the context of EU jurisprudence.[59] There is also the suggestion that the clause will have significant impact, on account of the power given by the Treaty to annul any EU action which does not conform with it.[60]

4.3 EU LAW AND POLICY ON PRECARIOUS WORK

It is possible to argue that early manifestations of employment law and policy at EU level were not grounded in the protection of vulnerability at all (or at least that the protection of vulnerability was a secondary aim to more pressing economic concerns). The difficulty was that the EU was formed as an economic entity focussed on economic integration through the removal of artificial obstacles to the free movement of labour goods and capital.[61] Policies pertaining to worker protection were seen as

---

[58] F Maupain, 'New Foundation or New Façade? The ILO and the 2008 Declaration on Social Justice for a Fair Globalization' (2009) 20 (3) *European Journal of International Law* 823, 842

[59] See the conclusion of Advocate-General, Pedro Cruz Villalon, in Case C-515/08 (*Santos Palhota and Others*) decided by the Court of Justice of the European Union in a ruling of 7 October 2010.

[60] Perulli (n 40) 41

[61] C Barnard, *EU Employment Law* (Oxford University Press 2012) 5

elements of social policy and therefore outside the ambit of EU competence. There was a lack of political will to introduce measures to address the vulnerabilities experienced by workers, as this kind of legislation was viewed as the preserve of member states. The result was that the first equality directives were introduced on the basis of a (pure) integrationist logic: that of creating a level playing field for actors and preventing unfair business competition.[62] This integrationist logic was, for example, clearly stated in Directives 75/117 on equal pay and Directive 76/207 on equal treatment. Both of these directives stated that their main aim was the 'harmonisation of living and working conditions' across the EU, although there was also reference to the need (for member states) to ensure the improvement of those conditions over time.

More recently, the EU has become increasingly willing to become involved in the regulation of vulnerable workers and precarious work. In this section, there will be an analysis of attempts to regulate 'atypical' work at EU level.[63] There have been three 'groups' of atypical workers which have been singled out for legislative action at this level: (1) part-time workers; (2) fixed-term workers; and (3) temporary agency workers. The first framework directive on part-time work was passed in 1997 (PTWD), followed by the framework directive on fixed-term work in 1999 (FTWD).[64] In 2008, the Temporary Agency Work Directive (TAWD) was finally approved by the European Parliament and became part of EU law.[65] These directives will be discussed in the next section.

---

[62]   M Bell, 'Between Flexicurity and Fundamental Social Rights: The EU Directives on Atypical Work' (2012) 37 (1) *European Law Review* 31, 31

[63]   'Atypical work' can be defined as work which falls outside the 'standard employment relationship' (full-time, year-round employment for a single employer). It therefore covers a wide range of employment forms including temporary, casual and part-time work, as well as disguised or illegal wage employment. For a full discussion of the meaning of this term see G Rodgers, 'Precarious Work in Western Europe: The State of the Debate' in G Rodgers and J Rodgers (eds), *Precarious Work Jobs in Labour Market Regulation* (ILO 1989) 1

[64]   Council Directive 1999/70/EC of 28 June 1999 concerning the Framework Agreement on Fixed-term work concluded by ETUC, UNICE and CEEP, OJ [1999] L 175/43; Council Directive 1997/81/EC of 15 December 1997 concerning the Framework Agreement on Part-time work concluded by ETUC, UNICE and CEEP, OJ [1998] L 14/9

[65]   Directive 2008/14/EC of the European Parliament and the Council of 19 November 2008 on temporary agency work OJ [2008] L329/9

4.3.1 The Regulation of 'Atypical' Work

The atypical work directives were designed to improve the position of atypical workers and the quality of their work through the imposition of a minimum standard of equal treatment (in contractual terms) between atypical workers and their 'full-time' or 'permanent' colleagues.[66] The commitment in the directives is to 'formal' notions of equality, but there is some indication of elements pertaining to more substantive equality. The introduction of these substantive elements accords with the under-standing under vulnerability theory (and social law) of the limitations of liberal formal equality. Under vulnerability theory, 'formal' notions of equality are at best a partial solution, and at worst can actually reinforce existing inequalities. It is hoped that more substantive notions of equality can more effectively reduce (social) inequalities and can aid more effectively in achieving mid-spectrum goals for the benefit of all (for example, the eradication of social exclusion). There are a number of examples of these elements of substantive equality in the atypical work directives. In the PTWD there are measures to promote equality of opportunity for part-time workers, by allowing part-time work at higher levels of the enterprise and by facilitating access to vocational training.[67] Similar provisions occur in the FTWD and the TAWD, although in the latter, refusal to allow equality of opportunity can be justified on objective grounds.[68] It might also be suggested that the interpretation of these provisions has aimed to restrict the scope of the objective grounds to ensure that the reference to non-discrimination does not undermine work quality.[69] The relationship of these directives to collective bargain-ing is also interesting. The PTWD and the FTWD were created through

---

[66]   Clause 1 (a) PTWD, Clause 1 (a) FTWD and Article 2 TAWD
[67]   Clause 5 (3) (d) PTWD
[68]   Clause 6 (2) FTWD and Article 6 (4) TAWD
[69]   At European level this is demonstrated well by the case of *Bruno v Pettini* (Cases C-395/08 and C396/08 *INPS v Bruno and Pettini, INPS v Lotti and Matteucci* [2010] 3 CMLR) which concerned access to pension rights for Italian part-time workers. The workers challenged an Italian statutory rule that qualifi-cation for pension rights depended on length of service on the basis that this was contrary to the PTWD. The Court held that this statutory rule was in breach of the PTWD for two reasons. The first was that it was directly discriminatory against part-time workers, and so was in breach of the anti-discrimination provisions of the PTWD. The arguments put forward by the Italian government in relation to the objective justification for this direct discrimination were rejected. The second reason was that this Italian statutory rule ran counter to the aim of the PTWD to promote work quality. This rule made part-time work less

the 'collective route' to legislation. This 'collective route' to legislation differs from the traditional legislative route, because the 'social partners' (employer organisations and trade unions) are much more involved in the process. Before proceeding with the drafting of legislation, the Commission first consults employer organisations and trade unions on the possible direction of Union action.[70] Once consulted, the social partners inform the Commission of their wish to deal with the issue by negotiation. If these negotiations are successful, the resulting agreement can be implemented by a directive, and therefore become part of EU law. It has been suggested that this method of framing directives is more sensitive to worker needs than command and control legislation.[71] Furthermore, in the atypical work directives there is some recognition that the power of negotiation of the atypical work groups needs to be maintained once they have gained legal protection. For example, there is reference in the atypical work directives to ensuring that workers are counted for the purposes of deciding union membership thresholds.[72] This reference to the importance of collective bargaining would also accord with the interests of vulnerability theory in promoting resilience among workers (although this theory would view collective bargaining in wide terms, not limited by trade union organisation). The argument is that building resilience among workers is more effective in the longer term at achieving mid-spectrum goals than one-off findings of discrimination. For example, democratic participation in the industrial sphere promotes democratic participation in a wider sense in other areas of social life.[73]

4.3.2   EU Law on Precarious Work and 'Flexicurity'

However, the effectiveness of the atypical work directives in meeting the aspirations of vulnerability theory has been affected by two different pressures: (1) political pressure which has led to the watering down of

---

attractive, because the effect of choosing part-time work was to postpone the date on which the worker would receive a pension. It was therefore contrary to the 'fundamental' quality objectives of the PTWD.

[70]   Article 154 (2) TFEU

[71]   S Smismans, 'The European Social Dialogue in the Shadow of Hierarchy' (2008) 28 (1) *Journal of Public Policy* 161, 162

[72]   Article 7 (1) TAWD

[73]   G Davidov, 'Collective Bargaining Laws: Purpose and Scope' (2004) 20 (1) *International Journal of Comparative Labour Law and Industrial Relations* 81

some of the provisions of the atypical work directives over time;[74] and (2) the association of the atypical work directives with the notion of 'flexicurity'.

In terms of the watering down of provisions, this is well illustrated by the original proposals for the TAWD as compared with the wording of the final version. The wording of the first draft directive on the regulation of temporary agency work reflects a desire to provide comprehensive protection for this group by addressing two concerns: (1) the potential for 'abuse' of temporary agency workers, which should be tackled through increasing the visibility of atypical work;[75] and (2) that temporary work should be 'supervised' and temporary workers should receive strong 'social protection'.[76] The coverage of the regulations was broader than the coverage of the final version of the TAWD. Under the first draft of the regulations, temporary agency workers were to be subject to 'the laws, regulations, and administrative and collectively agreed provisions, and the customary practices in force in the user undertaking as regards working conditions' for the duration of the assignment.[77] In the final version of the directive, the equal treatment of agency workers extended only to 'basic' working conditions, essentially working time and pay.[78] In the first draft, there was also a ban on the use of temporary agency work to fill vacancies due to strike action,[79] which was removed by the time of the drafting of the final version.

The association of the atypical work directives with the notion of 'flexicurity' is also problematic. Flexicurity was adopted as a guiding principle of both law and policy at EU level, as a response to pressures on the labour market brought about by globalisation. It stems from the concerns of efficiency theory that in order to be effective, regulation must be sensitive to economic developments. The idea was that in order to respond to economic change, the EU needed to adopt 'an integrated

---

[74] Indeed, the negotiation of the atypical directives was a long drawn out process. Of the nine draft directives to deal with the perceived problems of 'atypical work' put forward between 1982 and 1996, only one was adopted, concerning the (marginal) extension of existing health and safety regulation to temporary workers. The rest were rejected and had to be redrafted. M Jeffery, 'Not Really Going to Work? Of the Directive on Part-time Work, Atypical Work and Attempts to Regulate It' (1998) 27(3) *ILJ* 193, 201

[75] Proposal for a Council Directive concerning temporary work OJ C [1982] 128/2 (TAWD first draft) Preamble para 2

[76] Ibid Preamble para 1

[77] Ibid Article 9 (1)

[78] Article 3(1)(f) TAWD

[79] Article 11 TAWD first draft

strategy to enhance, at the same time, flexibility and security in the labour market'.[80] It was presented as a win-win scenario providing universalistic benefits for both employers and workers.[81] Furthermore, it was also thought that, for the first time, there could be a judicious combination of both employment policy and employment law. Employment law could help to reduce unemployment and improve equal opportunities (by allowing more women to enter the labour market) and thus further some of the aims of employment policy. Employment law would thus come to be seen as part of a strategy of increasing economic competitiveness, rather than stifling economic growth.[82] In the original formulations of flexicurity, the focus was on achieving a clear balance between flexibility and security, and it might be argued that these 'security' elements took the flexicurity agenda beyond pure efficiency concerns towards a greater focus on vulnerability. Under the flexicurity agenda, it was envisaged that 'flexible and reliable contractual arrangements' should be combined with 'comprehensive lifelong learning strategies' and 'active labour market policies' which fostered *employment* security. The idea was that regulation should focus on individual development (through training, for example) rather than protection of a particular job (*job* security). The focus on employment security would be the best means to provide worker protection in a changing economic environment. At the same time, the original flexicurity agenda promoted strong social security systems to provide adequate security for workers between jobs. This latter element is in line with the interest of vulnerability theory in recognising the threat to social exclusion which follows from a deregulatory (flexible labour market) strategy.

The flexicurity agenda is mentioned in the Preamble of all the atypical work directives. It is stated in these Preambles that the more flexible organisation of work corresponds to both the 'wishes of employees' and the 'requirements of competition'.[83] In the PTWD and the TAWD, the commitment to flexibility is clear, as in both directives there is a stated

---

[80]   European Commission, 'Towards Fundamental Principles of Flexicurity: More and Better Jobs through Flexibility and Security' COM (2007) 359 final, 5

[81]   M De Vos, 'European Flexicurity and Globalization: A Critical Perspective' (2009) 25 (3) *The International Journal of Comparative Labour Law and Industrial Relations* 209, 216

[82]   H Jorgensen and PK Madsen, 'Flexicurity and Beyond – Reflections on the Nature and Future of a Political Celebrity' in H Jorgensen and PK Madsen (eds), *Flexicurity and Beyond: Finding and New Agenda for the European Social Model* (DJØF, Copenhagen 2007) 7

[83]   Recital 5 PTWD and FTWD

recognition of the value of these kinds of work arrangements for economic development, and both of these kinds of contracts are actively encouraged. In clause 1 of the PTWD there is reference to the purpose of the legislation which is to 'facilitate the development of part-time work on a voluntary basis, and to contribute to the flexible organisation of working time', and in clause 5(1) member states are asked to 'review obstacles of a legal or administrative nature which may limit the opportunities for part-time work'. This is in alignment with Article 4(1) TAWD which requires member states to review prohibitions on the use of temporary agency work to ensure that they are justified. The position in the FTWD is more nuanced, and this directive is arguably more concerned with worker protection against the abuse of fixed-term work contracts than about the increase in use of these kinds of contract.[84] In practice however, this directive has been used to encourage some deregulation in the use of fixed-term contracts without adequate consideration of the quality of that work.[85] In the atypical work directives, the security elements are represented by the principles of non-discrimination and the idea of the improvement in the 'quality' of these forms of work. However, these security elements have also become imbued with elements of flexibility, so that their ability to promote security for workers has been brought into question. For example, in the atypical work directives, a level of flexibility is incorporated into the notion of equal treatment which is not normally permitted. This is illustrated by the fact that justification is permitted for *direct* discrimination (as opposed to indirect discrimination), and both the PTWD and the FTWD identify different instances in which justification is recognised.[86] These directives also appear to make little contribution either to job or employment security in practice.[87]

Indeed, it appears that since the financial crisis, the flexibilisation agenda has proceeded apace, while security elements have increasingly been left behind. Given high and increasing levels of unemployment, the central importance of employment policy has once again come to the fore. However, the Employment Guidelines which govern employment policy have increasingly been linked to economic targets and austerity measures rather than the achievement of labour law goals. The result is

---

[84] In Clause 1 (b) FTWD member states are required to set up 'a framework to prevent abuse arising from the use of successive fixed term contracts'.

[85] M Bell, 'Between Flexicurity and Fundamental Social Rights: The EU Directives on Atypical Work' (2012) 37 (1) *European Law Review* 31, 36

[86] See for example Clause 4 (4) PTWD and Clause 4 (4) FTWD

[87] Bell (n 85) 38

that the value of flexibility has been promoted over security in a number of member states. Member states governments have argued that flexibility can be viewed as achieving mid-spectrum goals (the development of employment and equal opportunities for men and women), so there is no need for labour law to supplement these goals (for example, by increasing work quality or reducing social exclusion). This position has been adopted in Spain with the instigation of the Labour Market Reforms of 2012. The goals of these reforms were stated as the reduction of unemployment through increasing flexibility and labour market efficiency.[88] Reference was made to the European economic/employment guidelines in this regard. Despite the reference in the Reforms to maintaining worker protection, the reform measures have facilitated the deregulation of atypical work contracts, leading to a worsened position for 'precarious' work groups and an increase in precarious work as a whole. For example, there are now enhanced opportunities for employers to manipulate the part-time/full-time contractual boundary to the detriment of workers. Contractual hours can be increased (to at or near full-time equivalent) without employers having to classify workers as full-time or standard workers for the purposes of the law, thereby denying a number of contractual and social security benefits to such workers.[89] There is also the increased possibility under the new Reforms for the use of 'training' contracts which fall outside mainstream regulation, and the use of successive fixed-term contracts without justification, despite the prohibitions and limitations on this kind of activity in the FTWD. As a result of these Reforms, the Spanish case has been labelled a 'flexi-precarity' model: promoting flexibility to create an increasingly precarious workforce. In fact, the experience in Spain and other countries of the EU is that increasing flexibility does not necessarily achieve employment policy goals or an increase in economic growth. There is certainly no evidence that the flexibility (or flexiprecarity) agenda has served to increase employment rates or speed up job creation. According to the ILO, three years after the crisis there were an added 27 million unemployed people in the global economy. The ILO's baseline projection shows no change in the global unemployment rate up to 2016.[90] In the Spanish case, a recent report of the Spanish Central Bank shows that the

---

[88]   J Lopez, A de la Court and S Canaldo, 'Breaking the Equilibrium between Flexibility and Security: Flexiprecarity as the Spanish Version of the Model' (2014) 5 (1) *European Labour Law Journal* 18, 22

[89]   Ibid 23

[90]   ILO, *Global Employment Trends 2012: Preventing a Deeper Jobs Crisis* (2012) 9

policy of flexiprecarity has not served to boost job creation or reduce job destruction.[91] It also has not served to boost labour market transitions from precarious into more permanent forms of work (a major end-game of European employment strategy). All this demonstrates the short sightedness of efficiency theory and the dangers of shifting the burden of the financial crisis onto labour.[92] These kinds of policies *create* vulnerability and stifle the resilience which allows individuals to build autonomy. The next section will further illustrate this point by reference to the law and policy on precarious work in the UK.

4.4 UK LAW AND POLICY ON PRECARIOUS WORK

4.4.1 Vulnerable Worker Policy

In 2006 the (then Labour) government in the UK introduced a parliamentary policy paper entitled *Success at Work*.[93] This paper introduced vulnerability as a policy tool in the field of employment for the first time. This policy showed a certain alignment with the precepts of vulnerability theory. For example, it showed a particular concern for precarious workers, but defined precarious work broadly and as part of a structure of vulnerability in employment. A vulnerable worker was defined in the following way:

> We have defined a vulnerable worker as someone working in an environment where the risk of being denied employment rights is high and who does not have the capacity or means to protect themselves from that abuse. Both factors need to be present. A worker may be subject to vulnerability, but that is only significant if an employer exploits that vulnerability.[94]

A number of sectors were singled out as being particularly problematic: retail, hotels, restaurants, care homes, textiles, construction, security and

---

[91]   Banco de España, 'La reforma laboral de 2012: un primer análisis de algunos de sus efectos sobre el mercado de trabajo', *Boletín Económico* (September 2013) 55–64 <www.bde.es/f/webbde/SES/Secciones/Publicaciones/InformesBoletinesRevistas/BoletinEconomico/13/Sep/Fich/be1309-art5.Pdf> cited in J Lopez (n 88) 27

[92]   S Marshall, 'Shifting Responsibility: How the Burden of the European Financial Crisis Shifted from the Financial Sector and onto Labour' (2013–14) 35 *Comparative Labor Law and Policy Journal* 449

[93]   DTI, *Success at Work: Protecting Vulnerable Workers, Supporting Good Employers. A Policy Statement for this Parliament* (March 2006)

[94]   Ibid 25

cleaning.[95] Furthermore, the vulnerable worker policy was aligned with vulnerability theory in that it promoted a number of mid-spectrum goals. The vulnerable worker policy was referred to in the context of wider policies to promote social inclusion.[96] In the *Success at Work* paper the government promoted the importance of work to social and personal empowerment, presenting work as allowing people to attain their potential. It was suggested that workers with a lack of capacity or means were unable to attain their potential through work and that this created vulnerability.[97] It also promoted the value of building resilience through union participation. The paper recognised that lack of union representation is a cause of vulnerability, and that unions should 'extend their reach into new sectors and industries' to ensure that they can provide help and support to the most vulnerable.[98]

Despite the fact that elements of vulnerability theory can be viewed in the aspirations of the vulnerable worker policy, the solutions actually suggested and enacted under this policy were relatively weak. From the outset it was made clear, in the *Success at Work* paper, that the vulnerable worker policy would not involve 'wholesale change to the current system' of labour regulation.[99] Following a consultation with stakeholders, the government concluded that:

> the present legal framework reflects the wide diversity of working arrangements and the different levels of responsibility and rights in different employment relationships. The Government believes that it meets the labour market's current needs and there is no need for further legislation in this area.[100]

The government, therefore, did not advocate the depth of change that would be required if following wholeheartedly the precepts of vulnerability theory. Rather, the main aims of the government's policy were to target specific instances of abuse (for example, of certain agency workers) as well as making sure that workers understood the rights to which

---

[95]   Ibid 30
[96]   For example, at page 8 in the *Success at Work* paper there is reference to the fact that the government aimed to create a 'new impetus to improve the position of vulnerable workers and promote social inclusion, using risk-based principles to avoid penalising good employers'.
[97]   DTI (n 93) 9
[98]   Ibid 49
[99]   Ibid 16
[100]   Ibid 17

they were entitled.[101] This very narrow focus on workers most at risk of abuse strikes a chord more with the aspirations of efficiency theory than vulnerability theory.

The actual policy adopted following the publication of the *Success at Work* paper involved three main strands. The first was the government's crackdown on 'rogue employers' announced in the Final Report of the Vulnerable Worker Enforcement Forum in August 2008.[102] In this Report, 'dark corners' of the labour market were identified, 'where more needs to be done to ensure that workers have access to the rights that Parliament intended'.[103] The second was a number of measures to strengthen the position of agency workers in the labour market. This policy was stated in the Vulnerable Worker Enforcement Forum report as follows:

> (1) revisions to the Employment Agency Conduct Regulations to give agency workers the right to withdraw from services provided without detriment; (2) government commitment to implementation of the Temporary Agency Worker's Directive; (3) strengthening the powers of the Employment Agency Standards inspectorate.[104]

Thirdly, a number of pilot projects were set up to bring together agencies (employers, trade unions, regulators, voluntary and community agencies, local authorities and ACAS) to 'offer a joint-up package of support that will reach out to vulnerable people'.[105]

4.4.2 Vulnerability and Agency Work

In large part, the solutions to the problems faced by agency workers in the *Success at Work* paper appeared to be aligned to the premises of efficiency rather than vulnerability theory (despite the reference to mid-spectrum goals in that policy). The government noted that agency work could be a locus of vulnerability, but restricted the policy reach to the 'most vulnerable agency workers'.[106] As these issues were specific and did not affect all agency workers they could be tackled 'in a manner most effective for workers and least burdensome for industry'.[107] The

---

[101] Ibid 17
[102] BERR, *Vulnerable Worker Enforcement Forum – Final Report and Government Conclusions* (August 2008)
[103] Ibid 3
[104] Ibid 4
[105] DTI (n 93) 32
[106] Ibid 17
[107] Ibid 19

identification of these issues, following consultation, led to minor legal changes to the Conduct of Employment Agencies and Employment Businesses Regulations 2003 (CEAEBR 2003).[108] By way of example, the government identified that a small number of agencies were mistreating work-seekers by making offers of work conditional on paying for services such as accommodation and transport. 'Rogue employers' were also giving loans to temporary workers, often from overseas, and then deducting loan repayments at high levels of interest from worker salaries.[109] Amendments were therefore made to Regulations 5 and 13 of the CEAEBR 2003 with the effect that (agency) workers taking up additional services could now withdraw from those services without incurring any detriment or penalty (Regulation 3 Conduct of Employment Agencies and Employment Businesses (Amendment) Regulations 2007[110] (CEAEBR 2007) in force April 2008). Agencies or employment businesses were required to give a work-seeker a statement of his right to cancel or withdraw from these services (Regulation 4 CEAEBR 2007). Further minor amendments were made to the Regulations simplifying the information agencies had to give employers in relation to workers supplied for short-term tasks (Regulations 5 and 6 CEAEBR 2007) and increasing the protection available for work-seekers where agencies proposed to charge fees for the inclusion of information about them in a publication (Regulation 7 CEAEBR 2007).

These changes were followed in August 2008 by the publication of the Vulnerable Worker Enforcement Forum's recommendations on the enforcement of employment rights. The measures to be implemented as a result of these recommendations included a doubling of the number of Employment Agency Inspectors by the end of July 2008, a campaign to promote awareness of the Employment Agency Standards Inspectorate (EAS), and a sharing of information between the Gangmasters Licencing Agency (GLA) and the EAS. Although these changes were welcomed, it was felt that they did not go far enough. For example, the GLA's coverage continued to be limited to certain sectors, and did not address agency worker status 'which stops their entitlement to many rights and allows an employer to sack them with no comeback if they attempt to

[108] SI 2003/3319. See BERR, *Protecting Vulnerable Agency Workers: Government Response to the Consultation* (November 2007)
[109] DTI (n 93) 18
[110] SI 2007/3575

enforce the limited rights they enjoy'.[111] Further, in the *Success at Work* paper, the government rejected the adoption of the European Agency Worker Directive (TAWD).[112] On the latter matter, of course, the government's position did change. In May 2008 an agreement was reached between the CBI and the TUC that agency workers should be given equal treatment after a 12-week qualifying period. On this basis, the government entered into consultation with the social partners about the implementation of the TAWD,[113] and drafted the Agency Worker Regulations 2010 (AWR), which came into force in the UK on 1 October 2011.[114]

The TAWD and the AWR will be discussed in more detailed in the case study on Temporary Agency Work in Chapter 5. That said, a few points should be noted here in terms of the application of the TAWD in the UK through the AWR. The 'right' for agency workers is limited in a number of ways. Firstly, the right is limited in scope as it applies only to 'basic working conditions'.[115] According to the TAWD, these 'basic working conditions' include: (1) the duration of working time; (2) overtime; (3) breaks; (4) rest periods; (5) night work; (6) holidays and public holidays; and (7) pay. The UK government defines the notion of pay narrowly, and excludes a number of 'payments or rewards' from the scope of application of the AWR (for example, occupational sick pay, pension payments, any payment in respect of maternity, paternity or adoption leave and expenses payments).[116] Secondly, the qualification period attached to the AWR dramatically reduces the number of agency workers who can use the regulations. Indeed, according to one survey in the UK, 55 per cent of the agency workforce had been on their assignment for less than 12 weeks.[117] This suggests that, in practice, the majority of agency workers would not benefit from the right to equal treatment. The effectiveness of these regulations for the 'group' of agency workers is therefore brought into question.

---

[111]   B Barber, 'TUC Response to BERR Vulnerable Workers Forum Report' (5 August 2008) <http://www.tuc.org.uk/newsroom/tuc-15161-f0.cfm> accessed 23 February 2014

[112]   Directive 2008/104/EC of the European Parliament and the Council on temporary agency work, OJ [2008] L329/9

[113]   BERR, *Implementation of the Agency Workers Directive: A consultation paper* (May 2009)

[114]   SI 2010/93

[115]   Article 2 TAWD; Regulation 5 (1) AWR

[116]   Regulation 6 (3) (a), (b), (c), (j) AWR

[117]   BERR, *Agency Working in the UK* (2008) 6–7

Furthermore, there is also a problem with these regulations for the protection of the most vulnerable agency worker. For example, there is the potential for 'unscrupulous' employers to manipulate the qualifying period to ensure that agency workers are excluded from the regulations. This kind of manipulation is most likely prevented by the regulations in relation to a particular agency worker operating on multiple assignments with one employer.[118] However, the employer remains at liberty to take on different agency workers for a series of 11-week assignments, despite the fact that none of those agency workers would be able to qualify for the AWR as a result.[119] There is also the possibility that agency workers may be excluded from the AWR because they cannot prove the requisite employment status. To qualify for the AWR, an agency worker must show that they are either an 'employee' or a 'worker' of a particular agency. It has traditionally been very difficult for agency workers to fall within these statutory definitions given the temporary and short-term nature of their work.[120] There is also the possibility that agencies could exploit this particular weakness by introducing contractual terms or creating contractual arrangements which defeat employment status. In fact, this concern was raised in the Consultation for the AWR, and the government pointed to judicial subversion of this trend in cases finding that the employment relationship (as constructed by the employer) was in fact a 'sham'.[121] The case law on sham contracts is, however, rather conflicted and does not guarantee protection for agency workers.[122] Arguably then, the result is that the AWR does not even meet the narrow premises of efficiency theory, because they do not protect the most vulnerable agency workers from abuse.

4.4.3   Vulnerability Policy and Trade Unions

Interestingly, part of the solution suggested in the *Success at Work* paper was to support the increase in union membership among vulnerable

---

[118]   Regulation 9 AWR

[119]   A Davies, 'The Implementation of the Directive on Temporary Agency Work in the UK: A Missed Opportunity' (2010) 1 *European Labour Law Journal* 307, 317

[120]   See for example *James v Greenwich London Borough Council* [2008] ICR 545

[121]   BIS, *Implementation of the Agency Workers Directive: Consultation on Draft Regulations* (2010) para 3.8

[122]   See for example the conflict in the case law between *Firthglow Limited (t/a Protectacoat) v Szilagi* [2009] ICR 835 and *Consistent Group v Kalwak* [2008] IRLR 505

workers. A London-based Vulnerable Workers Project (VWP) was established, which focused on the building services sector in the City of London and Tower Hamlet areas.[123] In this VWP, workers were given advice about how to join unions and encouraged to do so.[124] The project also aimed to help vulnerable workers to understand and secure their entitlement to employment rights, and to 'introduce vulnerable workers to opportunities for developing new skills'.[125] An employment rights advice and information service was set up in the Tower Hamlets Law Centre as a means to engage with vulnerable workers. It also collaborated with unions and provided support for non-unionised workers through the establishment of the 'Vulnerable Worker's Group'. This group gave workers the opportunity to discuss the issues they commonly faced and how those issues might be addressed.[126]

Furthermore, the Trade Union Congress (TUC) was involved in a number of ways in the vulnerable worker policy:

(1)   The TUC, an active proponent of the partnership approach[127] was involved in public consultation on the vulnerable worker policy through the Commission on Vulnerable Employment.[128]

(2)   Both the TUC and unions were involved in the Vulnerable Worker Enforcement Forum which was set up to 'consider evidence on the nature and extent of abuse of worker rights, examine the effectiveness of the existing enforcement framework, and identify possible improvements'.[129]

(3)   Trade unions have been co-opted to implement the vulnerable worker policy in the area of skills and training.

In the *Success at Work* paper, there is an explanation of the role of government-funded Union Learning Representatives who are involved in

---

[123]   Details of this project are available in TUC, 'Vulnerable Workers Project Final Report. Informing Strategies for Vulnerable Workers' (April 2009) <http://www.vulnerableworkersproject.org.uk/wp-content/uploads/2009/04/vwp_final_report_final.doc> accessed 23 February 2014

[124]   Ibid 12

[125]   Ibid 2

[126]   Ibid 2

[127]   K Ewing, 'The Function of Trade Unions' (2005) 34 (1) *ILJ* 1, 10

[128]   TUC, 'Hard Work, Hidden Lives: The Full Report of the Commission on Vulnerable Employment' (7 May 2008) <http://www.vulnerableworkers.org.uk/files/CoVE_full_report.pdf> accessed 23 February 2014

[129]   BERR, *Vulnerable Worker Enforcement Forum – Final Report and Government Conclusions* (August 2008) 4

helping workers with their training and development needs.[130] According to the government, 'basic skills are fundamental to getting a job, and to social inclusion, quality of life and improving and individual's position at work'.[131] Finally, trade unions have been involved in the 'partnership approach' of the Vulnerable Workers Projects. In the London-based VWP, the union Unite received government funding to train shop stewards to run advice surgeries in the field of employment rights.

In the vulnerability policy, the focus was on allowing worker-based groups (unions) to further the interests of worker members beyond immediate employment concerns. Unions were also integrated with other support services for non-unionised members, and groups outside the union structure were also encouraged. All of these elements appear to fit the model of vulnerability theory based around resilience. Unions and other worker groups are tasked with addressing individual concerns which will better enable those individuals to face employment and other challenges in the future. Unfortunately, however, this particular aspect of the vulnerable worker policy did not, in practice, prove to really increase the resilience or market power of workers. The projects under this policy were isolated and temporary in nature. The Vulnerable Workers projects ended in 2009, and the result was simply a policy report which included a set of generalised findings.[132]

4.4.4   Current Stance on Vulnerable Workers and Precarious Work

Following the onset of the financial crisis and the election of a Conservative/Liberal coalition and Conservative majority government in 2010 and 2015 respectively, the focus of employment law and policy in the UK has changed. Employment law and policy is more and more dominated by efficiency views, and the tendency has been towards deregulation rather than reregulation of the labour market. Although there has consistently been reference to a guarantee of minimum protection, that protection is only introduced or maintained on the basis that it does not undermine too far liberal values (such as freedom of contract) that efficiency views support. The result has been, like in other EU member states, the potential *creation* of vulnerability through legislative means. There has been both a reduction in existing protections, and also the

---

[130]   DTI (n 93) 23

[131]   Ibid 25

[132]   TUC, 'Vulnerable Workers Project: Informing Strategies for Vulnerable Workers' (2009) <http://www.vulnerableworkersproject.org.uk/> accessed 24 February 2014

creation of new legal elements which make workers more vulnerable, and increase precariousness within the workforce.

The Coalition introduced the Employment Law Review (ELR) in 2010 to run for the entirety of its Parliament (up until May 2015). Through this Review, the government promised a 'wide ranging examination of laws and regulations that affect the functioning of the labour market'.[133] The foundational premise of this Review was that labour law in the UK was 'not working' and needed to be restructured so that it was better equipped to support 'strong and efficient' labour markets. This follows the view from efficiency theory that employment law needs to stay in line with economic developments in order to be effective. According to the detail of the ELR, there were three elements to a strong and efficient labour market: flexibility, effectiveness and fairness.[134] A flexible labour market was defined according to job creation and job transition, effectiveness meant enabling productive workforce management, and fairness included some level of employment protection. At the outset of the ELR, the level of protection that the government wanted to achieve was stated as 'strong'.[135] However, as time has progressed, it has become clear that the commitment of the Coalition has been to a very minimum level of protection, and there is a preference for deregulation outside that minimum level. The Coalition increasingly presented employment law as an interference in the basic freedom of contract upon which the employment relationship is based. A good example of this position is provided in the recent Consultation entitled *Ending the Employment Relationship*, where it is stated that '[W]herever possible, the Government should keep out of individual employment relationships which are developed and managed by the two parties involved'.[136] The Review was very fast moving and involved a number of changes to labour law in the UK. There are three changes in particular, which are worthy of note, as they each demonstrate different elements of the government's attitude to vulnerability in employment. The first is the extension of the qualification period for unfair dismissal claims from one to two years, and the second is the introduction of employee shareholder status. The extension of the qualification period is interesting as a starting point because this represents a clear and direct deregulation of unfair dismissal law in the UK (and hence potentially a direct assault on the protection of vulnerable

---

[133] BIS, *Employment Law Review Annual Update* (March 2012) 5
[134] Ibid 5
[135] Ibid 5
[136] BIS, *Ending the Employment Relationship: A Consultation* (September 2012) 5

or precarious). It is also interesting in light of the rationale given for this deregulation. On the one hand, the government asserted that this measure was necessary in order to improve the flexibility and effectiveness of the labour market, as this would help companies to be able to make an assessment of their staff over a longer time period, without fear of costly employment tribunals. This was presented as a (universalistic) benefit to both employees and workers, as the employees would also benefit from an increase in investment in their training and other needs in the first two years of employment.[137] On the other hand, it was argued that this change would not result, in real terms, in a reduction in protection for workers. Those workers still had the benefit of anti-discrimination law, which was sufficient to ensure the minimum level of protection workers required. This assertion is a reference to the importance of fundamental human rights as the legal backstop of the liberal regime upon which the efficiency regime is based. Anti-discrimination law (based on the narrow premise of 'formal equality') falls neatly into this human rights category, whereas other employment law is more difficult to fit within this regime. This lays open the door for the deregulation of other employment laws (for example, unfair dismissal), despite the possibility of this deregulation having discriminatory effect.[138]

The second change of interest is the introduction of employee shareholder status (with effect from September 2013). This employee shareholder status is to exist alongside the other employment statuses of 'employee' and 'worker' in UK law. The basis of the scheme is that in exchange for a certain amount of shares in a company, a worker accepting this new status would forfeit certain employment rights, including the right to unfair dismissal (unless the dismissal was automatically unfair), the right to statutory redundancy pay, and certain rights to request flexible working and time to train.[139] The government explained that the reason for the introduction of this scheme was to increase the flexibility of the labour market, and introduce a further element of choice for employers in the organisation of their affairs. The government was clear (following protracted debate), that this would also be a genuine choice for the employee as well: 'no one would be

---

[137] BIS, *Resolving Workplace Disputes: Government Response to Consultation* (November 2011) 32

[138] Ibid 34. Here the government recognised the possibility of this discriminatory effect in relation to the extension of the qualification period for unfair dismissal.

[139] BIS, *Implementing Employee Owner Status – Government Response* (December 2012) 6

compelled to apply for or accept an employee shareholder job'.[140] This serves only to reinforce the comments made earlier concerning the commitment of the Coalition government to the maintenance of freedom of contract, and the understanding of the vast majority of employment relationships representing a meeting of two equal parties with equal power. In the discussion of the implementing law in the House of Lords, objections were raised to this understanding and the consequences that this would have for the most vulnerable workers.[141] As a result, the government was forced to concede amendments to its proposals to include certain protections for (vulnerable) workers. These concessions involved ensuring that workers were provided with a written statement detailing the rights forfeited under the scheme, the right to legal advice (at the expense of the employer) before agreeing to new status, and a seven-day cooling off period upon accepting the contract.[142]

There is a further strand of the UK Coalition's Employment Law Review which is of real interest in terms of the arguments put forward in this book. This is the introduction of a set of measures to amend procedural rules for employees/workers wishing to bring claims against their employers. One measure in particular will be considered here: the introduction of fees for bringing Tribunal claims.[143] These fees were introduced for all level of litigation, from issue of a Tribunal case to appeal. They applied to all categories of employment case, albeit stratified in terms of costs.[144] The government's rationale for the introduction of these fees was interesting.[145] First, the introduction was

---

[140] Vicount Younger of Leckie, in HL Deb 24 April 2013, col 1442

[141] Baroness Wheatcroft in HL Deb 20 March 2013, col 620 stated that: 'Throughout our debates, I have emphasised that we on this side strongly support wider employee share ownership... However, that is entirely different from trading shares for basic rights in what is an unequal employment relationship, which is the very reason why employment rights exist in the first place and why they have been built up by Governments of all parties over many decades.'

[142] These changes are implemented through the Growth and Infrastructure Act 2013, Section 31, which will occur in the Employment Rights Act as follows: s 205A (1) and (5) (a)-(j) ERA 96; 205A 6(a) ERA 96; s 205 A 6(b) ERA 96

[143] This was introduced in the Employment Tribunals and Employment Appeal Tribunal Fees Order 2013 (SI 2013/1893)

[144] There are two types of claims for the purposes of costs: A and B. Type A claims (theoretically more straightforward) attract lesser fees than Type B claims.

[145] A more detailed commentary on this rationale is provided in D Mangan, 'Employment Tribunal Reforms to Boost the Economy' (2013) 42 (4) *Industrial Law Journal* 409

presented as a cost measure: 'to ensure that the system is resourced to meet the needs of the economic climate with which we are all faced.'[146] Second, it was presented as necessary to reduce the 'burden on business' created by weak and 'vexatious' claims.[147] This presentation of the labour subject as 'vexatious' is worthy of note. It suggests that the labour subject has the power and potential to manipulate the Tribunal system essentially for economic gain. In the language of classical labour law, the inequality of bargaining power is reversed. It is no longer the employee who is vulnerable and needing to seek justice in order to strengthen that position. Rather, employers are presented as vulnerable to the vexatious litigant who will act to impose unnecessary and unfair costs on them. Tribunals are a cost and burden on economic functioning which can only be addressed by the reduction in access to justice. Although there may be discriminatory effects, these can be justified by the proportionality of measure in economic terms. Of course, this kind of argumentation complies only with a very extreme view of the operation of efficiency, and is an anathema to vulnerability theory. This kind of argumentation denies that workers are vulnerable and uses that denial to create further vulnerability for workers. This kind of policy will only increase the inequalities that exist (the weakest have even less access to rights) and will also serve as a barrier to the achievement of other mid-spectrum goals (such as social inclusion).

A final important point to make is the absence of any focus on strengthening representation or bargaining mechanisms for (precarious) workers in the Coalition reforms. In fact, some of the reforms could be detrimental to the bargaining position of precarious workers. For example, in the Employment Law Review, the government made changes to legislation on the transfer of undertakings and the operation of collective redundancies through the Collective Redundancies and Transfer of Undertakings (Protection of Employment) (Amendment) Regulations 2014 (CRATUPE). In CRATUPE it was provided that on the transfer of an undertaking, terms derived from collective agreements can be renegotiated to take effect one year post-transfer.[148] This is considerably less favourable than the position in relation to individual rights, where the restrictions on variation are more stringent.[149] A fear has been expressed that this could produce a 'two-tier' system of rights (with

---

[146]   BIS, *Resolving Workplace Disputes: A Consultation* (January 2011) 27
[147]   Ibid
[148]   Regulation 4 (5B) TUPE 2006
[149]   Regulation 4 (4) TUPE 2006

collective bargaining terms of lesser importance than individually negotiated terms).[150] It has also been suggested that this is in breach of international law.[151] There is also a weakening of the collective structure of negotiation in relation to collective redundancies. Not only has the time period for negotiation overall decreased with the advent of the new Regulations (and pre-transfer consultation negotiations now count for the purposes of calculating that time period),[152] small employers are no longer required to appoint employee representatives for the purposes of consultation. Consultation can now proceed 'directly' with the affected employees.[153]

Indeed, with the very recent election of a majority Conservative government, there is every indication that there will be a further weakening of support for trade union organisation and collective representation. On 15 July 2015 the Conservative government introduced a 'Trade Union Bill'[154] whose objective was to 'ensure that trade industrial action is only used as a measure of last resort and where there is clear and ongoing support' for that action.[155] The government proposed a new 50 per cent participation threshold for all trade union ballots. Instead of trade unions requiring a simple majority of votes cast to enable them to proceed legally to industrial action, this new threshold requires that 50 per cent of all trade union members registered to vote support the action in order for it to proceed. In addition, as part of the Trade Union Bill, the Conservative government proposed that trade union action in 'important public services' should require the support of 40 per cent of those entitled to vote in addition to the 50 per cent participation threshold. It is clear that both of these measures will reduce the ability of unions (and public service unions in particular) to proceed to strike action in the event of a dispute. This will weaken the bargaining power of unions in the ongoing negotiations for rights. There is the also the proposal as part of the Bill,

---

[150]   UNISON Scotland, 'Briefing 50: February 2014: Legislation Update TUPE 2014' <http://www.unison-scotland.org.uk/briefings/b050_Bargaining Brief_LegislationUpdateTUPE2014_Feb2014.pdf>

[151]   For example, in *Wilson and the National Union of Journalists: Palmer, Wyeth and the National Union of Rail, Maritime and Transport Workers: Doolan and others v United Kingdom* [2002] IRLR 128, the renegotiation of collectively agreed terms was deemed to constitute an offer to give up those terms and therefore to be in breach of Article 11 ECHR.

[152]   Section 198(A) TULR(C)A 1992

[153]   Regulation 13A TUPE 2006

[154]   Bill 58 (15 July 2015)

[155]   BIS, *Trade Union Reform: Consultation on Ballot Thresholds in Important Public Services* (July 2015) 3

that agency workers should be permitted to replace striking workers.[156] Again, this will significantly reduce the bargaining power of workers engaging in strike action, given that during the course of the strike action the employer's business needs would continue to be met.

The deregulation of employment law and the reregulation to impose greater vulnerability on workers illustrates the insight of vulnerability theory that vulnerability can be institutional, as well as economic and personal. Indeed, this kind of vulnerability creation can serve to reinforce already existing vulnerability at economic and personal levels. Individuals on the labour market are not autonomous beings best able to fend for themselves if stripped of their rights (employee shareholder status) or unable to access employment rights (previously) granted (the extension of the qualification period for unfair dismissal). They are not vexatious individuals with endless resources at their fingertips. Rather, they rely on sensitive policies which allow them to maximise their capabilities and develop their autonomy. These policies should also be multidimensional to reflect the multi-dimensional nature of vulnerability. That is not to say that they should be static and unresponsive to changing external conditions. However, there are certain basic vulnerabilities which will need to be addressed whatever the market conditions: for example, equality of opportunities, access to training to meet worker needs, a foundational social security network and access to means of representation and enforcement of the law. Without these guarantees, workers will be unable to build the resilience required under vulnerability theory and the overall development of society will be compromised.

4.5 CONCLUSIONS

It is theoretically possible that the law and policy on precarious work could share some of the concerns of vulnerability theory. On the one hand, that law and policy could be viewed as a response to particular economic/institutional vulnerabilities which need to be tackled at an individual level (to build resilience) as well as at the level of society (to create social progress through the development of mid-spectrum goals). Indeed, an analysis of the law and policy on precarious work at three different geographical levels (ILO, EU and UK), demonstrates that vulnerability concerns have informed the institutional response, albeit in different ways and at different times. At ILO level, the atypical work

---

[156] BIS, *Recruitment Sector: Hiring Agency Staff during Strike Action: Reforming Regulation* (July 2015)

Conventions displayed a concern for the particular vulnerability of atypical workers and the need to build resilience for those workers. This was repeated at EU level with the atypical work directives. At UK level, the vulnerable worker policy of the (previous) Labour government showed a concern for the different dimensions of vulnerability affecting workers. There was the identification of that vulnerability as both individual (relating to capabilities) and social (relating to the enforcement of rights). The importance of collective representation for tackling vulnerability was raised. The problem has been that the promise of vulnerability theory has not been met through these mechanisms for the regulation of precarious work. This can be attributed to a number of different factors. First, the theoretical underpinnings of the regulation for precarious work can often reflect the concerns of efficiency theory rather than the concerns of vulnerability theory. This is displayed at EU level by the manipulation of the 'flexicurity' agenda to meet the concerns of flexibility over the concerns of security for workers. This has translated into a watering down of directive provisions, or a focus on deregulation and promotion of atypical kinds of work rather than minimum standards for workers or increasing collective representation. Second, economic concerns have tended to take precedence over those of labour law, and this has particularly been the case in the wake of the financial crisis. Evidence of this is provided by the change in focus of employment law in the UK after 2010. The UK government (along with others) have argued that resources need to be reallocated away from employment law in order to ensure that the economy can continue to function. There has also been a continued pressure (contradictorily perhaps) to reduce the influence of collective bargaining and collective agreements on individual contracts. Finally, there is the question of institutional legitimacy and enforcement. For example, the ILO relies on maintaining legitimacy among its member states for the enforcement of its policies. This has meant that there has been a move away from setting strong legal standards towards other instruments. Furthermore, the enforcement mechanisms are weak, with the ILO relying on 'naming and shaming' of different governments in relation to their compliance with international standards. There is no mechanism for the ILO to force governments to change their domestic law (if that law is not incorporated automatically into the domestic legal system). This analysis suggests that a more coordinated response to the vulnerability arising from precarious work is required. This coordination might arise through the more comprehensive adoption of international standards, and the implementation of the EU social clause may provide some hope in this regard. This coordination might also involve a better and more committed approach to improving representation mechanisms for precarious workers. Indeed, these two elements are not mutually exclusive. Collective bargaining has always been central to the ILO's mission and forms one of the 'core labour standards'. The problem of course is that traditional collective bargaining mechanisms are difficult to access for precarious workers, and there is a distinct turn away from giving institutional support for collective bargaining. Furthermore, less traditional forms of help or representation for workers which rely on institutional support are also struggling. In the UK, there have been considerable cuts to public-funded representation and advice services in the wake of the financial crisis. Finally, the links between labour law and other social policy need to be further developed and explored. Social protection should become an element of international concern and should be taken away from employment policy and into law. Vulnerability will only be addressed through a focus on sustainable regulation which has institutional support. Only with this kind of stability can individuals start to build resilience and take control of their working lives.

5.   Temporary agency work

5.1 INTRODUCTION

The aim of this chapter is to investigate the themes identified in the previous chapters and apply them to one labour market group: temporary agency workers.[1] This group has been selected on the basis that temporary agency workers are generally considered among the most vulnerable on the labour market. This vulnerability has been presented as associated with a number of external pressures. These external pressures include the insertion of (all) workers into the capitalist system of production, as well as more specific economic elements such as the rise of 'new' forms of work following the advent of globalisation or the economic crisis of 2008. For example, temporary agency work has been presented as a typical example of one of the 'new' forms of work organisation associated with the globalisation of the economy.[2] Vulnerability arises when temporary agency work is used primarily as a cost-saving measure for firms seeking to maximise flexibility. The use of temporary agency work in this way means there is no incentive for companies to invest in these workers, which leaves the potential for temporary agency work to be poorly paid, low quality and lacking in job security. Temporary agency workers are also poorly organised as companies have become global players who have no incentive to invest in 'local' collective bargaining mechanisms (which often exclude agency workers in any event).[3]

---

[1]   Temporary agency work is characterised as a triangular employment relationship involving a temporary work agency, a client company and a temporary agency worker.

[2]   L Ratti, 'Agency Work and the Idea of Dual Employership: A Comparative Perspective' (2008–9) 30 *Comparative Labour Law and Policy Journal* 835, 838

[3]   It is argued that these pressures have created a particular set of vulnerabilities for temporary agency workers, as evidenced by the comment of the TUC that: 'It is our view that vulnerable employment cannot be discussed without reference to legally permissible inequalities in the treatment received by many atypical "workers" in the UK … Temporary workers are more likely than permanent workers to be low paid, and are much less satisfied with their job

In fact, this description may be rather simplistic and misleading. There is some evidence that temporary agency work is on the rise, as between September 2009 and May 2013, the number of agency workers as a percentage of the temporary workforce increased from 16.4 per cent to 18.9 per cent in May 2013.[4] It is difficult however to see temporary agency working as entirely 'new', as temporary agency working has long been a feature of the UK labour market,[5] and despite marginal increases in the number of temporary agency workers, the absolute number of these workers remains low (in the UK temporary workers made up only 6.3 per cent of the workforce in July 2013).[6] Furthermore, this character-isation of agency worker vulnerability does not take into account the diversity of temporary workers or of temporary agency work. Certainly, although some agency work is poorly paid and low skilled and associated with strategies of cost-saving and numerical flexibility, in fact, there is a growing demand for high-skilled or 'gold-collared' workers to meet the demands of the knowledge-based flexible economy.[7] These 'gold-collar' workers are able to attract high salaries for their specialist skills, and although it may be temporary, this work does not meet the stereotype of low quality work. Moreover, there is considerable diversity of contractual organisation within these two categories (low-paid workers versus gold-collar workers).

The 'economic' vulnerability of agency workers identified above has traditionally been coupled with a 'legal' vulnerability arising from the exclusion of (all) agency workers from legal rights. As a form of work

---

security. While some forms of temporary employment have been shown to act as stepping stones to permanent jobs, this is unlikely to be the case for those in low-paid and poorly protected posts.' TUC Commission on Vulnerable Employ-ment, 'Hard Work Hidden Lives: The Full Report of the Commission on Vulnerable Employment' (2008) 167 <http://www.vulnerableworkers.org.uk/files/CoVE_full_report.pdf> accessed 19 August 2011

[4]   Compare Office for National Statistics, 'Temporary employees' (May 2013) <http://www.ons.gov.uk/ons/rel/lms/labour-market-statistics/july-2013/table emp07.xls> and Office for National Statistics, 'Temporary employees (Nov 2011) <http://www.ons.gov.uk/ons/rel/lms/labour-market-statistics/december-2011/table emp07.xls> accessed 19 July 2013

[5]   P Leighton and M Wynn, 'Temporary Agency Working: Is the Law on the Turn?' (2008) 29 (1) *Company Lawyer* 7, 7

[6]   Office for National Statistics, 'Labour Market Statistics' (July 2013) <http://www.ons.gov.uk/ons/dcp171778_315111.pdf> accessed 19 July 2013

[7]   P Leighton, M Syrett, R Hecker and P Holland, *Out of the Shadows: Managing Self-employed, Agency and Outsourced Workers* (Butterworth-Heinemann 2007) 19

associated with the 'new economy', temporary agency work has a number of features which do not fit easily with the 'standard employment relationship' upon which labour law protection was established. As a tripartite rather than a traditional bipartite employment relationship, agency workers often have difficulty establishing employment status for the purposes of labour law. On a strict contractual analysis, there is the possibility that an agency worker will not have rights against either the agency (as an intermediary the agency has no mutuality or control) or the end-user (the company does not pay the worker).[8] Furthermore, even where the agency worker does establish a relationship in law against the end-user or the agency, the status of that relationship is far from clear. Certainly, agency workers have difficulty establishing 'employee' status, and may not even achieve the status of 'worker'. This is a function of the temporary nature of the assignments and, particularly for those at the lower end of the spectrum of agency workers in low-paid, low quality jobs, a function of the manipulation of contractual terms or arrangements by companies and agencies seeking to avoid costs.[9]

This presentation of the legal problems associated with agency work is not universally accepted. There is the argument that given the benefits that the 'knowledge' workers receive from agency contracts, and their market power, it is only right that they should be considered 'self-employed'.[10] Thus the problem is only for those at the lower end of the spectrum, who have no power to negotiate favourable contractual terms.[11] There is also the argument that legal protections for agency workers have dramatically increased over the last few years, and so the confusion in the case law on agency status is only a peripheral issue. For example, the passing of the Agency Worker Directive (TAWD)[12] means that in the EU agency workers will be entitled to equal treatment with permanent

---

[8]   M Wynn and P Leighton, 'Will the Real Employer Please Stand Up? Agencies, Client Companies and the Employment Status of the Temporary Agency Worker' (2006) 35 (3) *ILJ* 301, 303

[9]   Perhaps the most problematic group are those workers on zero-hours contracts. See Leighton P, 'Problems Continue for Zero-Hours Workers' (2002) 31 (1) *ILJ* 71

[10]   AL Bogg, 'Sham Self-employment in the Court of Appeal' (2010) 126 *Law Quarterly Review* 166, 166

[11]   Indeed, agency workers may not be the most vulnerable labour market group in this regard. Other groups, such as those on zero-hours contracts (rarely used by agencies) may be in a more vulnerable position. These will be discussed in more detail in Chapter 6, which deals with domestic work.

[12]   Directive 2008/14/EC of the European Parliament and the Council of 19 November 2008 on temporary agency work OJ [2008] L327/9

workers in terms of basic working terms and conditions. This is added to the already long list of protections for 'workers' who do not achieve 'employee' status.[13] Furthermore, in the UK, agency workers are protected by legislation which regulates the conduct of agencies. Although there have been problems with enforcement of this legislation in the past due to understaffing and underfunding of the Employment Agency Standards Inspectorate (EASI), there have recently been moves to increase the numbers and powers of the EASI inspectors with the hope that this will lead to a greater number of prosecutions against 'rogue' employment agencies.[14]

In any event, the literature on temporary agency work tends to concentrate on 'external' causes of worker vulnerability. There is less focus on the internal features of temporary agency worker vulnerability. In particular, the 'external' accounts of vulnerability tend to ignore important difficulties surrounding the identity and agency of temporary agency workers which lead to particular problems. On some accounts the problem is the presentation of temporary agency workers as a homogenous group, on others, the problem is that temporary agency workers are hardly considered a 'group' at all. All of these issues have implications for finding legal solutions for the vulnerabilities faced by these workers. It is suggested in this chapter that the search for legal solutions for temporary agency workers needs to start from the workers themselves, and to consider their dilemma in a relational sense. The legal structures need to be broken down and exposed as being themselves problematic; the solution not less regulation, but more helpful regulation to aid those workers to build agency and autonomy so that they can determine the best terms and conditions within the labour market.

5.2 OVERVIEW OF INSTRUMENTS

Before discussing in depth the possible application of the different views of vulnerability in the field of temporary agency work, it is perhaps just worth recapping the main legal and policy instruments in this field.

---

[13]   For example, workers are included within the scope of the National Minimum Wage Act 1998, and can also take advantage of the provisions on working time under the the Working Time Regulations 1998 (SI 1998/1833) and Working Time Regulations 1999 (SI 1999/3372).

[14]   BERR, 'Vulnerable worker enforcement forum: final report and government conclusions' (August 2008) 7 <http://www.bis.gov.uk/files/file47317.pdf> accessed 23 August 2011

Certainly, temporary agency work has been given considerable political and legal attention over the last few years, and the volume of new legal instruments is significant (in contrast to the position of domestic work which will be discussed in Chapter 6). The first instrument to emerge was the Private Employment Agencies Convention (PEAC) at ILO level.[15] This instrument aimed to ensure that private employment agencies were properly licensed, as well as ensuring a set of minimum standards for all temporary agency workers. These minimum standards were broadly defined, including access to training and maternity protection as well as 'basic' working conditions (pay, working time, and so on).[16] There was a particular emphasis on ensuring that temporary agency workers were given proper access to collective bargaining mechanisms and freedom of association.[17] Unlike other rights, the right to collective bargaining was not subject to the possibility of derogation by member states.[18]

The Private Employment Agencies Convention was not well ratified, possibly because of the breadth of its scope.[19] Certainly, the UK has not ratified the Convention, and for a long time, there was very limited regulation of agency work in this country. There were instruments regulating the conduct of employment agencies, which were strengthened during the Labour government's vulnerable worker policy from 2006 onwards. The vulnerable workers' policy also attempted to strengthen the relationship between (the most vulnerable) temporary agency workers and trade unions, and to improve access for agency workers to other centres of support and advice. But the introduction of legal protections and minimum standards for agency workers was largely resisted on economic grounds. Indeed, during the early stages of the vulnerable worker policy, the government made it clear that it was not in support of the introduction of EU-wide minimum standards for agency workers, and obstructed the introduction of the Temporary Agency Work Directive (TAWD) at EU level. It became clear, however, that the flexibilities within the TAWD meant that it could accommodate the UK position, and the TAWD was finally adopted in November 2008. The implementing

---

[15] ILO Convention 181, 'Convention Concerning Private Employment Agencies' (International Labour Office, Geneva 1997)

[16] Article 12 PEAC

[17] Article 4 PEAC

[18] The exclusion under Article 2 (4) (a) PEAC does not apply to Articles 4 (freedom of association) or Article 5 (non-discrimination).

[19] To date, only 30 countries have ratified this convention. This data is available at http://www.ilo.org/dyn/normlex/en/f?p=NORMLEXPUB:11300:0:: NO:11300:P11300_INSTRUMENT_ID:312326:NO> accessed 19 August 2015

legislation came into force on 1 October 2011, in the form of the Agency Worker Regulations (AWR).[20] The AWR guaranteed, for the first time, equal treatment rights for temporary agency workers with permanent employees in respect of certain 'basic' working terms and conditions.

5.3 CLASSICAL LABOUR LAW AND TEMPORARY AGENCY WORK

5.3.1 Characterisation of Vulnerability

According to the classical view of labour law, vulnerability is wide in that it attaches to all workers under the capitalist mode of production. Vulnerability is a function of the inequality of bargaining power between employers and (all) workers. Firstly, this inequality is created by the operation of the capitalist system under which labour becomes a 'commodity' to be bought and sold on the market. In Marxist terms, workers are exploited by capitalist employers, who use their superior economic bargaining power and ownership of the means of production to ensure that 'surplus value' created by those workers is siphoned off by employers for their own ends. Workers are forced into this relationship by the lack of real alternatives to meet their need for subsistence, and because they are alienated both from their own labour and from other workers, and are maintained in an inferior position compared to the 'bourgeoisie'.[21] Secondly, this inequality of bargaining power between workers and employers is created by the reality of the employment relationship which necessarily involves a 'power to command and a duty to obey',[22] aptly disguised by the institution of the 'contract of employment'. This contract of employment appears to be freely negotiated, but is in fact an 'element of subordination' which the worker has little power to change.[23] The existence of these inbuilt inequalities means that workers have the need, and in democratic societies, the right, to combine in autonomous trade unions to modify this imbalance of power by

---

[20]   SI 2010/93

[21]   R Belliotti, 'Marxist Jurisprudence: Historical Necessity and Radical Contingency' (1991) 4 (1) *Canadian Journal of Law and Jurisprudence* 145, 147

[22]   O Kahn-Freund, 'Some Reflections on Law and Power' in P Davies and M Freedland (eds), *Kahn-Freund's Labour and the Law* (Stevens and Sons 1983) 18

[23]   Ibid 18

collective action.[24] Indeed, it is only through the operation of collective power that there can be any autonomy or dignity achieved for the individual worker. The operation of this 'labour power' is essential in the recognition of workers as human beings rather than simply a commodity or article of commerce.[25]

On this view, agency workers would be seen as vulnerable. The classical view would adopt the Marxist perspective that like other workers of the 'proletariat', agency workers are subject to alienation and exploitation by the exigencies of a capitalist system co-opted by the 'bourgeoisie' for its own ends. Indeed, on this view, the characteristics of some agency work (low paid and lacking in job security) would be recognised as a typical example of the worst features of capitalist exploitation. More than this, agency workers would be seen as particularly vulnerable as they have been largely unable to organise to counteract the power of capital and management. Certainly, the statistics show that trade union density for temporary workers falls considerably below that for permanent workers. For example, in 2014, 26 per cent of permanent workers were members of trade unions, while this figure was only 15 per cent for temporary workers.[26] The difference was particularly stark in the private sector. Here, trade union density for temporary workers was only half that of permanent workers.[27]

5.3.2 Solutions to Vulnerability

According to the classical view, the solution to the vulnerability of agency workers is to increase the coverage of collective bargaining. Collective bargaining is preferred to the setting of legal standards as it achieves much more for workers. It has a role in establishing workplace democracy through the 'civilising' impact of collective agreements.[28] Under the collective agreement, management must conform to certain

---

[24] Lord Wedderburn, 'Collective Bargaining or Legal Enactment: the 1999 Act and Union Recognition' (2000) 29 (1) *ILJ* 1, 3

[25] Ibid 4

[26] BIS, 'Trade Union Membership 2014' (June 2015) 9 <https://www. gov.uk/government/uploads/system/uploads/attachment_data/file/431564/Trade_ Union_Membership_Statistics_2014.pdf> accessed 19 August 2015

[27] BIS, 'Trade Union Membership Statistics 2014' Table 1.4 <https://www. gov.uk/government/statistics/trade-union-statistics-2014> accessed 19 August 2015

[28] G Davidov, 'Collective Bargaining Laws: Purpose and Scope' (2004) 20 (1) *International Journal of Comparative Labour Law and Industrial Relations* 81, 89

rules, and therefore management actions are bound to be less arbitrary.[29] Another 'democratic' feature of well established collective bargaining mechanisms is the chance for workers to voice their views, and particularly to voice concerns which might otherwise carry the threat of dismissal.[30] This does not mean that there is no role for the 'law' and the setting of minimum legal standards for agency workers, but the argument is that standards alone cannot be effective because they 'cannot do much to modify the power relation between labour and management'.[31] Workers with no social power have no means to enforce them. Rather, in order for legal (or other) norms to be effective, they need to be backed by 'social sanctions', that is by 'the countervailing power of trade unions and other organised workers asserted through consultation and negotiation with the employer, and ultimately if this fails, through withholding their labour'.[32] Therefore, collective bargaining needs to be established *a priori* because without collective bargaining mechanisms there is no guarantee that legal standards can be enforced.

The central importance of collective bargaining in improving the position of agency workers (in line with the wide view of vulnerability) is given expression in the PEAC. Article 4 provides that 'measures shall be taken to ensure that the workers recruited by private employment agencies ... are not denied the right to freedom of association and the right to bargain collectively'. The fact that there is no derogation permitted from this article shows that these rights are considered foundational at ILO level, again in accordance with the argument on the wide view. At EU level, reference to collective bargaining is more nuanced, and there is no provision in the TAWD which (re)states the right of all temporary agency workers to bargaining collectively. That said, the TAWD is infused with the ethos of flexicurity, in which the social partners are deemed to have a central role. Article 5(3) TAWD is a good example of a provision which aims to involve the social partners in the furtherance of these flexicurity principles. It introduces flexibility into the legislation by allowing the social partners to negotiate terms and conditions for agency workers which 'while respecting the overall protection of temporary agency workers, may establish arrangements concerning the working and employment conditions which may differ' from the equal treatment principle. On the one hand, this provision has the potential to allow the social partners to obtain standards over and above those

---

[29]   Ibid 89
[30]   Ibid 89
[31]   Kahn-Freund (n 22) 19
[32]   Ibid 20

provided in the directive, and increase security for workers.[33] On the other hand, this provision allows the possibility for trade unions to *reduce* the protection of agency workers, and in practice, this has created real problems for agency workers. This also provides a real challenge to the theory of vulnerability on the classical view, and this will be discussed in more detail in the next section.

5.3.3 Criticisms of Classical Labour Law

The Marxist foundations of the classical view create severe problems when it comes to applying this theory in the real world and specifically to agency workers. Marxist theory tends to present all workers as part of the mass 'proletariat' and has no means of distinguishing between different individual situations. However, as we have seen, the labour market position of agency workers differs immensely. Some workers are indeed in low paid, low-skilled jobs and have little labour market power. Increasingly though, agency work is becoming a choice for highly qualified professionals who have considerable market power.[34] In this context, the (Marxist) metaphors of 'alienation' and 'exploitation' appear unsuitable. The metaphor of 'alienation' is best understood in terms of the factory system under which the creative and imaginative capacities of workers are reduced by mechanisation and repeated mundane tasks.[35] However, as far as the 'gold-collar' workers are concerned, they are part of the 'knowledge economy' and have the opportunity to use their creative and imaginative capacities. There is evidence that these workers

---

[33] M Schlachter, 'Transnational Temporary Agency Work: How Much Equality Does the Equal Treatment Principle Provide? (2012) 28 (2) *International Journal of Comparative Labour Law and Industrial Relations* 177, 194

[34] Evidence for this proposition is provided in B van Wanrooy, H Bewley, A Bryson, J Forth, S Freeth, L Stokes and S Wood, '2011 Workplace Employment Relations Study' 10 <https://www.gov.uk/government/uploads/system/uploads/attachment_data/file/210103/13-1010-WERS-first-findings-report-third-edition-may-2013.pdf> accessed 3 July 2014. In this study, it was found that as a result of the ongoing recession in the UK, only 3 per cent of workplaces had increased the use of temporary agency staff, whereas 16 per cent had reduced it. This suggests a reluctance to rely on 'numerical' flexibility strategies (using low paid temporary agency staff as a cost-saving measure in difficult economic circumstances). The profile of temporary agency worker bringing claims also suggests a set of 'gold-collar' temporary agency workers: see *Evans v Parasol Limited* [2011] ICR 37

[35] Belliotti (n 21) 145

have jobs which stimulate and challenge them.[36] It might also be difficult to argue that these workers suffer 'exploitation' on the labour market. 'Gold-collar' workers are highly mobile and arguably have a great number of labour market opportunities to choose from. They are therefore not 'forced' to stay in one position if the terms of that employment are not suitable. This takes away the power of employers to 'exploit' these workers, and to extract over and above the labour equivalent of what they produce.[37]

There are further theoretical problems for the classical view of labour law. As a general rule, this view assumes that workers have sufficient commonality of interest around which they can effectively organise, and that trade unions are effective at serving the interests of all these workers.[38] In the context of agency workers, these two assumptions are difficult to sustain. For a start, the commonality of interest under the classical view relies on an understanding of workers in a 'standard employment relationship'[39] supported by other labour and social institutions.[40] Agency working is a seminal example of a set of relationships which do not correspond with this standard employment relationship, and as such there is often no commonality of interest *within* the agency worker group. There is also a lack of communality of interest *between* agency workers and the wider working population. This poses difficulties for the placing of temporary agency workers within established traditional trade unions (assuming that permanent full-time workers still make up the core of those traditional unions). The interests of agency workers often conflict with those of permanent full-time workers, and so the trade union would not be able to serve both sets of interest. A particularly pertinent example is in relation to redundancy, where in times of economic crisis temporary agency workers tend to be the first to be dismissed. In this situation, if a trade union gives support to temporary agency worker members, the risk of redundancy would transfer to its permanent members, which would not be an acceptable situation for the union.

---

[36] Leighton and Wynn (n 5) 20
[37] Belliotti (n 21) 146
[38] J Fudge, 'Reconceiving Employment Standards Legislation: Labour Law's Little Sister and the Feminization of Labour' (1991) 7 *Journal of Law and Social Policy* 73, 77
[39] A Supiot, 'The Transformation of Work and the Future of Labour Law in Europe' (1999) 138 (1) *International Labour Review* 31, 33
[40] Ibid 35

The question is then whether specific unions could be formed outside the traditional union structure which would best serve the interest of just agency workers. Indeed, it has been argued by some modern authors that the establishment of collective bargaining in this way is essential for agency workers. As these workers often have very little market power, they have the least opportunity to take advantage of legal protection even where it exists.[41] They are particularly in need of collective bargaining to improve their market position. However, the evidence is that these kinds of specific unions have not been popular, and most agency workers, where they have become members of trade unions, are members of the most representative trade union in their sector.[42] Furthermore, there is evidence that where these specific trade unions have been established they have *reduced* the protection afforded to temporary agency workers. This position would clearly undermine the whole scheme of the classical labour law view. A good example is provided in Germany. Here, new legislation was introduced which included a provision in line with Article 5(3) TAWD (above), namely that equal protection rights for temporary agency staff could be avoided by collective agreement. This led to the establishment of a number of new unions, formed specifically for the purpose of maintaining lower wages and conditions in the temporary agency work sector.[43] The result was a reduction in standards for temporary agency workers across the sector, such that the original legislation had to be repealed.[44]

The above analysis lends weight to the argument that for temporary agency workers, collective bargaining simply cannot be an effective solution. Collective bargaining does not fit with temporary agency work as a new work form, and there is insufficient trade union membership among temporary agency workers for collective bargaining to fulfil its functions under the wide view (the increase in social power of workers vis-a-vis management). That said, there is some evidence that trade unions have been involved in increasing the visibility of temporary agency workers despite the low trade union density among these workers.

---

[41] N Smit and E Fourie, 'Extending Protection to Atypical Workers, Including Workers in the Informal Economy, in Developing Countries' (2010) 26 (1) *International Journal of Comparative Labour Law and Industrial Relations* 43, 53

[42] H Frenzel, 'The Temporary Agency Work Directive' (2010) 1 (1) *European Labour Law Review* 119, 130

[43] Schlachter (n 33) 195

[44] The new legislation is the Erstes Gesetz zur Änderung des Arbeitnehmerüberlassungsgesetzes, 28.4.2011, BGBl.I.642

This action is rather difficult to explain on the classical view, and will be discussed further in the section on the vulnerable subject approach to temporary agency work in Section 5.6.

5.4 EFFICIENCY THEORIES AND TEMPORARY AGENCY WORK

5.4.1 Characterisation of Vulnerability

On labour law views sympathetic to efficiency regulation, there would certainly be some agency workers who would be seen as vulnerable (at least among those taking the new institutional economic view of regulation). This vulnerability would be interpreted narrowly; attaching to workers recruited by companies as part of a strategy of numerical flexibility, with no investment in the employability of those workers. They are trapped in low quality, low skilled jobs which offend the principles of the knowledge economy and do not allow them to progress.[45] On the other hand, certain agency workers would not be seen as vulnerable. These agency workers would be represented by 'gold-collar workers' who use their knowledge and expertise to command high salaries and favourable working conditions. Such workers have high level of autonomy and are able to use their skills and knowledge to ensure that a job is performed efficiently. They have a high level of employment security and are able to ensure continued investment in their expertise. This kind of 'flexible employee'[46] is the most valued on the narrow view, as both a contributor to and beneficiary of the flexible knowledge economy.

There is a recognition on this narrow view of vulnerability that labour law fails to recognise the diversity of agency workers, and neither supports vulnerable agency workers nor encourages the advancement of gold-collar workers essential to the new economy. Labour law regulation is based on an outdated understanding of the functioning of the contract of employment represented by the 'standard employment relationship'. Agency work contracts do not correspond to this kind of relationship, because they are for a limited period, and they are also characterised by a trilateral employment relationship between an agency, an agency worker and company end-user. There is also a wide diversity of agency

---

[45]   H Collins, 'Regulating in the Employment Relation for Competitiveness' (2001) 30 (1) *ILJ* 29

[46]   Ibid 24

work situations within the agency work category. Therefore, regulation associated with traditional contractual analysis based on the standard employment relationship fails to support agency workers, and also fails to recognise the different positions in which *individual* agency workers find themselves.

5.4.2 Solutions and Criticisms of Efficiency Theories

The difficulty is the kind of reregulation which should follow from this analysis on the efficiency view of labour law. These difficulties are both theoretical and practical. On a theoretical level, the efficiency view is a liberal view, and hence tied into a contractual analysis which upholds freedom of contract for the majority of workers (although this freedom may be modified where there is evidence of severe abuse). There are real flaws in this contractual analysis for agency workers. On a purely contractual analysis, agency workers are denied the employment status required to gain access to any employment rights. In terms of the relationship between the agency and the agency worker, the pure contractual analysis can be used to argue that the agency simply acts as a recruitment vehicle with no long term control over (or mutuality of obligation with) the agency worker.[47] This kind of argument has been used in the UK courts to deny any contractual status between agency and agency worker.[48] In terms of the relationship between the end-user and the agency worker, it can be argued through a contractual analysis that the fact that the end-user does not pay the agency worker means there is no 'work-wage' bargain on which to found mutuality of obligation.[49]

In the UK, recent court decisions have followed this approach, calling into question previous decisions which suggested that a contract could be implied between temporary agency worker and end-user.[50] In

---

[47] Leighton and Wynn (n 5) 303

[48] *Montgomery v Johnson Underwood Ltd* [2001] IRLR 269, *Brook Street Bureau (UK) v Dacas* [2004] IRLR 358 and *Bunce v Postworth Ltd* [2005] IRLR 557. These cases appear to call into doubt the earlier case of *McMeecham v Secretary of State for Employment* [1997] IRLR 353 in which the Claimant successfully argued that he had achieved employee status with the agency. The decision of the Court of Appeal was based on a rather elaborate construction consisting of two contracts: one in existence during assignments and the other in existence between assignments.

[49] Leighton and Wynn (n 5) 301

[50] Historically, there have also been instances where the courts have been open to the argument that an employment relationship exists between an agency worker and client or end-user. Prior to 2006, there was no direct authority for this

James v Greenwich Council the court held that there should be no assumption of a contract between an agency worker and end-user, unless there was some particular action over and above 'normal' conduct by either the agency or the company to justify that assumption.[51] A contract should only be implied where it was necessary to do so to reflect the business reality of the relationship.[52] This case served to affirm the contractual analysis and has been referred to consistently in later cases. For example, in the case of *Tilson v Alstom Transport*[53] the court applied the 'necessity' test outlined in *James* to conclude that there was no contract between the agency worker and client. The court was keen to point out that employment status could not be found simply on the basis of 'public policy' or because the arrangement resembled an employment contract. Something more was needed. Furthermore, in the case *of Eric Muschett v HM Prison Service*,[54] the Claimant failed to establish status with the end-user (or the agency) on the basis that there were insufficient facts upon which to infer that the implication of contract for services was necessary.[55] This position was also adopted in the recent case of *Smith v Carillion*, in which the agency worker was not found to have a contract of any kind with the end-user company.[56]

The necessity test may be avoided where there is evidence of a 'sham agreement' deliberately created to avoid statutory protection for the worker. This may aid agency workers in establishing worker status, although it has not necessarily been helpful to agency workers in the past. In the case of *Consistent Group v Kalwak*[57] for instance, the agency

---

position, although *Franks v Reuters Ltd* [2003] IRLR 423 did suggest that an implied contract could be found between an agency worker and client where there was a relationship which proceeded for a considerable time. There were also obiter comments in *Dacas v Brook Street Bureau* [2004] IRLR 358 that a finding of a contractual relationship between an agency worker and client was possible. In 2006, the courts moved from suggesting a possible relationship between client and agency worker to finding a relationship as a matter of fact. However, In *Cable & Wireless v Muscat* [2006] IRLR 354 the court held that Muscat was an employee of the end-user, based on the specific facts (a highly paid worker in the IT services industry who provided his services through a limited company to the client via an agency).

[51]   [2008] ICR 545, para 51
[52]   Ibid para 52
[53]   [2010] EWCA Civ 1308
[54]   [2010] EWCA Civ 25
[55]   Ibid para 38
[56]   (2014) WL 16572
[57]   [2008] EWCA Civ 430

workers were unsuccessful in proving that their contract with the agency was a sham (and therefore establishing contractual status) because the Court of Appeal required proof that both parties intended to paint a false picture as to the true nature of their respective obligations. This followed the approach adopted in relation to commercial contracts, where the 'freedom' of the parties of the contract was considered paramount. However, in the later case of *Firthglow Limited (trading as Protectacoat) v Szilagi*,[58] the Court required only that one party intended to misrepresent the relationship (that is, the employer) in order to show that there was a sham contract, and the worker was able to prove status in this case. Furthermore, in the recent case of *Autoclenz v Belcher*,[59] the Court of Appeal suggested that the vulnerability of the worker should be taken into account when considering the existence of a sham agreement:

> So the relative bargaining power of the parties must be taken into account in deciding whether the terms of any written agreement in truth represent what was agreed and the true agreement will often have to be gleaned from all the circumstances of the case, of which the written agreement is only part.

This suggests that if agency workers are considered particularly at risk in the labour market, the court may look beyond the contractual documentation to avoid agency workers being excluded from labour law rights. Despite the fact that this denies freedom of contract, this solution may be acceptable to the narrow view, given that it is only activated in certain extreme cases where there is a real risk of abuse.

On a practical level, it is very difficult to create policies which recognise the diversity of agency worker situations: to simultaneously support 'gold-collar' workers and protect vulnerable agency workers. One attempt to provide this simultaneous support and protection has been to institute training programmes which improve employment security for all (agency) workers. This falls under the ambit of 'regulation for competitiveness' or regulation for 'flexicurity'; the idea is that a reduction in rigid employment protection mechanisms associated with 'jobs for life' operates within a framework consisting of strong social security systems and investment in 'lifelong learning' which allows workers to achieve their (individual) goals and ensures they are adequately supported in a 'flexible' knowledge-based economy.[60] In practice however, 'flexicurity'

---

[58]   [2009] IRLR 365
[59]   [2011] IRLR 820
[60]   European Commission, 'Towards Common Principles of Flexicurity: More and better jobs through flexibility and security' COM (2007) 359 final, 6

policies which have attempted to improve 'employment' security for all
(agency) workers in the knowledge economy have, at best, tended to aid
gold-collar workers and neglect the more vulnerable agency workers. In
Denmark, which is viewed as having a progressive government training
policy compliant with the ethos of 'flexicurity', there is a wide disparity
between workplaces and the type of workers receiving vocational training. There seems to be reluctance here among companies to invest in
training for unskilled workers, with most of the training budget reserved
for top managers, skilled workers and salaried employees.[61] In the UK, a
legal right to request training came into force on 6 April 2010.[62]
However, this right was restricted to 'employees' with 26 weeks'
service[63] and agency workers were specifically excluded from the legislation.[64] The effect of this exclusion was to increase rather than reduce
the vulnerability of some agency workers, and undermine the provisions
of the AWR. For example, although under the AWR, agency workers are
to be given the same opportunities as permanent staff to apply for
vacancies in the user undertaking, if they are excluded from training
opportunities (within the firm), they are perhaps less likely to obtain a
permanent position even if aware of a vacancy.

The difficulty of addressing all agency workers might lead to the
conclusion that it is the vulnerable agency workers who should be given
targeted support to ensure that they can take advantage of the benefits of
the knowledge economy. In the UK, a number of specific measures
targeting particularly vulnerable agency workers were introduced in the
vulnerable worker policy. A 'Vulnerable Worker Enforcement Forum'
was set up to make a number of policy recommendations and reflect on
strategies to improve the position of the most vulnerable agency workers.
The main recommendations consisted of improving institutional structures to ensure the most vulnerable workers were fully aware of their
employment rights (rather than suggesting that they needed new rights).[65]

---

[61]   Ibid 201

[62]   The main provisions are contained in a new Part 6A of the Employment
Rights Act 1996 comprising sections 63D to 63K. These Regulations are
supplemented by two statutory instruments: the Employee Study and Training
(Procedural Requirements) Regulations 2010 (SI 2010/155) and the Employee
Study and Training (Eligibility, Complaints and Remedies) Regulations 2010 SI
2010/156

[63]   Regulation 2 (1) Employee Study and Training (Qualifying Period of
Employment) Regulations 2010 SI 2010/800

[64]   Section 63 D (7) (d) Employment Rights Act 1996

[65]   BERR (n 14) 28

There were also a number of measures to try to improve the regulation of 'rogue' agencies through increasing the number and power of inspectors connected to the EASI. However, the 'pilot' projects implementing the new institutional structures were temporary and never fully followed through,[66] and the regulation measures have only had a minor influence on improving the position for agency workers. Furthermore, any positive outcomes of these pilots have now been severely undermined by the reduction in funding for the Citizens' Advice Bureau and the closure of some branches as a result of public sector funding cuts.[67]

5.5 SOCIAL LAW AND TEMPORARY AGENCY WORK

5.5.1 Characterisation of Vulnerability

According to the sociological or social law view of vulnerability, workers are vulnerable if they are not organised as a 'group' and if they are not recognised as a group in need of protection (by the state). This is because, as we have seen, under the social law scheme it is groups rather than individuals that are the subject of the law. The law is not merely a formal 'right' based on high philosophical or moral ideals, but rather is a policy response recognising a particular settlement reached between social groups. Therefore, if the state has intervened to guarantee a certain level of protection to a group, it is because the state has recognised that the maintenance of the *relationship* (that is, between employers and agency workers) is important for society, and therefore it is in the interest of the state that the 'burdens and profits' produced by their activities are equally distributed.[68] The pervasiveness of the state and the law under the social law scheme means that rights have far more 'power' for groups in a practical sense than rights under a liberal regime. They can be utilised on a day-to-day basis to gain advantage: rights are a 'weapon, a strength,

---

[66] Ibid 49. This provides information on the pilots. They were commissioned in 2007 and ran for two years. One was based in London (City and Docklands) and focused on the cleaning and building services sector. The other was based in Birmingham and focussed on the hospitality sector.

[67] C Jayanetti, 'Exclusive: More than 2000 charities and community groups face cut' (2 August 2011) <http://falseeconomy.org.uk/blog/exclusive-more-than-2000-charities-and-community-groups-face-cuts> accessed 23 August 2014

[68] F Ewald, 'A Concept of Social Law' in G Teubner (ed), *Dilemmas of Law in the Welfare State* (Walter de Gruyter 1986) 43

an advantage one should seek to have'.[69] Therefore under the social law scheme, groups that are the subject of legislation have significantly more power than those outside the law. Of course, as the law is simply the recognition of social compromise between groups, it is subject to manipulation and change, but association remains the only way to achieve status and power and to neutralise social conflict.

As far as agency workers are concerned, it has already become clear that agency workers have not been particularly successful at forming specific groups to represent their interests at work. However, more traditional unions have been involved in promoting the interests of these workers, and the 'visibility' of the group has increased in this way. In the UK for example, the TUC promoted the adoption of the TAWD and negotiated for a reduction in the length of the qualification period for these rights.[70] Furthermore, the Communication Workers Union (CWU) has been involved in highlighting the 'exploitation' of agency workers in the UK, and promoting the correct implementation of the TAWD in the UK.[71] Under the social law view, the development of the rights under the TAWD and subsequently the AWR would indicate the success of group action in increasing the visibility of temporary agency workers vis-a-vis the state and reducing their vulnerability.

However, the social law view would be uncomfortable with the *nature* of the equality granted by the agency legislation. The TAWD and the AWR are founded on the notion of formal equality; that is 'likes must be treated alike'.[72] The idea of formal equality is inspired by liberal notions of state neutrality, individualism and the promotion of autonomy.[73] This formal equality does not guarantee any particular outcome for agency workers, and particularly it does not guarantee the improvement of the position of agency workers generally. This is because all that formal equality demands is consistency of treatment; there is no distinction between treating agency workers just as *badly* as other workers as

---

[69]   Ibid 46

[70]   TUC, 'The EU Temp Trade': Temporary Agency Working Across the European Union' (2005) <http://www.tuc.org.uk/extras/eu_agency.pdf> accessed 19 July 2014

[71]   L Peacock, 'Protests begin over agency workers cheated on pay' *The Telegraph* (16 January 2013) <http://www.telegraph.co.uk/finance/jobs/hr-news/9803866/Protests-begin-over-agency-workers-cheated-on-pay.html> accessed 19 July 2013

[72]   B Hepple and C Barnard, 'Substantive Equality' (2000) 59 (3) *Cambridge Law Journal* 562, 562

[73]   S Fredman, 'Equality: A New Generation' (2001) 30 (2) *ILJ* 145, 154

opposed to treating them equally *well*. This problem is compounded in the AWR by the requirement that the 'comparator' for determining the terms and conditions for agency workers need only be an 'employee' engaged in the 'same or broadly similar work'. In theory, then the comparator could be a worker engaged on a (short) fixed-term contract who may in fact be working under less favourable conditions than a full-time worker.[74] Therefore, there must be serious doubt as to whether this legislation will achieve social law ideals, which aim for group empowerment and the correction of inequality through granting previously 'passed over' groups a level of material or substantive equality with other social groups.

The second problem is that the equality granted in the TAWD and the AWR is limited not only in terms of type, but also in terms of its scope.[75] According to the provisions of the TAWD and AWR, agency workers are entitled to the same 'basic working and employment conditions' as 'employees' at the end-user. These basic working conditions refer to pay and working time benefits.[76] However, the definition of 'pay' adopted in the AWR is very restricted and excludes a long list of benefits available to company employees. Benefits excluded in the definition of 'pay' are (among others):

(1)　occupational sick pay;
(2)　pension payment;
(3)　payment in respect of maternity, paternity or adoption; and
(4)　payment in respect of redundancy.[77]

The TAWD and AWR further provide that agency workers should have the same right of access as 'comparable workers' to collective facilities and amenities, which include canteen, childcare and transport services.[78] These rights are also limited however, as less favourable treatment of agency workers as regards access to these services can be justified on objective grounds.[79] Finally, the provisions in the TAWD and AWR do not guarantee equality of *status* for agency workers. In the TAWD,

---

[74]　N Countouris and R Horton, 'The Temporary Agency Work Directive: Another Broken Promise?' (2009) 38 (3) *ILJ* 329, 333

[75]　Indeed, the TUC lodged a formal complaint with the European Commission that the AWR failed to properly implement the directive

[76]　Article 3 (1) (f) TAWD and Article 6 (1) AWR

[77]　Article 6 (3) AWR

[78]　Article 6 (4) TAWD and Regulation 12 AWR

[79]　Article 6 (4) TAWD and Regulation 12 (2) AWR

Article 2 provides that the directive aims to 'ensure the protection of temporary agency workers and to improve the quality of temporary agency work … by recognising temporary-work agencies as employers'. It is possible to argue from this statement that there is a presumption that agency workers are employees of their temporary work agency.[80] However, the directive is drafted 'without prejudice to national law as regards the definition of pay, contract of employment, employment relationship or worker'.[81] On translation of the provisions of the TAWD therefore, the UK government has not used this opportunity to clarify the status of agency workers. The AWR simply provide that an 'agency worker' is an individual who works either under a contract of employment with the agency or has 'any other contract to perform work or services personally for the agency.[82] The result is that agency workers will continue to be denied a range of rights associated with 'employee' status (for example, rights to claim unfair dismissal).

From the above discussion, it appears that the equality legislation in place for agency workers does not meet the premises of social law. The liberal foundations of this legislation and its reliance on formal equality mean that it is unable to guarantee any level of substantive equality. The question is how substantive equality for agency workers could be achieved without *over* compensating some agency workers, given the diversity in their situations. Certainly, some agency workers already receive the same or better conditions than permanent workers. Furthermore, the idea of privileging agency workers is controversial in the context of scepticism about the desirability of this particular form of working. This scepticism is exemplified by comments at European level that 'stable' employment contracts of indefinite duration are the 'general form of employment relationship' in the EU, and that protecting workers against instability of employment is a valid aim of EU law.[83] It could therefore be suggested that reducing the ability of companies to resort to agency work could be more in line with achieving substantive equality than creating conditions favouring it. Perhaps the solution that would best

---

[80]   E McGaughey, 'Should Agency Workers be Treated Differently?' (July 2010) LSE Law, Society and Economy Working Papers 07/2010, 5 <http://papers.ssrn.com/sol3/papers.cfm?abstract_id=1610272> accessed 12 August 2014

[81]   Article 3(2) TAWD

[82]   Regulation 3 (b) AWR

[83]   Joined cases C-378/07 to C-380/07 *Kiriaki Angelidaki and Others v Organismos Nomarkhiaki Aftodiikisi Rethimnis and Dimos Geropotamu*, [2009] ECR I-03071, para 99

fit in practice with the ethos of social law is the regulation of employment agencies rather than agency workers. This involves state interference in 'private' affairs, a situation which would be objectionable by a liberal view, but which fits well with the socialisation of economic processes promoted by social law. The tighter regulation of agencies would also presumably go some way to levelling the playing field *between* agency workers, rather than between agency and permanent workers. Indeed, it has been recognised at both national and international level that there is the potential for agencies to 'abuse' workers. At international level, the PEAC was set up on the basis of the 'need to protect workers against abuses'. The PEAC recognised, in particular, the often poor treatment of migrant workers by employment agencies. In Article 8, the PEAC provides that ratifying countries should ensure that, in relation to agencies dealing with migrant workers, there are 'laws or regulations which provide for penalties, including prohibition of those private employment agencies which engage in fraudulent practices in abuses'.

In the UK, the government does regulate private employment agencies to a certain extent. As early as 1973, the Employment Agencies Act (EAA) prohibited the charging of upfront fees to agency workers (with a number of exceptions).[84] The EAA also gave discretion to the Secretary of State to ban agencies for regulatory breach.[85] More recently, the EAA was amended by the Conduct of Employment Agencies and Employment Businesses Regulations 2003 (CEABR 2003)[86] which (further) restricted the activities of employment agencies. For example, there are now restrictions on agencies selling other services, using agency workers during industrial disputes and giving false information to agency workers about the nature of their business.[87] However, by 2006 it was clear that 'while the majority of agencies treat their workers fairly' there were still a significant number of agencies which were mistreating agency workers.[88] Further amendments were made to the CEABR 2003 in 2007 and again in 2010. The Conduct of Employment Agencies and Employment Businesses (Amendment) Regulations 2010[89] made it easier for agency workers to withdraw from agency contracts and provided specific

---

[84]   s 6 EAA
[85]   s 13 EAA
[86]   SI 2003/3319
[87]   Regulations 5, 7 and 9 CEABR 2003
[88]   DTI, *Success at Work: Protecting Vulnerable Workers, Supporting Good Employers. A policy statement for this Parliament* (March 2006) 18
[89]   SI 1782/2010

requirements for information to be given to agency workers on commencement of their contracts.[90] However, despite these amendments, there remain serious problems with the package of legislative measures for agency workers. The first problem is that there is no consistency on the issue of licensing. Licensing is required only in certain restricted industries and licences are regulated by the Gangmasters Licensing Agency rather than the EASI. This is unfortunate, given that the threat of licence revocation is a real incentive for agencies to comply with the regulations.[91] The second problem is that there remain exceptions to the prohibition on agency fees. Fees can still be charged in relation to actor, modelling, musician and sports jobs. These fees are detrimental as they 'can reach high levels without any promise of work' and can be a barrier to jobs.[92] The third problem is that of enforcement. The enforcement of the agency regulations traditionally relies on public bodies which are understaffed and underfunded, although some moves have been made to increase the productivity and number of inspectors in recent years. It also appears to be inefficient to have two public bodies (GLA and the EASI) operating in this field.[93]

5.5.2   Criticisms of the Social Law Approach

On the social law view, it is assumed that agency workers have achieved a certain negotiation status because of their inclusion in (equality) legislation, and therefore a certain equality of bargaining power. What is clear however from the AWR is that the negotiation position of groups favouring industry has been preferred (by the state) over groups favouring agency workers. This is particularly apparent in the compromise reached on the 'qualifying period' for the application of the AWR. Despite the fact that, in the consultation for the AWR, groups representing agency workers felt that there should not be a qualifying period for

---

[90]   Regulation 4 and Regulation 6 CEABR 2010
[91]   McGaughey (n 80) 12
[92]   Ibid 12
[93]   The CEABR 2010 are again subject to consultation under the Employment Law Review in the UK: BIS, 'Consultation on Reforming the Regulatory Framework for Employment Agencies and Employment Businesses' (January 2013) <https://www.gov.uk/government/consultations/consultation-on-reforming-the-regulatory-framework-for-employment-agencies-and-employment-businesses> accessed 30 May 2013. Although this consultation closed on 11 April 2013, the government has not yet produced a response to the consultation.

this legislation,[94] the UK government conceded to industry pressure and drafted the AWR on the basis of a qualifying period of 12 weeks.[95] The evidence is that this qualifying period will automatically exclude over half of agency workers from benefitting from the provisions of the legislation.[96] The negotiation problems faced by agency workers and their supporters are further illustrated by the formal complaint made by the TUC to the European Commission in 2013. In this complaint, the TUC argued that the AWR failed to implement the TAWD properly into domestic law. For example, the TUC pointed out that the definition of pay in the TAWD was in fact narrower than that used in other employ-ment and tax legislation (for example, s.27 Employment Rights Act 1996), and that they did not agree with some of the exclusions set out in Regulation 6(3). The TUC admitted that they did agree that occupational sick pay and occupations pensions should be excluded, but they did not agree to the exclusion of bonuses not directly applicable to the amount or quality of work done, share options and contractual maternity, paternity and adoption pay. Indeed, it is possible to argue that the whole ethos of the TAWD and AWR is rather industry focussed. The Preamble to the TAWD is dominated by references to 'flexicurity', which in theory seeks a balance between employer flexibility and worker security, but in practice allows employers to proceed unhindered with practices which undermine job (and other types of) security for workers.[97]

The problem with the social law scheme then is the assumed relation-ship between negotiating power and rights. It is assumed that in achieving certain rights, a particular group is no longer vulnerable because they have achieved recognition by the state. The experience of temporary agency workers suggests that this is not the case. There is also the problem that under the social law scheme there is nothing permanent about groups or group protection. The law is consistently up for grabs. Although this might seem empowering, in fact it suggests that there is nothing systemic about vulnerability, or that vulnerability is not the most interesting line of enquiry in relation to workers generally or precarious work specifically. Again vulnerability is under-theorised. It appears that

---

[94] BIS, 'Agency Workers Directive Consultation: Summary of Responses to Consultation' (October, 2009) 15 <http://www.bis.gov.uk/files/file53185.pdf> accessed 19 August 2011

[95] Regulation 7 (1) AWR

[96] Countouris and Horton (n 74) 333

[97] M De Vos, 'Flexicurity and Globalization: A Critical Perspective' (2009) 25 (3) *International Journal of Comparative Labour Law and Industrial Rela-tions* 209, 217

what is needed is a theory which places vulnerability at the heart of all employment regulation. This would allow the possibility for the recognition of the importance of negotiation for vulnerable groups/individuals but provide more support to vulnerable groups and individuals in achieving those strategies and maintaining rights. The potential of the 'vulnerable subject' approach in this regard will be considered in the next section.

5.6 THE VULNERABLE SUBJECT AND TEMPORARY AGENCY WORK

Under the vulnerable subject approach, vulnerability is pervasive. Vulnerability attaches to all workers by virtue of their humanity. For all workers there is the ever present possibility of dependency, as abilities and capacities shift through a lifecycle. According to the vulnerable subject approach, this vulnerability needs to be at the heart of the law. It is argued that currently, the law fails (vulnerable) individuals for a number of reasons. First, that law is based on an understanding of the 'liberal subject': an atomised, economically rational individual. Autonomy of that individual is assumed. As a result, governments argue for restrained intervention on the basis that the autonomy of individuals needs to be respected. The result is minimalist intervention in, for example, employment relationships. Second, the law is based on 'formal' equality premised on the idea of sameness of treatment (between equally rational, autonomous individuals). This formal model of equality relies on designated distinguishing characteristics which have limited value in protecting individuals. Designating these distinguishing characteristics means that divisions between different groups are emphasised over their sameness, with the result that those groups are pitted against each other in the struggle for limited resources.[98] This focus on individual and group characteristics also obscures distributions of power, wealth opportunity or social goods which have affected the organisation of interest groups and legal protections. As a result, the equality legislation does little to disrupt persistent forms of inequality.[99]

In relation to temporary agency work, it is clear that formal modes of equality in the law do not reach all agency workers, or deal with all lines

---

[98]   M Fineman, 'The Vulnerable Subject and the Responsive State' (2010) 60 *Emory Law Journal* 251, 253

[99]   M Fineman 'The Vulnerable Subject: Anchoring Equality in the Human Condition' (2008) 20 (1) *Yale Journal of Law and Feminism* 2, 3

of vulnerability. More than this, there is a problem with the identification of temporary agency workers as a group. There is a problem with this in an economic sense, in terms of the wide diversity of agency workers that exists. Some agency workers may be highly paid knowledge workers, while others will be low-paid workers holding low status positions. There is also a problem with temporary worker identity in another sense. The regulations pertaining to temporary agency work regulations divide more than they unite. Examples are provided by the provisions of the TWR in the UK. For a start, there are status and qualification requirements which it is very difficult for the majority of agency workers to fulfil. More generally, the requirement that there must be an 'agency' relationship means that the temporary agency work legislation can help only a very narrow range of vulnerable temporary workers. Likewise, the requirement that the work must be 'temporary' also limits the extent of the legislation to really help vulnerable individuals. This is illustrated by the recent case of *Moran v Ideal Cleaning Services Limited.*[100] In this case a number of cleaners were employed by ICS for a number of years but then placed with a second company. They argued that they were agency workers and therefore entitled to be treated equally to the second company's permanent employees in accordance with Regulation 5 AWR. The EAT held that they could not fall within the scope of the AWR because they were placed on a permanent basis with the second company and were therefore not 'temporary'. The EAT recognised the potential for injustice but pointed out:

> Insofar as that may be thought by some to leave a lacuna in the scope of protection of the legislation that is a lacuna that was deliberately left by the legislative organs of the European Union, which in this context included the Parliament, which of course is the only directly elected institution of the European Union.[101]

More broadly, the identity of temporary agency workers has been constructed as economically determined (that is, through economic processes of globalisation). This is a problem for the development of the law in this area because the presentation of this kind of work as an economic choice creates a deregulatory pressure.[102] Furthermore, the

---

[100] [2014] 2 CMLR 37

[101] Ibid para 48

[102] A particular example of this is provided in relation to a recent consultation on the regulation of zero-hours contracts. Zero-hours contracts are problematic because not only do they fail to guarantee any level of income, the employment status of individuals employed on these kinds of contracts is very

economic identity of temporary agency workers might be viewed as not only a constraint on the development of the law, but also the development of mechanisms outside of the law which might enable agency workers to promote their concerns and build resilience. Temporary agency workers do not appear to have been able to mobilise behind a common concern. This can be contrasted with the position of domestic workers, who have (to some degree) been able to mobilise behind different and intersecting identities to the purely economic (for example, gender, immigration status, and so on).[103]

On the vulnerability analysis, it is suggested that significant progress could be gained from a move away from identity-based considerations towards wider enquiries into privilege and disadvantage. It is suggested that this would allow a set of more fundamental questions about the current organisation of wealth and work to be asked.[104] As privilege and disadvantage cross different (identity) categorisations, then the structures and institutions which support our current organisation come under scrutiny, and particularly the ways in which those institutions produce or exacerbate existing inequalities.[105] For example, it may be possible to see the problem of agency work as a much wider problem concerning the separation in law which is made between dependent employment relationships and those of self-employment. It is possible to argue that many of the identity-based qualifications and considerations in the law are based around this distinction. The idea that temporary agency workers must work for 12 weeks before qualifying for equal treatment imbues the

---

uncertain. However, the government's consultation did not address either of these particular concerns. Only a very minor amendment was made to the law, banning exclusivity in the use of these contracts (inserting a new Section 27A into the Employment Rights Act 1996). The justification given by the government was as follows: 'Zero hours contracts have been used responsibly in some sectors for many years. They can support business flexibility, making it easier to hire new staff and providing pathways to employment for young people. These contracts and other flexible arrangements give individuals more choice and the ability to combine their work with their other commitments.' BIS, *Consultation: Zero Hours Contracts* (December 2013) 4

[103]   This will be discussed in more detail in Chapter 6.

[104]   Fineman (n 99) 21 suggests a number of questions including: Why do we privilege contract over status, market over family or individual? Why does law divide up the market analytically and put its various parts in competition with each other: corporation versus workers versus consumers versus government? Why do we have a fictitious public/private divide imposed on the family and in employment?

[105]   Ibid 21

idea that for shorter periods it is the temporary agency worker who is enjoying the benefits of a large amount of work flexibility and therefore must take on the risk of that work. Another (paradoxical) example is that an agency worker is only protected by the legislation if they are employed on a temporary basis. Once they are more permanently placed, then the assumption is that they have taken on an 'employee' or 'worker' type relationship and are therefore covered by core employment laws. Once an agency worker is permanently employed, the risk should shift to the employer rather than remain with the individual. In fact, at each of these points there will be workers who suffer inequality and disadvantage. The temporary agency worker who is employed by the agency for less than 12 weeks may in fact be the most vulnerable in terms of pay and conditions and therefore in the need of most protection. The 'permanent' agency worker may suffer the same disadvantage compared to directly employed employees that 'temporary' agency workers suffer, but find themselves unprotected by the law. Arguably, it is only by reconsidering the categories of 'employee', 'worker' and 'self-employed', whether they are needed and what they stand for that the real inequalities faced by temporary agency workers can be addressed.

There is also a need to consider the relationship between vulnerability and agency. This in itself is bound up with questions of identity. One insight of vulnerability theory is that autonomy among workers is not a natural state. Individuals are not autonomous rational individuals. They are vulnerable, dependent individuals, whose vulnerability and dependency varies throughout their lifecycle. The benefit of this analysis is that it exposes the multi-dimensional and relational nature of the creation of advantage and disadvantage for workers, and allows for thinking about how strategies of resilience can be formed. Certainly, the legislation on agency workers does not sufficiently consider institutional support for temporary agency workers beyond the agency worker legislation. For example, in the UK, the government has enacted the 'Swedish derogation' of the TAWD into UK law. This Swedish derogation provides that agency workers who are employment on a permanent contract with the agency and continue to be paid during assignments may be exempted from the right to equal treatment. In Sweden, where this clause was conceived, collective bargaining is strong and workers have a set of institutional supports, which mean that this derogation does not put these temporary agency workers at a significant disadvantage. Workers still receive equal pay on placement and 90 per cent of pay between assignments. However, in the UK (in the absence of strong institutional supports), it has been argued that workers employed on 'Swedish derogation contracts' often experience pay discrimination, and can be paid up to £135 a week less than permanent staff.[106]

Moreover, there is evidence that wider mechanisms are at work which threaten the institutional support granted to temporary agency (and other non-standard) workers. In a number of European countries, regulations have been passed which decentralise collective bargaining from the national level to the firm-level. With this process of decentralisation, provisions have been introduced to the effect that firm-level collective bargaining agreements can disregard or derogate from industry wide agreements and national labour legislation, particularly in relation to non-standard work. For example, in 2011 there was a reform which provided for the decentralisation of collective bargaining in Italy.[107] As part of this reform (introduced as a late amendment by the government), there was the opportunity for firm-level agreements to regulate non-standard work, including fixed-term, part-time or temporary agency work. It has been argued that this kind of reform could encourage opportunistic conduct against non-standard workers and worsen their position.[108] This must also be seen in the context of the difficulties temporary agency workers have in joining trade unions and making their voices heard.

5.7 CONCLUSIONS

It appears from this analysis that while significant progress has been made in the protection of agency workers as a matter of law, there are still considerable gaps in the coverage and effectiveness of legal rights in relation to this group. It is argued in this chapter that this failure stems from the particular way in which the problems of agency workers are constructed in a theoretical sense or the failure of our current theoretical mechanisms within labour law to adequately account for this group. Classical labour law theory does not appear to deliver an adequate framework for the consideration of the problems faced by agency

---

[106] C Churchard, 'Ban Swedish Derogation to End Pay Abuses Says TUC' (2 September 2013) <http://www.cipd.co.uk/pm/peoplemanagement/b/weblog/archive/2013/09/02/ban-swedish-derogation-to-end-pay-abuses-says-tuc.aspx> accessed 14 August 2015

[107] Decree 138/2011-Law 148/2011

[108] V De Stefano, 'A Tale of Oversimplification and Deregulation: The Mainstream Approach to Labour Market Segmentation and Recent Responses to the Crisis in European Countries' 10 (4) (2014) *Industrial Law Journal* 253, 272

workers, or the solutions to those problems. This kind of theory is based on a general account of inequalities of bargaining power between capital and labour, and the problems of commodification engendered by the insertion of all workers into the capitalism system. The problem in relation to temporary agency workers is that not all workers could be considered vulnerable in this way. Some of these workers are highly skilled, well paid and have a certain autonomy in the direction of their employment relationship. Furthermore, the solutions suggested in the classical scheme appear inadequate. The reliance on traditional forms of collective bargaining has a number of flaws in the context of the real difficulty that temporary agency workers have in accessing trade unions, or the mismatch between the concerns of these unions and the workers themselves.

More modern labour law theories have attempted to address the concerns of temporary agency workers and their diversity more specific-ally. Reference has been made to the economic changes which have 'produced' these temporary agency workers and the different needs within this group. There have been laws particularly drafted to try to ensure that these precarious workers are treated equally as opposed to more traditional workers on 'standard' employment contracts. However, there are a number of flaws with the theorisation of the problems in relation to temporary agency workers and the laws which have been produced as a result of these theories. These more modern labour law theories appear dominated by economic models. They appear to accept that temporary agency work is economically created, that temporary agency work serves important economic purposes for both employers and employees. The legislation produced is underscored by the acceptance of this economic position and (related) liberal understandings of the proper operation of law. The result is that the law contains a series of exclusions designed to protect economic independence but which in fact create difficulties for the least economically independent workers in accessing rights (for example, the qualification period of 12 weeks).

It appears then that there is a need for a theorisation which is neither bound by the constraints of history or by the economic and liberal approaches to law. This chapter investigated the potential of the social law approach in this regard. It appears that this approach is useful as it rejects the constraints of the liberal approach to equality and suggests the need for more substantive equality ideals in the law. However, this approach tends to accept that temporary agency workers have achieved a certain status and power as a result of the allocation of specific rights to this group. It does not provide a real insight into the group's enduring vulnerability. It is suggested in this chapter that such an insight can only be provided by an approach which investigates vulnerability itself and puts vulnerability at the heart of the law. It is argued that the vulnerability approach promotes an investigation into different modes of identity, and how those modes of identify create or reinforce disadvantage. Moreover, the vulnerability approach links the problems faced by (certain) agency workers to wider institutional and relational modes of disadvantage. For example, it exposes how the enduring divisions of employment status in labour law reinforce vulnerability and how the economic constitution of the agency work status itself restricts the ability of the group to access collective modes of representation which would improve their position. It is only when these deep-seated elements are addressed that the different vulnerabilities of agency workers can be exposed and a law built that can really allow the development of independence, autonomy and agency among these workers.

6. Domestic work

6.1 INTRODUCTION

This chapter considers the vulnerability in theory and practice of a second labour market group: domestic workers. This group has been chosen because in a similar way to temporary agency workers, domestic workers have been identified in academic and political literature as one of the most vulnerable groups on the labour market. Conversely, this group has also been chosen because it provides an interesting contrast to the previous case study on temporary agency work: the position of domestic workers raises particular challenges both in terms of legal theory and practical legal regulation, which differ from the challenges raised by temporary agency work. Indeed, domestic work can be viewed as representing a more significant departure from the 'standard employment relationship' than even temporary agency work. First of all, domestic work is carried out in private homes, and domestic workers are often employed not by companies but by private individuals.[1] Secondly, this type of work is largely carried out by women rather than men: of 18 countries surveyed by the ILO, women represented over 90 per cent of total domestic employment.[2] Men tend only to be involved in those tasks less likely to be viewed as 'women's work', such as gardening or driving.[3] Thirdly, the percentage of domestic workers with permanent contracts tends to be very low. This is either because of the very casual nature of the work, or because the contracts exist only informally.[4] Finally, the consideration of domestic work is complicated by issues of race, class and citizenship which are not considered in the standard employment relationship model.

---

[1] ILO, *Report IV – Decent Work for Domestic Workers – Fourth Item on the Agenda* (Geneva 2010) 28

[2] Ibid 6

[3] MA Chen, 'Recognising Domestic Workers, Regulating Domestic Work: Conceptual Measurement and Regulatory Challenges' (2011) 23 *Canadian Journal of Women and the Law* 167, 169

[4] In Latin America, only 20 per cent of domestic workers have a labour contract compared to 58 per cent of the total urban workforce. Ibid 171

Domestic work is extremely heterogeneous in form. Workers may be employed directly by private employers or may be self-employed and work for more than one employer. Workers may be hired by an agency to carry out domestic work, in which case the employer-employee relationship becomes more formal and less personal than those hired directly. Occasionally, domestic workers are members of cooperatives who jointly negotiate contracts to provide domestic services. Of these groups, it is the 'live-in' domestic workers who are considered most at risk of abuse. Live-in domestic workers face greater isolation and more limited mobility than other domestic workers and are potentially subject to longer hours for less pay. They are also at greater risk of physical and sexual abuse by their employers. Live-in *migrant* domestic workers face even greater challenges. Not only do they have to endure the conditions of live-in domestic workers, they are also subject to abuses within the recruitment system and from the police and immigration authorities. According to a report by Kalayaan in 2010, 65 per cent of Migrant Domestic Workers stated that their passport had been withheld and 18 per cent reported physical abuse by their employer, while 3 per cent claimed they had been sexually abused.[5] The difficulties faced by these workers are compounded by the transnational nature of their recruitment and placement, which makes regulation difficult. This has allowed unscrupulous practices of employment agencies to proliferate, including the charging of advance commission fees.[6]

The low status of domestic work is reinforced by the exclusion of domestic work from many areas of regulation of the employment contract. The reason for this exclusion is not only the lack of economic value associated with this type of work, it is also because of the 'personal relationship' of domestic workers and their employers in the 'private sphere'.[7] Under liberal theory, which has been very influential in the development of both national and international legislation, the private sphere is not suitable for legislative intervention. This is because under this theory, individuals should be 'free' to pursue their own view of the 'good life' (in the private sphere), as long as those actions do not infringe someone else's rights (as defined in the public sphere). This separation of

---

[5]   M Lalani, *Ending the Abuse: Policies that Work to Protect Domestic Workers* (Kalayaan, May 2011) 13

[6]   J Fudge, 'Global Care Chains, Employment Agencies, and the Conundrum of Jurisdiction: Decent Work for Domestic Workers in Canada' (2011) 23 *Canadian Journal of Women and the Law* 235, 236

[7]   E Albin and V Mantouvalou, 'The ILO Convention on Domestic Workers: From the Shadows to the Light' (2012) 20 (2) *ILJ* 67, 76

the public and private sphere is essential to the operation of liberal theory, as it allows liberals to demonstrate that the law in the public sphere is determined by universal, rational and neutral principles and is not affected by arbitrary desires of individuals or groups (in the realm of the private sphere).[8] Furthermore, it is argued that the distinct separation of the public and private sphere is necessary to preserve the functioning and characteristics of the private sphere. Just as the private sphere should not inform public legal rights, 'public' legal regulation should not govern the 'private sphere', because this risks harming the institution of the family by contaminating this 'safe haven' with economic interests. This 'commodification anxiety' has resulted in the low coverage of domestic workers by protective employment legislation, and also the low enforcement of legal rights by domestic workers where they do exist. If domestic workers are instituted as 'one of the family', this tends to make employment law seem irrelevant or inapplicable to the relationship.[9] Labour inspections are also uncommon in the field of domestic work, because of the potential for such inspections to conflict with the rights to privacy held by the domestic employer.[10]

The aim of this chapter is to consider the particular situation of domestic workers in the context of the theories and practices of the regulation of vulnerability in the earlier chapters of this book. Perhaps more than any other group, domestic workers present challenges to the theorisation of vulnerability and its regulatory solution. There are a number of 'new' issues that these views need to deal with in respect of domestic work. For the classical views of labour law, the isolation of domestic workers and the intimate relationship with their employers means that the organisation of these workers is potentially difficult. The effectiveness of the efficiency views is to be questioned in the context of domestic work. Under this kind of ideology, the construction of legal subjects is bound up with liberal and economic ideology, which largely excludes domestic work from legal consciousness. To some extent this visibility has been improved by the recourse to human rights law, but this resort to human rights law has also further obscured the need to deal with domestic work as a distinct and vulnerable group. In relation to social law (as understood in this book), there are major challenges to the

---

[8]   JW Singer, 'The Player and the Cards: Nihilism and Legal Theory' (1984) 94 (1) *The Yale Law Journal* 1, 42

[9]   G Mundlak and H Shamir, 'Bringing Together or Drifting Apart? Targeting Care Work as "Work Like No Other"' (2011) 23 *Canadian Journal of Women and the Law* 289, 296

[10]   Ibid 297

construction of 'equality' for domestic workers, because of the diverse identities and situations faced by this group. There is also the challenge of deciding what 'equality' means for a group with such specific and historically embedded problems. It appears that progress will only clearly be made by an approach which moves towards a consideration of the complexity of the position of domestic workers both personally and institutionally. It is to this end that the potential of the vulnerable subject approach for the regulation of domestic work is analysed in the final section of this chapter.

6.2   OVERVIEW OF INSTRUMENTS

In contrast to the position in relation to temporary agency work, domestic work has not traditionally been the subject of specific regulation at any geographical level. At the national level, domestic workers have, on occasion, been implicitly included in legislation, but in many countries these workers have been either explicitly or implicitly excluded.[11] In the recent ILO Report on Domestic work, the following countries were found to explicitly exclude domestic workers from legislation: (1) Jordan, (2) Lebanon, (3) Yemen, (4) Egypt, (5) Turkey, (6) Bangladesh and (7) Korea. Those countries implicitly excluding domestic work were found to be (among others): (1) China, (2) Switzerland, (3) India, (4) Indonesia and (5) Pakistan. Furthermore, even where domestic workers are considered to be implicitly included in legislation, there are often a number of exceptions which mean that domestic workers are not, in practice, fully included in labour law. A good example is the case of the UK, which is classified by the ILO as implicitly including domestic workers within its legislative scheme. In the UK jurisdiction, domestic workers are in fact explicitly excluded from legislation on working time and health and safety.[12] They are also exempted from the national minimum wage if they are treated as family members, and are entitled to be paid less than the

---

[11]   ILO (n 1). In this report the following countries were included in those explicitly excluding domestic workers from regulation: Jordan, Lebanon, Yemen, Egypt, Turkey, Bangladesh and Korea. Those countries implicitly excluding domestic work were found to be: China, Switzerland, India, Indonesia and Pakistan.

[12]   Regulation 19 of the Working Time Regulations 1998 (SI 1998/1833); Section 51 of the Health and Safety at Work Act 1974

minimum wage if they live in tied accommodation.[13] These provisions have been the subject of a number of recent controversial (and rather conflicting) decisions in the UK courts.[14] These decisions will be discussed in more detail later in the chapter.

At EU level, there has also been no specific regulation of domestic work, although the EU has advocated for the inclusion of domestic workers in national legislation, and has voiced its support for the ILO Conventions and Recommendations on domestic work (discussed below).[15] The European Court of Human Rights (ECHR) has also considered the scope of Article 4 ECHR in relation to domestic work. The ECHR has found not only that the actions of employers towards domestic workers may breach the human rights protection under the Convention, but also that (domestic) workers may be entitled to compensation where governments fail to provide sufficiently for sanctions against employers in breach of their Article 4 obligations.[16] Furthermore, there are a number of measures which have been introduced under the EU's recently reinvigorated anti-trafficking policy, which may have relevance for the protection of some domestic workers. Firstly, there is a directive providing for minimum standards on sanctions and measures against employers of third country nationals staying in the country illegally.[17] As many domestic workers are migrant workers, this directive may be relevant. Where employers are found to be guilty of employing third country nationals illegally, they are to be subject to a fine, and are required to pay the worker back pay (in accordance with the relevant minimum wage requirements) and cover costs of repatriation. It must be noted, however, that the UK, Ireland and Denmark are not parties to this directive. Secondly, there is a new directive on the prevention and

---

[13] Regulations 2 (2) and 2 (3), 36 and 37 National Minimum Wage Regulations 1999 (SI 1999/584)

[14] Cf *Ms T Nambalat v Mr Taher and Mrs S Tayeb* [2012] EWCA Civ 1249 and *Ms P Onu v Mr O Akwiwu, Ms E Akwiwu* 2013 WL 1841654

[15] The European Commission states that: 'Domestic workers are often excluded from the protection of labour laws or are treated less favourably than other wage workers. National labour laws should be better assessed and strengthened implementing the basic principles embodied in Convention No. 189 [the Domestic Work Convention].' It has posted the ILO publication 'Effective Protection for Domestic Workers: A Guide to Designing Labour Laws' on its Together for Trafficking website <http://ec.europa.eu/anti-trafficking/entity.action?path=percent2FPublicationspercent2FEffective+Protection> accessed 18 June 2013

[16] See for example *CN v United Kingdom* (2013) 56 EHRR 24

[17] Directive 2009/52/EC, OJ L 198

combating of trafficking of human beings,[18] which requires member states to instigate criminal sanctions against those persons found to be traffickers under the directive. This directive has a wide definition of trafficking, and specifically includes (domestic) servitude.[19] The date for implementation of this directive was 6 April 2013, and the UK government made amendments to the Asylum and Immigration Act 2004 to comply with this directive.[20]

However, by far the most comprehensive regulatory proposals in relation to domestic work have come from the ILO. At its 100th International Labour Conference, the ILO proposed a Convention[21] and Recommendation[22] providing for decent work for domestic workers. The aim of these texts was to ensure that employment standards reached as many domestic workers as possible, leading to the 'improvement of domestic workers' working and living conditions and access to social security'.[23] It was also hoped that the Convention and Recommendation would provide 'sufficient guidance and incentives to enable the provisions to be meaningfully implemented in practice'.[24] By 5 September 2012, this Convention had been ratified by two countries (Uruguay and the Philippines), and therefore came into force on 3 September 2013,

---

[18]   Directive 2011/36/EU, OJ L101/1

[19]   Article 3 defines trafficking as including 'the recruitment, transportation, transfer, harbouring or reception of persons, including the exchange or transfer of control over those persons, by means of the threat or use of force or other forms of coercion, of abduction, of fraud, of deception, of the abuse of power or of a position of vulnerability or of the giving or receiving of payments or benefits to achieve the consent of a person having control over another person, for the purpose of exploitation'.

[20]   Whether these amendments have gone far enough to comply with the Directive are to be questioned, as there is still no reference to the specific offence of 'servitude' in the Asylum and Immigration Act. However, there are provisions in the Coroners and Justice Act 2009 (Section 71) which do bring into force criminal sanctions for the offence of 'servitude'. For a discussion of the failings of the UK in having criminal sanctions for servitude (prior to the entry into force of s 71 CJA) see *CN v United Kingdom* (2013) 56 EHRR 24.

[21]   ILO Convention 189 'Domestic Workers Convention' (International Labour Office, Geneva 2011)

[22]   ILO Recommendation 201 'Domestic Workers Recommendation' (International Labour Office, Geneva, 2011)

[23]   ILO (n 1) 95

[24]   Ibid 95

according to ILO convention. By July 2015, a further 19 countries had also ratified the Convention countries.[25]

6.3 CLASSICAL LABOUR LAW AND DOMESTIC WORK

6.3.1 The Nature of Vulnerability

The classical labour law view represents the constitutive narrative of employment and labour law, namely that labour law exists to counteract the inequality of bargaining power 'which is inherent and must be inherent in [any] employment relationship'.[26] Advocates of this view differ as to the acceptable balance to be struck between 'auxiliary' legislation (legislation which permits and encourages collective bargaining) and 'regulatory law' (statutory rights), and some advocates (particularly Kahn-Freund) question the effectiveness of the law at all in equalising power relations. However, it is possible to say that with this view it is understood that the equalisation of power between employee and employer is the only way in which dignity, fairness and freedom can be achieved for workers. Underlying this understanding is the recognition of the worker as a human being; that 'labour is not a commodity'. To this extent the working relationship is characterised as one of subordination, and is bound up with the operation of the capitalist economy. The classical view pursues the Marxist notion that the ownership of the means of production on the part of employers means that they are able to maintain workers in an inferior position and continually exploit them. This relationship of exploitation is obscured by the 'contract of employment' which, although on the face of it freely negotiated, is in fact simply a means by which workers can be maintained in their inferior position. The aim of the law, and more importantly collective bargaining, is to free workers from this subordinate relationship and enable them to recapture their status as human beings (rather than legal persons).[27]

[25] This information is available on the ILO website at <http://www.ilo.org/dyn/normlex/en/f?p=NORMLEXPUB:11300:0::NO:11300:P11300_INSTRUMENT_ID:2551460:NO> accessed 28 July 2015

[26] P Davies and M Freedland, *Kahn-Freund's Labour and the Law* (Stevens 1983) 18

[27] H Sinzheimer, *Arbeitsrecht und Rechtssoziologie* (Europäische Verlagsanstalt 1976) 117

In the context of domestic work, it is obvious that only some elements of the classical view of vulnerability will be useful, and that the situation of domestic workers was not contemplated within this theory (this will be discussed in more detail in criticism of this approach below). However, it is still useful to analyse the classical view of vulnerability in the context of domestic work, because it provides insights which have perhaps been forgotten with the modernisation of labour law and the attempt to find a normative underpinning which does not rely on the conjunction of the ideas of 'inequality of bargaining power' and 'labour is not a commodity'.[28] In fact, the conjunction of these two normative insights appears relevant to the situations for some domestic workers. Certainly, 'subordination' and 'exploitation' are experienced on a daily basis by some members of this group, and this is profoundly bound up with inequality and power relationships (although not necessarily, in the economic sense, understood in the wide view). In the most extreme situations, the commodification of domestic labour has extended to every area of a domestic workers' life, and has been designated 'slavery',[29] which brings to mind Marx and Engels' description of the situation for the working classes in the factory system in the nineteenth century:

> Everyone who has served as a soldier knows what it is to be subjected even for a short time to military discipline. But these operatives are condemned from their ninth year to their death to live under the sword, physically and mentally. They are worse slaves than the Negros in America, for they are more sharply watched, and yet it is demanded of them that they shall live like human beings, shall think and feel like men![30]

The case of *Siliadin v France*[31] provides a stark example of the 'slavery' to which some domestic workers are subjected. In this case Ms Siliadin, a Togolese national, worked as a general housemaid for a French couple. She worked seven days a week and was never allowed a day off. Her working day began at 7:30am and ended at 10:30pm. She slept on a mattress in the same room as the couple's baby, and was required to look after him if he woke up. She was not paid for the work that she carried out. The French couple confiscated Ms Siliadin's passport and her

---

[28]   B Langille, 'Labour Law's Theory of Justice' in G Davidov and B Langille (eds), *The Idea of Labour Law* (Oxford University Press 2011) 105

[29]   V Mantouvalou, 'Servitude and Forced Labour in the 21st Century: The Human Rights of Domestic Workers' (2006) 35 (4) *ILJ* 395, 395

[30]   F Engels, *The Conditions of the Working Class in England in 1844* (Cambridge University Press 2010) 180

[31]   (73316/01) (2006) 43 EHRR 16 (ECHR)

situation only came to light after she spoke to a neighbour about her treatment. Proceedings were brought against the French couple under the French Criminal Code, and they were sentenced to 12 months' imprisonment, a conviction which was later quashed. However, the case was also pursued in the civil courts and the couple were ordered to pay Ms Siliadin damages for her unpaid work, and she was also awarded an amount for her salary arrears, notice period and holiday leave. Likewise, the abusive treatment of domestic workers was reported in the UK case of *R v K (S)*.[32] In this case the Claimant alleged that she had been made to work almost 24 hours by the employer, was poorly fed, was never allowed out on her own and seldom with others, and had little contact with her family. Of the 10 pounds a month she was supposed to receive while in the UK, she in fact received very little.

Both of these cases considered whether the treatment of the domestic workers in this way amounted to 'slavery', 'servitude' or 'forced or compulsory labour' under Article 4 of the European Convention on Human Rights. In *Siliadin*, the Court held that Ms Siliadin's labour was 'forced' because she had no option but to carry out the work (her passport having been withheld) and she was effectively 'under the menace of penalty' because she feared arrest by the police if she did not continue to work (on the grounds of her illegal immigration status).[33] The Court also found that Ms Siliadin had been subject to 'servitude'.[34] She was under an obligation not only to provide her services but also to stay with her employer, and was not in a position to change this situation. The Court stopped short of a finding that Ms Siliadin was a 'slave'. Such a finding would require that Ms Silidain's employers exercised a right of ownership over her, rather than simply a finding that her personal autonomy had been restricted. The Court held that, in this case, the restriction of the applicant's autonomy did not amount to a reduction of her status to that of an object and therefore did not amount to 'slavery'.[35]

Central to the classical view is the understanding that, in order to challenge the 'slavery' of work, workers have to have the opportunity to equalise the power relations to which they are subject. The most effective way in which to do this is to join together with other workers so that workers can effectively negotiate with their employers, and ultimately impose the 'social sanction' of withholding labour if that negotiation fails. With this view, domestic workers would be seen as particularly

---

[32] [2011] EWCA Crim 1691
[33] *Siliadin* (n 31) para 118
[34] Ibid para 129
[35] Ibid para 122

vulnerable where they have not been successful at organising in trade unions and therefore have not had the opportunity to equalise power relations at work. In terms of evidence for this 'vulnerability', gathering statistical evidence for the low trade union density of domestic workers is challenging. For example, in the UK, 'domestic work' does not appear as an occupational category for the purposes of measuring trade union density. However, there is value for 'home workers', which could include domestic workers (but could also include a number of other professions). The trade union density for home workers is very low and in 2010 was at 10.6 per cent overall. For women home workers that value was only 7.3 per cent, and there was no value entered for part-time home workers.[36]

The obstacles that domestic workers face in attempting to organise are both practical and legal. In some countries, domestic workers are specifically excluded from the right to organise. For example, the National Labour Relations Act in America, which gives employees the right to organise and join a trade union, excludes this group.[37] Even where domestic workers are not specifically excluded, trade union density often remains low, either because domestic workers are implicitly excluded (for example, the casual nature of their work means that they do not have 'employee' status) or because of other practical issues. Those practical issues include the fact that domestic workers work in one-on-one relationships with their employer and so it is difficult to have 'collective' negotiation for terms and conditions. There is also the associated problem that trade unionism may not seem relevant in a household setting where the domestic worker is designated as 'one of the family'.[38] Coupled with the isolation of domestic workers from one another, it is easy to see why traditional trade union organisation among domestic workers has remained low.

The classical view pursues the idea that despite these difficulties, trade union organisation is the most effective way in which vulnerability can be challenged. Indeed, outside the UK, there is some evidence that domestic workers have been able to take advantage of trade union

---

[36] BIS, 'Trade Union Membership 2010' (April 2011) 25 <http://web archive.nationalarchives.gov.uk/+/http://stats.bis.gov.uk/UKSA/tu/TUM2010.pdf> accessed 18 January 2014. The home workers' classification disappears in later UK trade union membership statistics, and is not present in the latest 2014 statistics.

[37]   29 U.S.C. s 152 (3)

[38]   P Smith, 'Organizing the Unorganizable: Private Paid Household Workers and Approaches to Employee Representation' (2000) 79 *North Carolina Law Review* 45, 54

support. In some instances, domestic workers have been able to join with the main unions to gain legal rights and advantage (in accordance perhaps with the vision of the wide view). For example, domestic workers have been able to join unions with a wider focus in Kenya (the Kenya Union of Domestic, Hotels, Educational Institutions, Hospitals and Allied Workers) and India (the Self Employed Women's Association). Furthermore, in terms of outcomes, there are a number of instances where traditional trade unions have taken up the cause of domestic workers to considerable effect. In Brazil, the affiliation of FENETRAD (the National Federation of Domestic Workers) to one of the main trade unions (CUT) has boosted its political influence and has resulted in a number of improvements to the legal regime for domestic workers.[39] In Spain, two of the main trade unions – the UCT (the General Workers Union) and the CCOO (Trade Union Confederation) – have achieved significant legal improvements for domestic workers. They obtained the Spanish government's commitment to the reform of social security law to include domestic workers, and negotiated with the government and employers' association to achieve the Royal Decree 1620/2011. This Royal Decree is important as it includes provisions for the inclusion of domestic workers in minimum wage provisions and advocates a certain amount of annual leave for these workers. It also potentially guarantees greater job security for domestic workers because it ensures that (temporary) domestic work contracts must be terminated with just cause.[40]

Specific domestic workers' unions have also been formed to further the domestic worker cause. These kinds of worker unions exist in South Africa (the South Africa Domestic Service and Allied Workers Union) and in Hong Kong (the Hong Kong Domestic Workers General Union).[41] Moreover, some groups of domestic workers have formed outside the confines of trade union status. Increasingly evident on a global scale are member-based organisations, which like trade unions are democratic and representative and have due-paying members but have not achieved trade

---

[39] A Gomes and IB Puig, 'Domestic Work after Labour Law: the Case of Brazil and Spain'. Paper prepared for the Labour Law Research Network Inaugural Conference at Pompeu Fabra University, Barcelona, 13–15 June 2013 <http://www.upf.edu/gredtiss/_pdf/2013-LLRNConf_GomesxBaviera.pdf> accessed 19 June 2013

[40] Ibid 16

[41] C Bonner, 'Domestic Workers around the World: Organising for Empowerment' (30 April 2010) 9 <http://www.dwrp.org.za/images/stories/DWRP_Research/chris_bonner.pdf> accessed 20 January 2012

union recognition. An example of such an organisation is the Mujeres Unidas Y Activas or Women United and Active in California. This group was formed by a group of immigrant women to provide support for immigrant, women and workers' rights. Although these groups do not have the membership base or credibility of union organisation to effect national changes, they provide a platform for the mobilisation of (domestic) workers and, and can provide information and advocacy at the local level.[42] However, these groups are perhaps better analysed in terms of other vulnerability theories. They do not fit with the classical view's position that trade unions provide the best means of organisation, and the outcomes sought for these groups extend beyond the labour law field. They therefore look more like the 'occupational associations' of social law than the trade unions of the classical view.

6.3.2   Criticisms of the Classical Labour Law Approach in relation to Domestic Work

It is clear from the above discussion that the classical view does not provide an immediate 'fit' to the problems of domestic work. To understand this lack of 'fit', it is important to look at the conceptual underpinning of the theory of vulnerability in the classical view. As has been explained, the classical view relies on a Marxist view of exploitation: exploitation arises through the operation of the institutions of the capitalist system. This capitalist system creates power relations which act to subordinate workers. As the 'bourgeoisie' own the means of production they have a 'right of command' over workers who rely on wages to live.[43] However, for many domestic workers and their employers, the idea of 'inequality of bargaining power' seems very alien. Although that inequality is perhaps in evidence for live-in domestic workers, many domestic workers are now employed in day work and job work. They work for many different employers and for a very low number of hours every week, and the amount of control that employers have over this work is low. The main problems with this type of work are not 'exploitation' at all, but the extreme informality and precariousness of this work which leaves workers 'vulnerable to abuse and the whims of

---

[42]   Ibid 6

[43]   R Dukes, 'Hugo Sinzheimer and the Constitutional Function of Labour Law' in G Davidov and B Langille (eds), *The Idea of Labour Law* (Oxford University Press 2011) 59

employers'.[44] These workers share the problems of isolation and invisibility of live-in domestic workers, and the lack of coverage of legal rights, but this is a problem of informality rather than exploitation as such.

The conceptual problems of the classical view in relation to domestic work extend not only to the way in which vulnerability is characterised but also to the preferred solution to counteract that vulnerability. As we have seen, under the classical view, the preferred solution to vulnerability is collective organisation to counteract the social power of the owners of capital and to therefore exact economic justice for workers. However, the tangential and indirect relationship between domestic workers and the wider economy creates problems for both of these theories. More than this, the diversity and informality of domestic work contracts mean that the unity of interests assumed under this industrial relations model is subject to challenge (parallels can be drawn here in relation to the situation with temporary agency work). These conceptual problems with collective organisation are only compounded by the practical problems associated with the isolation of domestic workers from each other. Moreover, collective organisation may be seen as a very low priority for a number of domestic workers, particularly those migrant workers whose interest lies in obtaining as many jobs as possible in order to send money back to their home countries.[45] It may also be that collective organisation may be a disadvantage for some workers, as this would act to change the relationship from 'one of the family' to a more formalistic and contentious relationship and so it may be a conscious decision among domestic workers to avoid this organisation.

It is also possible that the classical view is overly sceptical about the ability of the law to aid the plight of domestic workers. According to the classical labour law view, the law cannot be central to the equalisation of power relations between employers and workers because law is itself a social power which is made by the ruling classes and is used to 'subordinate' weaker members of society. It replicates rather than counteracts the social power imposed on workers by capitalist employers. Furthermore, the law is the law of individuals and 'knows nothing of a balance of collective forces'.[46] It can therefore never control absolutely

---

[44] Smith (n 38) 56

[45] P Smith, 'The Pitfalls of Home: Protecting the Health and Safety of Paid Domestic Workers' (2011) 23 *Canadian Journal of Women and the Law* 309, 328

[46] P Davies and M Freedland, *Kahn-Freund's Labour and the Law* (Stevens 1983) 12

the 'orderly development of labour relations'.[47] This is useful in the modern context of domestic workers, as it is clear that even where the law implicitly includes domestic workers, they are often excluded in practice. It is also clear that currently the law has been ineffective at addressing the myriad of specific problems encountered by domestic workers, because these problems are not seen as legal problems at all. However, it is possible to argue that certain legal guarantees are necessary in order for workers to start to counteract the equality of bargaining power enforced over them. Indeed, in practice, trade unions organisations sympathetic to the plight of domestic workers have tended to try to include domestic workers in the legal regime.

6.4 EFFICIENCY THEORIES AND DOMESTIC WORK

6.4.1 Characterisation of Vulnerability

Economic efficiency views relating to labour market regulation seek to understand how current market processes (particularly processes of globalisation and the flexibilisation of work relations) have acted to marginalise certain workers and how far institutions of the 'old' regime are implicated in this process. In particular, a number of labour lawyers are sceptical of the value of continuing to base labour law on the 'standard employment relationship'. To these lawyers, this standard employment relationship represents the traditional bilateral, full-time permanent employment relationship of the Fordist factory regime. It no longer corresponds to the majority of work contracts in the flexible knowledge economy. Rather, developments in the global economy have, on the one hand, resulted in greater opportunities for individuals to enter into tailored work arrangements which more effectively meet the needs of employers and workers. On the other hand, processes of globalisation and the flexibilisation of work contracts have resulted in some workers being employed in more precarious jobs, which are of low quality, low paid and are not recognised in law.

On efficiency views of vulnerability, domestic workers would be viewed as vulnerable where they are unable to take advantage of the opportunities of the flexible knowledge economy and therefore end up in precarious jobs of low quality. The disadvantages faced by domestic workers would not be viewed as systemic. For if the vulnerability of

---

[47]   Ibid 12

domestic workers were to be systemic, then this would mean that the whole foundation of the efficiency view in the premises of liberalism would have to be reassessed. The efficiency view is complicit in the distinct separation of the public (economic) and private (non-economic) spheres. In terms of gender issues, the lawyers sympathetic with the efficiency view are far more likely to point to the advantages of the growing labour market participation of women as a whole (both for individuals and for the economy) rather than the plight of domestic workers as women. Indeed, it is possible to argue that those supporting efficiency views of regulation would fail to make the connection between the increased labour market participation of women and the problems faced by domestic workers. As stated in the UK government's *Success at Work* paper, the main gender issue is that 'there are still too many whose skills and potential are not realised. For instance, if more women were to participate in the labour market and make full use of their talents, the UK would be up to £23 billion better off.'[48] With this view, unemployment is seen as a greater problem than any faced by those in work: 'There is still more that needs to be done to break down the barriers that prevent many people from moving off benefits and into work.'[49]

The foundations of efficiency views are represented in the solutions that it presents to worker vulnerability. The vulnerability of domestic workers is neither systemic, nor does it extend to the whole group. Rather the argument is that, for many domestic workers, this kind of arrangement will be a choice which is useful, rational and deliberate. Some workers will choose and gain advantage from the informality of domestic work arrangements. The position on the efficiency view would therefore not be to attempt to 'improve' the position for all domestic workers. Rather, the idea would be to tackle those at particular risk of abuse. On the efficiency view, the human rights regime is especially useful because it not only captures a liberal conception of rights (these rights are individualistic and enforceable through the courts), but those rights are only applicable in the most extreme instances of abuse. Indeed, in the domestic worker field, human rights are more easily engaged than in the field of temporary agency work for example, because of the close and personal nature of many domestic relationships, which make the connection between employment and personal dignity both obvious and pertinent. There have been a number of instances of domestic workers

---

[48]   Department of Trade and Industry, *Success at Work: Protecting Vulnerable Workers, Supporting Good Employers. A Policy Statement for this Parliament* (March 2006) 8
[49]   Ibid 8

successfully having reference to the human rights regime, and these were discussed in Section 6.3. Domestic workers have also used human rights to argue that a government needs to do more to ensure those human rights are respected.

There have also been other instruments which may aid those domestic workers at particular risk of abuse. As stated in Section 6.2, there are two main directives at EU level which are worthy of discussion. The first is the directive providing for minimum standards on sanctions and measures against employers of third country nationals staying in the country illegally.[50] There is the argument that migrant domestic workers are particularly vulnerable because of the coincidence of the lack of resi-dence status, as well as the often very personal and isolated notion of the domestic employment relationship. Arguably this directive is useful as it encourages member states to have proper criminal and civil sanctions for harbouring illegal immigrants, and therefore ensures that employers aid domestic workers in the achievement of both residence and employment status. The second directive concerns criminal sanctions for the traffick-ing of human beings.[51] This includes the 'harbouring' of domestic workers for the purposes of servitude. Of course, neither of these statutes are specifically employment statues designed to improve the working conditions of domestic workers. They are essentially part of the criminal law, and are short-term measures to eliminate abuse. Their effect may be to make domestic work even more insecure than it might otherwise be.

6.4.2   Criticisms of the Efficiency Approach

The first failing of the narrow or efficiency view in the context of domestic work is its reliance to the premises of liberal theory. Running through liberal theory is the distinct separation of 'public' and 'private' spheres of action. In the public sphere, the concern is for a freely functioning market supported by a set of universal, rational and abstract legal rules. By contrast, the private sphere is neither determined by economic or legal rules; these rules become important only when private functions become public. The problem is that domestic work acts precisely at the juncture between 'public' and the 'private', and does not fit neatly into either of these categories. The second failing of the narrow view, which is connected inevitably with the first, is the characterisation of all legal and economic subjects as individuals, who act rationally and

---

[50]   Directive 2009/52/EC, OJ L 198
[51]   Directive 2011/36/EU, OJ L101/1

according to their choice. In this sense, the narrow view upholds the idea that domestic workers make a choice between the flexibility and informality of domestic work in the private sphere (and the benefits of a 'safe haven', and so on) and formal contractual arrangements which are subject to legal rules. This suggests that informality is not a problem per se, as there are usually 'economic reasons for the tendency to employ informal workers and to take on informal work, as this kind of work is more favourable than registered work for both sides'.[52]

In the same way, the illegality of work contracts is presented as a choice which is simultaneously undertaken by both parties. This argument was essentially presented in the case of *Hounga*.[53] This case concerned a domestic worker, Ms Hounga, who arrived in the UK on a visitor visa which was illegally obtained (and did not in any event give her the right to work). She claimed that her employers treated her less favourably because of her status as a (Nigerian) illegal immigrant and sought to rely on the provisions in the Race Relations Act 1976. The case turned on whether Ms Hounga's status as an illegal immigrant barred her from making a statutory claim (clearly she was barred from making a contractual claim because the contract was illegal). The question was essentially whether Ms Houga's claim was so inextricably linked with her illegality in obtaining and continuing employment that her claim should be barred (on the grounds of public policy). The EAT found that the involvement of Ms Hounga in the illegality of her actions was outweighed by the illegal action of her employers. This decision was overturned on appeal, with the Court of Appeal holding that there was a direct link between her claim of discrimination and her illegal conduct: her discrimination case was based on her particular vulnerability as a result of her illegal employment contract.

When the *Hounga* case reached the Supreme Court, the Court was asked to consider whether the Claimant's claim for the statutory tort of discrimination (as opposed to other statutory employment claims) was barred for illegality. In seeming contrast to the comments in the Court of Appeal, Lord Wilson stated that the Claimant's illegal employment contract provided only the 'context' in which the Respondent then perpetrated the physical, verbal and emotional abuse against the Claimant.[54] Any connection between the illegal act and the abuse was therefore insufficient to bar the claim. Furthermore, public policy considerations

---

[52] European Economic and Social Committee Opinion on 'The Professionalisation of Domestic Work' OJ [2011] C21/39 para 3.1.4.3

[53] *Hounga v Allen* [2012] EWCA Civ 609

[54] [2014] UKSC 47 at para 39

could not be applied to defeat the Claimant's complaint. On the face of it, this judgement appeared to move away from the (liberal) assumption of the nature of choice in relation to illegal and informal contracts. In the Court of Appeal, it was argued that Ms Hounga and Ms Allen were 'equal participants' in the illegal contract of employment.[55] As a result, both parties should bear the consequence of that choice. For Ms Hounga this meant that she could not rely on any claims which were 'inextricably linked' with this contract. Lord Wilson questioned this (liberal) position in relation to the construction of (illegal) contracts as equal, and suggested that the greater responsibility of the Respondent in the exercise of this contract should be a relevant consideration. The liberal notions of choice were therefore nonsensical in this context.[56]

This appears to be a progressive stance and a direct affront to efficiency views. However, a number of words of caution should be raised in this respect. In the dissenting judgement, it was made clear that the findings of the judgement were limited to its particular facts. In this case, there was no inextricable link between illegality and the Claimant's claim because the claim was for a statutory tort and the illegality was her immigration status. As a result, if the claims had been based more squarely on the contract of employment (including statutory claims relating to the contract) then these claims would be barred for illegality. The Claimant also could not rely on claims of trafficking or slavery where 'she was well aware of what [she] was doing and voluntarily did it'. Furthermore, a differently constituted Supreme Court took the opposite position to the majority in *Hounga*. In *Les Laboratoires Servier v Apotex*, Lord Sumption rejected the approach taken by Lord Wilson in *Hounga*. According to Lord Sumption, this approach reflected a move away from the treatment of illegality as a 'rule-based' doctrine toward an approach based around judicial discretion.[57] The case also demonstrates the difficulties of relying on discrimination law in these instances, a fact

---

[55] *Hounga* (n 53) para 60

[56] *Hounga* (n 54) para 39. Indeed, in the EAT, it was demonstrated that Ms Hounga's choice was compromised by a number of elements, including her age (she was only 14 when she came to the country) and her status in Nigeria. Furthermore, the EAT found that the obtaining of an illegal passport and visa was 'masterminded' by her previous employers in Nigeria in conjunction with her employers in the UK. She would not have known on her own how to get the documentation to get to the UK.

[57] [2014] UKSC 55, para 14. See also the commentary in A Bogg and S Green, 'Rights are Not Just for the Virtuous: What Hounga Means for the Illegality Defence in the Discrimination Torts' (2015) 44 (1) *ILJ* 101

reiterated in the case of *Ms P Onu v Mr O Akwiwu*.[58] Here, it was decided that there could not be race discrimination because the real cause of discrimination was immigration status rather than race. This was a 'socio-economic' characteristic rather than a protected characteristic under the Race Relations Act 1976.

The case also demonstrates the difficulties of the reliance of individuals on the human rights regime. Such claims are not immune from considerations of illegality, immunity and so on. This appears to undermine the view, seemingly accepted under economic efficiency arguments, that this regime provides reliable protection for the most vulnerable workers. Furthermore, the cases referred to in Section 6.3 demonstrate the difficulty of bringing human rights claims, and the length of time involved in their enforcement (Ms Siliadin only became aware of her rights after interference by her neighbour). These cases also demonstrate the very specific function of human rights in dealing with the most extreme forms of abuse. For example, despite the clear restriction on Ms Siliadin's liberty in the case of *Siliadin v France*, she did not fall within the definition of a 'slave' because her personal autonomy was not sufficiently compromised. It might therefore be suggested that it is only with a more systematic approach to the regulation of domestic work that their working conditions may be improved in practice.

6.5 SOCIAL LAW AND DOMESTIC WORK

6.5.1 Characterisation of Vulnerability

Under the social law view, labour, and society in general, is seen as consisting of a series of (more or less vulnerable) sub-groups who are, or should be, in a continuous battle to 'win' social and labour rights. It envisages a major role for the state as the arbiter of these competing interests and the guarantor of group rights (for example, in the guise of discrimination law). However, social law is sceptical of a strict 'top-down' approach to the constitution of labour rights; the social law ideal is to allow social groups the power to effectively bargain for their own rights. There are thus two elements to counteracting vulnerability with this view:

---

[58] [2013] WL 1841654

(1)   the recognition of the interests of vulnerable groups by the state (as the guarantor of group rights); and
(2)   the recognition of those interests in a way which promotes the empowerment of those groups and allows them to bargain for their own interests.

On the face of it, this social law view provides insight into the vulnerable position of domestic workers in relation to the law. On the one hand, domestic workers have not been recognised as a group in need of protection and have been explicitly excluded from the law. On the other hand, the construction of legislation can act to implicitly exclude these workers, because the categories of 'employment' do not cover these workers. Examples of these types of exclusions are present in a number of jurisdictions throughout the world, but this section will focus on the EU, because there are relevant examples of both implicit and explicit exclusion of domestic workers here, and because the EU legislation has had a very great impact on the structure of UK law. At EU level, the explicit exclusion of domestic workers is evident in the European Framework Directive on Health and Safety at Work (EFDSH).[59] This sets the benchmark for health and safety standards across the EU, and forms the basis of a number of more specific individual health and safety directives (in relation to chemical agents and chemical safety,[60] physical hazards[61] and biological agents[62]). Article 5 of the EFDSH states that 'employers shall have a duty to ensure the safety and health of workers in every aspect related to the work'. However, in Article 3(i) domestic workers are specifically excluded from the scope of the worker definition. In the more specific individual health and safety directives, the term worker is not further defined, and so it is assumed that the definition in the EFDSH applies, and domestic workers are also excluded from these

---

[59]   Directive 89/391/EC on the introduction of measures to encourage improvements in the safety and health of workers at work OJ [1989] L 183/1
[60]   For example, Directive 2009/148/EU of 30 November 2009 on the protection of workers from the risks related to asbestos at work OJ [2009] L 330/28
[61]   For example, Directive 2003/10/EC of 6 February 2003 on the minimum health and safety requirements regarding the exposure of workers to risks involving physical agents (noise) at work OJ [2003] L 48/32
[62]   Directive 2000/54/EC of the European Parliament and of the Council on the protection of workers from risks related to exposure to biological agents at work OJ [2000] L 262/21

directives. Domestic workers are also specifically excluded from UK health and safety legislation in line with the EU position.[63]

On the social law view, this explicit exclusion would lead to the identification of domestic workers as a vulnerable group, as their interests have not been recognised, or recognised as important by the state. With this view, the exclusion of domestic workers is recognised as political, and bound up with liberal ideology and the separation of the public and private spheres. Liberal ideology represents the 'private' world of the family (and the domestic workers who serve them) as outside the scope of 'public' law, and presents the home as a 'safe haven' free of environmental risks. In fact, the view of the domestic work environment as a 'safe haven' has been questioned by a number of empirical studies, which demonstrate the very real risks to health and safety faced by domestic workers. Workplace hazards have been shown to include exposure to harmful cleaning chemicals, faulty electrical wiring, as well as verbal, physical and sexual harassment.[64] For live-in domestic workers, these problems are compounded by unsuitable and unsafe living accommodation which provides further threats to their health, safety and well being. It may be therefore that the social view of vulnerability is useful as a starting point to analyse the vulnerability of domestic workers.

As well as facing explicit exclusion from legislation at EU level, domestic workers are also implicitly excluded. In the Working Time Directive[65] derogations are permitted 'when, on account of the specific characteristics of the activity concerned, the duration of the working time is not measured and/or predetermined or can be determined by the workers themselves'. Specific examples of permitted derogations under this section are stated as managing executives (Article 17 (a)), family workers (Article 17 (b)) and workers officiating at religious ceremonies (Article 17 (c)). Domestic workers are not mentioned specifically, but are implicitly included within the scope of possible derogations. This is demonstrated by the specific exclusion of 'domestic' service from the scope of the Working Time Regulations 1998, which implement the EU Working Time Directive.[66] Domestic workers could also be deemed to be

---

[63] Section 51 Health and Safety at Work Act 1974 provides that: 'Nothing in this Part shall apply in relation to a person by reason only that he employs another, or is himself employed, as a domestic servant in a private household.'

[64] Smith (n 45) 310

[65] Directive 2003/88/EC concerning certain aspects of the organization of working time OJ [2003] L299/9

[66] SI 1998/1833, Regulation 19

implicitly excluded from the definitions of 'employment' and 'worker' at EU level. The definition of employment requires both some element of subordination and 'control' by the employer.[67] 'Workers' must also show that they are engaged in a 'genuine and effective' economic activity. Domestic workers will often face difficulties in satisfying these criteria, although the jurisprudence is not clear cut.[68] For example, in *Levin*,[69] the Court held that a chambermaid who worked part-time could be a 'worker' despite earning less than the subsistence wage. By contrast, in the case of *Raulin*,[70] the Court doubted whether an on-call worker who was not guaranteed a particular level of work, and often only worked a very few days per week would satisfy the definition of worker for the purposes of EU law.

In any event, the social law view of vulnerability predicts the failings of laws based on general and abstract legal categorisations to provide adequate protections for vulnerable groups. According to this view, the 'natural' distribution of rights according to such general categorisations acts only as a smokescreen to obscure dominant social and political interests. As rights are sociologically determined, such exclusion simply represents the fact that a certain set of interests (workers engaged in the 'standard employment relationship' perhaps) hold sway over others (those of domestic workers). Therefore, the only way in which domestic workers will gain access to 'justice' is to have their own specific rights protected. What domestic workers should aim for then, is the recognition by the state that their interests are so important that they should be specifically protected.

One attempt to develop specific rights for domestic workers is demonstrated by the ILO's Convention and Recommendation on Decent Work for domestic workers (the DWC and the RDW respectively). The Convention recognises that in some ways, domestic work is 'work like no other' and there are specific structural and cultural issues which have led to domestic workers experiencing particular sectoral disadvantage. Such specific issues require specific and tailored regulation. Article 10 of the Convention and paragraphs 8–13 of the Recommendation recognise the

---

[67]   'Employment' was defined in the case of *Lawrie-Blum* as existing where 'for a certain period of time a person performs services for and under the direction of another person in return for which he receives remuneration'. Case 66/85 [1986] ECR 2121, para 17

[68]   C Barnard, *EC Employment Law* (OUP 2006) 173

[69]   Case 53/81 *Levin* [1982] ECR 1035

[70]   Case C-357/89 *Raulin v Minister van Onderwijs en Wetenseur* [1992] ECR I-1027

particular problems domestic workers experience over the allocation of 'working time'. Many domestic workers, particularly live-in domestic workers, find that there is insufficient distinction between work and rest time and that they have little access to annual leave or weekly rest. This is a function of their work as 'one of the family' inside the home and their personalised relationship with those in their care.[71] Article 10 seeks to address this by requiring member states to ensure that annual leave, hours of work and overtime compensation are regularised and that 'periods during which domestic workers are not free to dispose of their time as they please and remain at the disposal of the household in order to respond to possible calls shall be regarded as hours of work'.

The DWC also seeks to deal with the particular problems experienced by domestic workers in terms of occupational health and safety, by requiring that members take appropriate measures 'with due regard to the specific characteristics of domestic work' to protect domestic workers from workplace hazards. The particular problems associated with 'live in' accommodation are dealt with in paragraph 16 of the Recommendation, which provides the minimum conditions that should be fulfilled in this respect (access to suitable sanitary facilities, adequate lighting, heating and/or air conditioning and the provision of adequate and good quality meals). Finally, the Convention also seeks to deal with the particular problems that domestic workers experience in terms of access to justice. Article 14 of the Convention provides that members should take measures which ensure that domestic workers have easy access to courts, tribunals and other dispute resolution procedures. This is recognition that, even where domestic workers are covered nominally by (equality) law, there are many hurdles for domestic workers in obtaining redress.

The ILO Convention is an important milestone in the recognition of specific rights for domestic workers and addresses vulnerability in many of the ways envisaged by the social law view. For a start, domestic workers are recognised as a group in need of protection. Having a specific piece of legislation for domestic workers means that not only are they no longer excluded from the law, they also do not have to attempt to fit into legal categorisations designed by a liberal system (which is blind to domestic work as a valuable economic activity). However, it is to be remembered that justice under the social law scheme requires groups not only to have their rights recognised but to be empowered to maintain those rights. Therefore, it is to be questioned whether standard setting at international level can ever achieve the aims of social law. For this

---

[71]   Albin and Mantouvalou (n 7) 13

legislation to be effective it would have to be enacted at a local level and adopted by the domestic workers themselves as a basis for their own empowerment. Arguably, this requires the specific encouragement of the trade union and member-based organisations identified in the previous section.[72]

6.5.2   Criticisms of Social Law

The social law scheme can be criticised for its reliance on the idea that the state should act (only) *a posteriori* in order to guarantee the relationships and hence compromises between groups. It could be argued that, in order for groups to form successfully, some principles of justice already need to be established (freedom of association, for example). For 'special' rights to be granted to groups, they need to be treated in the first instance like any other group. This is the argument made by the ILO in the design of its Convention on domestic work. The ILO's Convention recognises that in order for employment protection to be extended effectively to domestic work it must be recognised not only as 'work like no other' but also as 'work like any other'.[73] Therefore, the ILO seeks to ensure that domestic workers are covered by human rights in the same way as other individuals and employment rights in the same way as other workers. The ILO Convention refers to human rights instruments in its Preamble, and Article 3(1) seeks to ensure 'effective protection of the human rights of all domestic workers'. Indeed, it has been argued that this human rights focus complements the sectoral focus of the instrument, and it is only in the combination of these two approaches that the plight of domestic workers can be addressed.[74]

This is, of course, a very optimistic view of this instrument, and there is a danger that the inclusion of human rights prevents further thinking about the way in which the specific rights of the instrument can be improved. Certainly, it could be argued that the specific rights in the Convention need to be extended to cater for the particular vulnerability of

---

[72]   The ILO Convention does recognise the importance of freedom of association and in Article 3 (2) requires ratifying nations to 'respect, promote and realize freedom of association and the effective recognition of the right to collective bargaining' for all domestic workers. However, such 'rights' must be successfully and positively enacted at local level if they are to be meaningful for this group.

[73]   ILO (n 1) 13

[74]   Albin and Mantouvalou (n 7) 11

certain *elements* of the domestic worker group. For example, the Convention also does not consider the complexities and implications of 'cash-for-care' schemes for domestic workers. These schemes, which exist in various forms throughout Europe and the United States, allow the users of social-care support to receive cash in place of services and to spend that money on the direct employment of 'personal assistants' who deliver care for them in their own homes.[75] In some parts of Europe, the work of these carers is highly regulated, and they require specific qualifications in order to be engaged by the service users.[76] However, in the UK under the Direct Payments scheme, service users recruit their 'personal assistants' directly, and they can therefore choose the skills and qualifications that they wish their personal assistants to possess. There is no formal requirement for these 'personal assistants' to have any formal caring qualifications, despite the fact that they often perform caring functions. Furthermore, under the Direct Payments scheme, personal assistants are often employed just by one employer, due to their care needs.[77] This situation can work very well, and service users and personal assistants can build strong relationships. However, this organisation of work can subject domestic workers to real difficulties and there are real problems with the enforcement of legal rights if the relationships break down.

Certainly, the very close and personal relationship with the service user can create major problems for personal assistants. A good example of this is given in the case of *Mr MP Cooper v Monzur Miah t/a Monty's Care*.[78] In this case, Mr Miah, the service user, employed two personal assistants to help with basic personal care, housework, shopping and general physical assistance. They were also tasked with carrying out general administrative duties and dealing with Mr Miah's financial affairs. However, after a year, the relationship started to break down because Mr Miah felt that the personal assistants were being 'overbearing' towards him and that they were threatening his independence (he cited the fact that he had stopped feeding himself and was letting them do it for him). He also stated that there were irregularities in his financial affairs, and that this was due to the fact that the personal assistants were

---

[75] C Ungerson, 'Whose Empowerment and Independence? A Cross-national Perspective on "Cash for Care" Schemes' (2004) 24 *Ageing and Society* 189, 190

[76] In France for example, the Prestation Spécifique Dépendance can be used to employ carers, but because of the limitations of this dependency benefit, the workers are largely employed through agencies which require a basic care qualification. Ibid 200

[77] Ibid 203

[78] Case ET/1305328/2006

not paying his bills on time. The personal assistants disputed these allegations, but the vulnerability of the service user and the personal nature of their duties greatly increased their potential liability. Furthermore, the personal assistants did not have any independent qualification or training as care professionals to fall back on and to show that they had followed the correct procedures in dealing with this service user.

There are also often problems for personal assistants in relation to the governance of the employment relationship and difficulties of communication between the parties. Contracts are often poorly constructed and often do not reflect the nature of the duties involved. Disciplinary procedures may not be used effectively; this was one of the complaints raised by the personal assistants in the *Miah* case above. Variation of contracts may proceed informally, which causes problems when these variations are challenged. Furthermore, in some situations problems arise because of the involvement of a number of different parties in the employment relationship, all giving different accounts about agreements reached. This involvement is a function of the extreme vulnerability of some service users, who rely on a number of different parties for their overall care (for example, the service user's support worker, independent living centres, friends and relatives who also undertake care work). This only serves to exacerbate communication difficulties. This is well demonstrated by the case of *Mrs S Bicknell v Miss I Hughes*.[79] This case concerned an extremely vulnerable service user with a complex of disabilities which affected her ability to communicate both orally and in writing. She was assisted by a number of friends, as well as a number of personal assistants, including Mrs Bicknell. Mrs Bicknell contended that she was told by other personal assistants and Miss Hughes' relatives that her day shift activities were changing and she was not happy with these changes. She decided that she had no option but to relinquish her day shifts, and this led her to claim constructive dismissal against Miss Hughes.

The *Bicknell* case also illustrates a final point: the difficulty of enforcement of legal rights against service users, particularly in a Tribunal setting. For a start, the nature of Miss Hughes' disability meant that she was not able to attend the Tribunal and relied on a friend to represent her. Secondly, it is clear that the Tribunal saw Mrs Bicknell's claim against Miss Hughes as rather unsavoury and in the mediation on this case, the Tribunal chairman commented that the Tribunal was not the

---

[79]   Case ET/1305506/2007

proper place for the resolution of such disputes.[80] Thirdly, direct payment recipients have only a very restricted income (the direct payments money and other benefit needs to cover often complex needs) and so would have difficulty paying any compensation awarded. Indeed, in the *Miah* case, Mr Miah had so overspent his income that he was technically insolvent and repaying his creditors under a voluntary agreement.

This analysis of the particular problems faced by direct payment personal assistants highlights a number of (further) difficulties with the social law view. In order for domestic workers to achieve protection under this view, they need to be recognised as a group in need of protection and have available instruments which empower them to maintain their status. However, domestic work is extremely heterogeneous in form, and the interests of different 'groups' of domestic workers varies considerably. This is a considerable problem for the solutions to vulnerability in the social law view. It is a problem for the recognition of domestic workers as a 'group' with similar interests. It also creates a problem for the design of instruments which lead to their empowerment. Even if instruments are designed with the intention of creating specific rights for these workers, it could be argued that even specific rights will never cover all the situations in which domestic workers find themselves. Furthermore, there is the problem of their empowerment. Labour law instruments may allow these workers 'freedom of association' and the right to collective bargaining, but the question is how to encourage associations outside the traditional trade union structure, given the massive practical and administrative hurdles associated with trade union organisation. This may involve legislation beyond the scope of labour law, and 'positive' action which goes beyond the scope of traditional labour law instruments. This will be discussed further in the next section.

6.6 THE VULNERABLE SUBJECT AND DOMESTIC WORK

6.6.1 Characterisation of Vulnerability

It is argued in this chapter, and more widely in this book, that vulnerability theory is potentially a very useful tool in highlighting the

---

[80] These comments were made in the mediation of this case in December 2007.

problems with the current conceptualisations of vulnerability and precarity in employment relationship and in suggesting how those failures have underscored the failure of our current laws to really address precarious work. In some senses, this view builds on some of the insights of the social law tradition in seeking to move beyond liberalism as the foundation of our law, and also to consider the social construction of vulnerability in all its different dimensions and what this means for the effective building of law which is responsive to individual needs. It does however differ from the social law position in some important respects (discussed in more detail in Chapters 2 and 3 particularly). For example, it does not rely on group identity to the same extent as social law, and takes a different stance on the question of rights. These elements will be discussed in more detail during the course of this section.

According to vulnerability theory, our current legal conceptions fail because they are based around the 'liberal subject'. This liberal subject is a de-personalised being who acts in an autonomous, rational or independent way. In the liberal subject both agency and autonomy are assumed. It is argued that having the liberal subject at the heart of our law means that it is deprived of its usefulness for a number of reasons. First, the default position in relation to law is that of deregulation. As all liberal subjects are deemed to act independently and rationally, there is a fear that (too much) regulation will constrain and impair the agency of individuals and will not allow them to pursue their own autonomous ends. This deregulatory stance posits the state in a very negative relationship to the law. Second, the law is unresponsive to vulnerability and fails to address real need. The law does not address actual vulnerability because it is vulnerability-blind or assigns vulnerability only to a certain set of identity categories which can be reasonably dealt with within the bounds of certain categories (for example, the bounds of discrimination law). Finally, where vulnerability is considered, it is addressed in very negative terms. Vulnerability is associated with individuals who posit excessive dependence on the state or who deliberately try to subvert its (legal) structures. Vulnerability is viewed as both anti-legal and anti-economic.

In relation to the first of these failings, this can be illustrated by the lack of comprehensive instruments regulating domestic work in the majority of nation states, and indeed, the exclusion of domestic workers from a multitude of labour law instruments at domestic level.[81] The DWC

---

[81]   There are a number of exceptions to this. In South Africa, the South African Basic Conditions of Employment Act 1997 (BCEA) includes domestic workers in at least some of its provisions. Furthermore, the Domestic Worker

attempts to rectify this exclusion, but carries its own set of barriers. One significant problem is the set of qualification criteria that domestic workers need to fulfil to come within the scope of the Convention.[82] Under the DWC, a domestic worker is defined as 'any person engaged in domestic work within an employment relationship'.[83] Individuals who perform domestic tasks 'only occasionally or sporadically and not on an occupational basis' are specifically excluded from the scope of the Convention.[84] It may be argued that this need to prove an employment relationship is a particular example of the failure of this law to deal with the particular vulnerabilities of domestic workers. Arguably it is an example of the liberal position that in order to claim legal rights, individuals must already have a level of independence and autonomy. Furthermore, in Article 2 of the Convention it is provided that ratifying countries can exclude 'limited categories of workers in respect of which special problems of a substantial nature arise'. Again, this suggests that there is a reluctance to create a law which is excessively burdensome for regulators, or which might be viewed as having an excessive negative impact on other areas of regulation.

The multi-factoral and the multi-dimensional nature of domestic work and its surrounding institutions also continue to cause problems for domestic workers, despite the enactment of the Domestic Workers Convention. A good example is provided in relation to migrant domestic workers. This group is recognised as particularly vulnerable and is given specific reference in the provisions of the Convention. Article 8 requires that migrant domestic workers who are recruited in one country for domestic work in another receive a written job offer or contract of employment that is enforceable in the country in which the work is to be performed. That contract must set out the terms and conditions of the employment in an easily understandable manner, and must be received prior to the appointment of the worker. Furthermore, under Article 9 each member is tasked to approve measures to ensure that domestic workers are free to reach agreement with their employer on whether to reside in

---

Sectoral Determination 2002, introduced under the auspices of the BCEA, makes considerable specific provision for domestic workers in relation to the law. See commentary in S Fredman, 'Home from Home: Migrant Domestic Workers and the ILO Convention on Domestic Workers' in C Costello and M Freedland (eds), *Migrants at Work: Immigration and Vulnerability in Labour Law* (Oxford University Press 2014)

[82] Ibid 399
[83] Article 1 (b) DWC
[84] Article 1 (c) DWC

the household, and are not obliged to remain in the household during periods of rest or annual leave. According to this provision, domestic workers must also be entitled to keep their travel and identity documents in their possession to prevent abuse. Members are required to cooperate with each other to ensure that the provisions of the Convention are applied effectively to migrant domestic workers.

The problem is that the institutional vulnerability of domestic workers means that such provisions are potentially ineffective. For example, it might be suggested that providing a contract of employment to domestic workers does little to tackle their vulnerability if that contract is not genuinely agreed and just imposes certain terms and conditions.[85] Furthermore, the Convention does not dig deeply enough into the specific institutional problems experienced by domestic workers (which may differ from other workers), and so their vulnerabilities are perpetuated. For example, in terms of migrant domestic workers, the Convention does not tackle problems of tied employment status. This tied employment status, whereby a domestic worker may not change employer, makes it very difficult for domestic workers to make demands for certain of the rights and freedoms promoted in the Convention. For example, in the UK, a specific overseas domestic worker visa was introduced on 6 April 2012. Under this visa domestic workers are not entitled to change employer or to renew their visa beyond six months. This makes domestic workers employed under these visas extremely vulnerable. It increases the potential for abuse, as the employer is aware that if a domestic worker leaves, that worker is at risk of deportation. Indeed, in evidence collected by the charity Kalaayan, it was reported that domestic workers on these visas all received less than £100 per week and 62 per cent were paid no salary at all. 85 per cent of domestic workers did not have their own room and 95 per cent were not allowed out unsupervised.[86] This evidence suggest that Article 9 of the Convention is not a reality for this group of domestic workers in the UK.

The 'momentous' Modern Slavery Act enacted in the UK in March 2015 has not addressed this particular problem.[87] Indeed, during the course of the agreement of the Modern Slavery Act, the government specifically rejected an amendment to the Act which would have allowed

---

[85]   Fredman (n 81) 412

[86]   Kalayaan, 'Slavery by another name: the tied migrant domestic work visa' (May 2013) <http://www.kalayaan.org.uk/wp-content/uploads/2014/09/Slavery-by-a-new-name-Briefing-7.5.13.pdf> accessed 13 August 2015

[87]   Home office minister Lord Bates, quoted in K Nguyen and K Guilbert, 'Human Traffickers may face life sentence under Britain's tough new slavery

overseas migrant workers to change employers.[88] The government also rejected the proposal that domestic workers should attain a three-month temporary visa permitting them to live in the UK for the purposes of seeking alternative employment as an overseas domestic worker where there is evidence of modern slavery. Instead, a clause was inserted into the Act to the effect that migrant domestic workers may attain a six-month visa as a domestic worker if they approach the government's National Referral Mechanisms and are found to have been subject to slavery or trafficking.[89] This provision does not effectively tackle the problems and vulnerabilities of workers under the tied visa system. It requires that overseas domestic workers approach public authorities when their immigration status is insecure, and in circumstances where their protection is not guaranteed. This places the risk firmly on the worker and, as such, domestic workers are unlikely to attempt to take the benefit of this provision.[90]

6.6.2   Solutions to Vulnerability

The question is whether there are any solutions which could be suggested to address these vulnerabilities and to allow domestic workers to build resilience. Of course, the inclusion of domestic workers in legislative instruments is important, particularly where that inclusion recognises (some of) the diversity of the situations in which domestic workers find themselves. But it is suggested that a purely legal response in this way does not totally fulfil the aims and aspirations of vulnerability theory. The key is to promote collective association of domestic workers because it is through this association that domestic workers can really make visible the issues that affect them in practice. This promotion of collective association cannot just rely on increasing trade union membership, although this strategy has helped domestic workers in some

---

bill' *The Guardian* (27 March 2015) <http://www.theguardian.com/global-development/2015/mar/27/human-traffickers-face-life-sentence-britain-slavery-bill> accessed 13 August 2015

[88]   This amendment was proposed by Lord Hylton as an amendment to Clause 51 of the Modern Slavery Act. Full details of the proposed amendment available   at   <http://www.publications.parliament.uk/pa/bills/lbill/2014-2015/0069/amend/am069-f.htm> last accessed 13 August 2015

[89]   Clause 53 (1) Modern Slavery Act 2015

[90]   Kalayaan, 'Lost opportunity as the Modern Slavery Bill leaves migrant domestic workers tied to their employers' (23 March 2015) <http://www.kalayaan.org.uk/news/final-chance-for-the-modern-slavery-bill-to-protect-migrant-domestic-workers/> last accessed 13 August 2015

instances. For example, the Domestic Workers and Allied Trade Union in South Africa has been active in campaigning for domestic workers on a national level, and was at the forefront of demanding a specific Convention for domestic workers at international level. This Trade Union was also active in the consultations on the proposals for the Domestic Workers Convention, and ensuring that the Convention met the needs of these workers as far as possible.[91] However, traditional trade union organisation has its limits for domestic workers. As discussed earlier in this chapter, this kind of organisation is often difficult to access for domestic workers, and trade union membership can increase the vulnerability of domestic workers.[92] Therefore, for collective association to work for domestic workers, organisations outside the trade union structure must be created or engaged.

There are examples of innovative arrangements by groups outside the trade union structure to engage and assist domestic workers. In New York, Domestic Workers United has established a neighbourhood shop steward system. Under this system, DWU ambassadors (themselves domestic worker members of the organisation) are trained to provide information on the rights of domestic workers and connect them to the service of DWU.[93] In Ghana, a non-governmental organisation, LAWA (Leadership and Advocacy for Women in Africa) has established a number of domestic workers' associations in a number of cities. Local contact persons facilitate dialogue with the employers of domestic workers where problems occur.[94] Often these organisations work in tandem with trade unions. These groups and schemes benefit greatly from state support. In Belgium for example, there is a state-subsidised scheme of service vouchers. These vouchers enable private individuals to have domestic tasks performed by a worker from a recognised firm. As soon as a firm employs at least 20 workers, Belgian unions have the right to set up a trade union delegation, which is equivalent to union local committee. Each union delegate has the right to take five days' leave per year for trade union meetings or training.[95]

---

[91]   Fredman (n 81) 410
[92]   ILO, Domestic Workers across the World, Global and Regional Statistics and the Extent of Protection (ILO 2013) 70
[93]   ILO, Achieving Decent Work for Domestic Workers: An Organizer's Manual to Promote ILO Convention 189 and Build Domestic Workers' Power (ILO 2012) 16
[94]   Ibid
[95]   Ibid

It is through these kinds of associations and the links between them and the state that there appears to be significant potential for institutional change. Importantly, these groups recognise the particular issues faced by domestic workers, and can provide support mechanisms for individuals. They can also ensure a more effective operation of the law, not only through lobbying processes but also through innovative methods of legal enforcement. One possible methodology is that of regulatory 'layering', through which new (non-legal) rules are attached to existing ones. These non-legal rules not only have the potential to change the operation of existing legal rules, but also involve a number of new actors or agents into the regulatory process. This can in turn create institutional change. Indeed, an example of the effectiveness of this layering effect is given by Marshall.[96] She outlines how the actions of the Textile Clothing and Footwear Union of Australia worked together with an alliance of community groups to develop a Code of Practice to bolster the existing legal system and make it more inclusive. This Code of Practice aimed to enhance the operation of labour law, through creating incentives for manufacturers to comply with the Code (those who complied were licensed to display the Ethical Clothing Australia mark), and also ensured that a greater number of agencies were involved in regulatory enforcement. According to Marshall, the result is a 'complementary networked regulatory system' under which the state draws on the power of non-state and quasi-state actors who are allies in increasing compliance.[97]

6.7 CONCLUSIONS

The case study on domestic work illustrates well the challenges facing labour law theories of worker vulnerability. In particular, domestic work presents profound theoretical challenges to the efficiency views of regulation, which arguably represents the basis for current assessments of worker vulnerability and the protection which workers should be afforded. The reasons for the blindness of the efficiency view to the particular problems of domestic workers relates to a number of factors. Firstly, the efficiency view relies on liberal theory which separates private family activity from public economic activity. It therefore cannot deal with private family activities which have an economic basis and a public function. Secondly, the efficiency view relies on the notion of rational

---

[96] S Marshall, 'How Does Institutional Change Occur? Two Strategies for Reforming the Scope of Labour Law' (2014) 43 (3) *ILJ* 286
[97] Ibid 303

choice, and does not sufficiently take into account restraints on that choice (for example, immigration rules and lack of resources). Thirdly, the efficiency view sees the law as acting best as a universal guarantor of 'human' rights. With this view, there is nothing special about the 'social' considerations in labour law rights to distinguish them from other social rights considerations (the right to social assistance, and so on), and labour law rights have a secondary status to more important political and civil rights considerations. In practice, although domestic workers have been able to use human rights to some degree to improve their position, this can only ever be a partial solution, given the difficulties in access-ibility of human rights law, and the very specific problems displayed in the vast diversity of situations in which domestic workers find them-selves.

The benefit perhaps of the classical view over the narrow view is that it can incorporate the extremes of exploitation experienced by some domestic workers into the labour law consciousness. It does not rely on the regime of human rights to protect workers against such exploitation. The problem is that the exploitation envisaged on the wide view relies on a Marxist interpretation of the functioning of the capitalist system, and does not directly translate to the situation of domestic workers. Further-more, the solution offered by the classical view, namely the equalisation of power relations by the organisation of workers into trade unions, does not appear to be feasible for many domestic workers. There are many practical barriers for domestic workers seeking to organise, including their isolation and employment in a 'family' setting seemingly outside the sphere of industrial relations. That said, there are a number of instances of the successful organisation of domestic workers outside the confines of the trade union system. This appears to show that power does indeed stem from collective organisation, and that this collective organisation can help to improve the terms and conditions of domestic workers generally (particularly where the law fails).

It appears that the social law view has considerable potential as a framework for the consideration of the vulnerability of domestic workers. It completely rejects the liberal foundations of the efficiency view of regulation and exposes the dangers of the reliance on liberal theory for groups historically passed over by the liberal regime. As the law on the social view is not formulated as a system of abstract ideals created by the political elite, but as a 'social' law determined by social groups them-selves, it is potentially empowering for domestic workers. According to this theory, domestic workers do not have to fit within legal structures to enforce their rights (which is problematic where those legal structures do not support them), rather they can create their own rights simply by joining together and making it clear that their position is one that should be protected by the state. Furthermore, the social view allows the potential for domestic workers to claim certain resources for themselves, so that rights are of immediate practical use. The danger of course is that the administrative resources needed to sustain this redistribution and the constant conflict of the claims of domestic workers with all the other interests that people have, leads to an unwieldy and unworkable system which ultimately controls more than it empowers.

The vulnerable subject view complements the social law approach in a number of ways. It recognises the importance of identity in the formation of the law, and the importance of institutions in building resilience. It suggests that vulnerability is always multi-factoral and multi-dimensional. It is also institutionally embedded. The value of this approach is in capturing the wide diversity of domestic worker situations, and the recognition that there are a number of factors outside the confines of labour law which affect particular domestic workers' vulnerabilities. This approach also recognises that vulnerability itself must be accounted for in the design of the law if workers are really to build a sustainable system of law which responds to worker needs and which is actively enforced. This requires that institutions are effective for workers and that the state plays an active part in building and supporting those institutions which aid workers. If workers are to have agency then all institutions need to be directed towards developing that agency which allows wider mid-spectrum goals to be achieved.

7.   Conclusions

7.1 ON VULNERABILITY

The context of this book is the move in labour law to create and consider regulation for precarious work and precarious workers. This move has been spurred by the identification of a number of economic changes which present a real challenge to the traditional design and functions of labour law. For example, it is argued that labour law is traditionally based on the idea of an inequality of bargaining power between employees and employers in the labour market. This presumes a standard employment relationship under which an employee carries out full time, year round work for a single employer. However, in the 'knowledge economy', workers select flexible strategies which mean that relationships with employers are diffuse, or short term, and many have much more labour market power than ever before (based on the acquisition of skills which are transferable between employers). These relationships no longer correspond to the 'standard employment relationship' upon which labour law is based. Furthermore, 'inequality of bargaining power' is not present in all cases in these flexible relationships: some of these strategies make workers vulnerable (precarious workers) and others do not (gold-collar employees). It follows that labour law based on inequality of bargaining power in standard employment relationships is necessarily both over- and under-inclusive, and fails to capture those precarious workers in need of protection (who are not able to take the benefits of the flexibilisation of work relations).[1]

It is certainly possible to argue that classical labour law is wedded to a particular economic and social moment, and that the institutions of that labour law need to be (constantly) reconsidered, redeveloped and re-designed. However, it is the contention of this book that the particular direction that this reconsideration has taken has been lacking in a number of respects. First and foremost, the theorisation of the need to regulate

---

[1]   G Davidov, 'The Reports of my Death Are Greatly Exaggerated: "Employee" as a Viable (Though Over-used) Legal Concept' in G Davidov and B Langille (eds), *The Boundaries and Frontiers of Labour Law* (Hart 2006)

precarious work starts from an economic perspective. This economic perspective dominates the regulatory view. Regulation has become determined by considerations of efficiency, and compliance with the institutions of liberal law. In the context of modern liberal political thinking about the need for a light touch in the labour market, regulation for precarious work has gained acceptance, but the economic perspective of this view has resulted in limited and restricted solutions for precarious workers. For example, there has been a reliance on equality legislation which promotes equality between precarious and permanent workers. However, that equality legislation has been limited in both scope and effect. Other 'solutions' have involved deregulatory changes which supposedly allow precarious workers greater freedom to take advantage of economic changes, but which in fact are likely to maintain workers in a situation of precariousness or disadvantage. Second, the precarious work theorisations miss the opportunity for a full and proper reconsideration of the value and institutions of classical labour law. In fact, the precarious work theorisations adopt the weaker elements of that classical labour law, and reject some of its major strengths. For example, the precarious work theorisations tend to under-theorise vulnerability in a similar way to the theories of classical labour law. In both accounts, vulnerability is economically determined and so it is economic systems which are deemed worthy of scrutiny rather than the labour subject itself. Vulnerability is also under-theorised in both accounts because they assume a 'liberal' labour subject: an autonomous rational and rarefied individual. By contrast, the precarious work theories do not consider the stronger elements of classical theory. They do not consider, for instance, the claim by classical labour law that problems in labour relationships are systemic rather than momentary. They also do not consider the influence of social law on these classical theories and the potential of this more social bent to explain or counteract vulnerabilities in employment relationships.

The aim of this book is not only to consider this development in a negative sense. The aim is to draw on this recognition of the failings of precarious work theorisations and to suggest alternative solutions (which do reflect the positive elements of classical labour law). This book attempts to put 'vulnerability' centre stage. It is argued that this is useful in a number of ways. It allows a move away from the 'liberal subject' foundation of classical labour law and more modern economic theory and towards a more complete examination of the labour subject. This, in turn, leads to a reconsideration of the economic determinism which has dominated labour law thinking. Under this (new) account, labour law starts from the 'vulnerable' subject of labour. This 'vulnerable' subject' is a complex individual with a complex set of relationships with other subjects and surrounding (economic, social, legal) institutions. This changes the priorities and insights of labour law theory. It means that issues of identity and agency become much more important: the aim of labour law institutions is now not to 'reflect' individual autonomy but actually to create it. Labour law also becomes part of the pattern of advantage and disadvantage experienced by labour subjects, and those patterns themselves become the subject of scrutiny. This brings the analysis full-circle: to the criticisms of social law in the institutions of the liberal state.

The aim of this book is also to provide insight into and analysis of the regulations for precarious work and precarious workers, and how the areas might be developed in light of the perspective of the vulnerable subject approach. The next section brings out some of the conclusions which might be drawn from the link between the different views of vulnerability outlined in this book and how these have impacted on our current regulatory pattern. The final section outlines some practical suggestions for the development of the law in the light of the insights gained from a greater examination of the theory of vulnerability in employment relationships as outlined in this book.

7.2 DIFFERENT VIEWS OF VULNERABILITY AND PRECARIOUS WORK

7.2.1 Classical Labour Law Views and their Application

On the classical labour law view, worker vulnerability is created by the combination of 'inequality of bargaining power' and the commodification of labour. This vulnerability is systemic and applies to all workers; there is no automatic distinction between precarious workers and the general vulnerability of the working population as a whole. It is a function of, firstly, the operation of capitalism, which serves to alienate workers from their own labour; labour is simply a commodity to be bought and sold on the labour market. This draws on Marxist theories of exploitation and subordination of the 'proletariat' by the bourgeoisie. The second factor is the '*fictio juris*' of the contract of employment. Although this contract appears to be freely negotiated, it is in fact just a tool through which employers can maintain their position of power over workers.[2] The

---

[2]   P Davies and M Freedland, *Kahn-Freund's Labour and the Law* (Stevens and Sons 1983) 17

notion of 'vulnerability' outlined here constitutes the traditional narrative of the labour law's foundation: inequality of bargaining power between employer and employee and the commodification of labour result in the subordination and exploitation of workers, which must be addressed by legal intervention.

However, under classical labour law, the solution to worker vulnerability is not (simply) the application of legal standards to the labour market. Indeed, authors on this view tend to be sceptical about the power of the law, on its own at least, to really improve working conditions. Rather, the aim is a solution through which all workers can be involved in the management of their working lives. Therefore, first and foremost, the solution lies in the constitutionalisation of labour relations, and particularly allowing workers to have a voice through institutionalised collective bargaining to boost their social power. Authors with this view differ on the particular form of this constitutionalisation, and how far this should involve state intervention and legislation. At the one extreme, Kahn-Freund suggests a system of 'collective laissez-faire', whereby collective negotiation operates almost exclusively in the private sphere. Under this system, legislation is only required as 'auxiliary law' to support collective bargaining, rather than as a means to create labour standards through 'regulatory law'.[3] At the other extreme, Sinzheimer suggests that the system of industrial relations should be entirely governed by an economic constitution, which is backed by the state acting in the public interest.[4] Between these two positions, authors suggest systems of collective bargaining rights which support the proper operation of trade unions and promote trade union membership.[5]

In theoretical terms, there are a number of useful elements to the classical view. At the very least, it sets out the 'basic' position with which other theories of labour law can be contrasted; namely that labour law is underpinned by the conjunction of the ideas of 'inequality of bargaining power' and 'labour is not a commodity'. Moreover, it does not shy away from highlighting the failings of capitalism (and the institutions which support it) in providing support for workers. Indeed, there is a concern that, if left unchecked, the combination of economic and social power

---

[3] Ibid 37
[4] H Sinzheimer, 'Zur Frage der Reform des Schlichtungswesens' (1929) in H Sinzheimer *Arbeitsrecht und Rechtssoziologie: Gessammelte Aufsätze und Reden* (Europäische Verlagsanstalt 1976) 226
[5] K Ewing, 'The Implications of the ASLEF case' (2007) 36 (4) *ILJ* 425; Lord Wedderburn, 'Collective Bargaining or Legal Enactment: 1999 Act and Union Recognition' (2000) 29 (1) *ILJ* 1

which comes to be exerted by capitalists is both bad for the economy and for workers as part of society as a whole. This view reminds us that economic order cannot be separated from social order, and that labour law cannot just be about the private relations between parties.[6] In Sinzheimer's 'economic constitution', for example, both employers and workers organisations make decisions together, so that workers are not only economically involved in production, but are also democratically involved. This means that workers are not only economic but also political subjects, and become 'labour citizens' imbued with real social power.[7] The classical labour law position is also critical of liberalism law based on liberal ideology. It only goes so far in this, of course, because the theorists in this position do not suggest that this capitalist system should be replaced (in the Marxist sense), and some of the ideas promoted by authors under the classical view have, in practice, turned out to be compatible with liberal ideology.[8] Furthermore, the classical labour law view is firmly complicit in the liberal view of the labour subject. The humanity of the labour subject is considered in contrast and apart from the de-humanising processes of capitalism. The aim of labour law is to counteract the deleterious processes of capitalism to allow humanity to shine through. This means that the vulnerability of workers, their complex interaction with others and all the legal, social and economic institutions which affect them are not properly considered.

There are also questions about the practical relevance of the classical labour law view. The reliance of this view on trade unionism is problematic. The density of trade unions has declined in many nation states in recent years,[9] and there is also the problem of the very national focus of trade union bargaining, which does not fit with the need for supranational regulation of global production processes.[10] These two

---

[6]   R Dukes, 'Hugo Sinzheimer and the Constitutional Function of Labour Law' in B Langille and G Davidov (eds), *The Idea of Labour Law* (Oxford University Press 2011) 65

[7]   Ibid 64

[8]   A good example is Kahn-Freund's system of collective laissez-faire. R Dukes, 'Otto Kahn-Freund and Collective Laissez-Faire: An Edifice without a Keystone?' (2009) 72 (2) *MLR* 245, 277

[9]   By way of example, in the UK a report for the Department of Business, Innovation and Skills in 2015 found that trade union density had declined in the period of 1995 to 2014, from 32.4 per cent in 1995 to 29.8 per cent in 2000 and 25.0 per cent in 2014. BIS, 'Trade Union Membership Statistics 2014' (June 2015) Table 1.2b <https://www.gov.uk/government/statistics/trade-union-statistics-2014> accessed 19 August 2015

[10]   Dukes (n 8) 66

factors, among others, explain the lack of reference to the classical labour law view at either UK or EU level. At UK level, the decline in trade union membership has reinforced the argument that it is not practical for worker issues and rights to be determined through collective bargaining and, in any event, there has been no political will to engage with collective action as a meaningful bargaining tool.[11] At EU level, there has been the problem of the lack of a transnational social dialogue process, so that collective bargaining issues are dealt with in an isolated fashion, in terms of individual breaches of human rights to freedom of association. This is dogged with problems, given the complexity of the proportionality tests involved when determining the balance to be struck with these 'rights' to freedom of association in contradistinction to other EU rights (particularly under the ambit of the fundamental freedoms of the EU constitution).[12] This is not to say that the development of transnational solidarity is non-existent, but it is certainly at an early stage.[13]

By contrast, the classical view is fundamental to the establishment and polices of the ILO. The first of the 'fundamental principles' stated in the ILO's constitution is that 'labour is not a commodity', and the starting point of the ILO is to address 'conditions of labour [that] exist involving such hardship and privation to large numbers of people'.[14] In terms of solutions to vulnerability, the ILO has also traditionally aligned itself with the classical view in espousing the fundamental importance of collective bargaining: the second fundamental principle of the ILO's constitution states that 'freedom of expression and of association are essential to sustained progress'. However, the ILO has also faced difficulties in maintaining its commitment to the classical view, given a number of factors. The first is the difficulty of coordinating and maintaining a programme which attempts to deal with all the diverse

---

[11] On the strikes planned by teaching unions over pay and conditions in late 2013, Michael Gove, Secretary of State for Education, stated that the 'direction of travel' on the issue of pay and pensions was 'fixed', implying a lack of willingness to seriously negotiate change. See A Harrison, 'Teachers announce one-day national strike' <http://www.bbc.co.uk/education/-23285445> accessed 15 July 2015.

[12] P Syrpis and T Novitz, Economic and Social Rights in Conflict: Political and Judicial Approaches to their Reconciliation' (2008) 33 (3) *European Law Review* 411

[13] S Sciarra, 'Notions of Solidarity in Times of Economic Crisis' (2010) 39 (3) *ILJ* 223

[14] ILO, 'Preamble' of the Constitution of the International Labour Organization, 1919 <http://www.ilo.org/ilolex/english/iloconst.htm>

situations in which workers find themselves. For example, the ILO's Decent Work programme[15] has faced a number of problems of legitimacy, and in 2008, the ILO Declaration on Social Justice for a Fair Globalization[16] was introduced to reassert the importance of the decent work agenda and to promote the more successful coordination of its different elements. Furthermore, the tripartite structure of the ILO (and its commitment to traditional trade union membership) has hindered the progress of its programmes. A good example is the resistance of both employers and governments to the decent work programme, and the resistance of employers, governments and trade unions to involving organisations outside the tripartite structure in the coordination and management of its programmes.[17] The result has been to fall back on the set of core labour standards as set out in the Declaration of Fundamental Rights and Principles at Work.[18] On the one hand, it has been argued that these core labour standards allow the effective reassertion of the ILO's message (in the classical view) because there is a focus on the 'procedural' right to collective bargaining. On the other hand, it has been argued that the concentration on a narrow range of core labour standards reduces the protection afforded to workers by the international (human rights) regime.

In terms of the two case studies, there are a number of difficulties of application in terms of the classical labour law view. The first is the relevance of the particular version of vulnerability espoused by the classical view. The idea of 'inequality of bargaining power' is fundamentally linked to the model of the 'standard employment relationship', which is difficult to apply to employment relationships which are flexibly designed. Secondly, the classical view of vulnerability assumes homogeneity of employment relationship types, whereas both domestic work and temporary agency work exist in extremely heterogeneous forms. Finally, the classical view assumes that all forms of work relationship can be adequately represented through collective bargaining. For temporary

---

[15]   ILO, *Decent Work* Report of the Director General, International Labour Conference (87th session, Geneva 1999) <http://www.ilo.org/public/english/standards/relm/ilc/ilc87/rep-i.htm> accessed 10 August 2015

[16]   ILO, *Declaration on Social Justice for a Fair Globalization* (August 2008) <http://www.ilo.org/wcmsp5/groups/public/@dgreports/@cabinet/documents/publication/wcms_099766.pdf> accessed 10 July 2015

[17]   G Rodgers, E Lee, L Swepston and J van Daele, *The ILO and the Quest for Social Justice 1919–2009* (International Labour Office 2009) 227

[18]   ILO, *ILO Declaration on Fundamental Principles and Rights at Work and its Follow-up* (International Labour Office, Geneva 1998)

agency workers and domestic workers, both face great difficulty in accessing and joining the traditional trade union organisations with which the classical view is associated.[19] However, the classical view does maintain some useful analysis of both of these work types. There is some evidence in both of these case studies that affiliation with trade unions can achieve improvements in work conditions for precarious workers, and provide some means by which to counteract the degrading processes of commodification associated with the global capitalist system.[20]

7.2.2 Economic Efficiency Views and their Application

It is argued in this book that modern thinking about precarious work has largely been dominated by the efficiency discourse, or is at least complicit in it. This has tended to eclipse other ways of thinking about precarious work and the challenge of precarious work to labour law. This dominance can be explained in a number of ways. The first is that this view introduces the problems of precarious work as a new problem, and therefore a focal point for the development of labour law. Second, the efficiency view attaches itself to 'modern' ways of thinking about labour law. It is sympathetic to the concerns within labour law to move away from a concentration on collective bargaining as the main way to resolve the problems workers face. It recognises the strategic importance of this move, and the need for workers to attach themselves to 'human' rights, given the global hegemony of human rights language. Finally, the efficiency view of vulnerability is politically legitimate, in that it fits with the neo-liberal political outlook shared by the most influential global actors. The efficiency view advocates that the problem of vulnerability is not a general failure of the economic system; it is the failure of certain individuals to take advantage of that system. Solutions can therefore be introduced which do not unduly interfere with economic functioning, and are broadly in line with liberal ideals.

Under the efficiency view, there is a rejection of the twin foundations of classical labour law: that labour law is not a commodity and there is

---

[19] Figures suggest that in 2014, 26 per cent of permanent workers were members of trade unions, as opposed to 15 per cent of temporary agency workers. BIS, 'Trade Union Membership 2014' (June 2015) 9 <https://www.gov.uk/government/uploads/system/uploads/attachment_data/file/431564/Trade_Union_Membership_Statistics_2014.pdf> accessed 19 August 2015

[20] See for example the influence of trade unions in Brazil and Spain in improving work conditions discussed in Chapter 6.

an inequality of bargaining power between employers and their employees. It rejects these ideas on the basis that they fit neither with economic theory nor economic reality. In terms of economic theory, it is possible to argue that neither of these foundational arguments make sense. Under economic arguments, labour is necessarily a commodity as it is bought and sold as other commodities on the open market. Likewise, inequality of bargaining power is nonsense in the context of contracting parties freely entering into mutually beneficial arrangements. Furthermore, inequality of bargaining power does not make sense in the current economic climate. Some market actors in the knowledge economic area have a high amount of power to determine their own (favourable) terms and conditions. Under the efficiency view, there is a (related) rejection of the idea that labour necessarily requires regulation. Under this view, the market is the most efficient allocator of resources. Labour law necessarily disrupts this allocation and creates inefficiencies. The only exception is in the instance of labour market failure, of which precarious work may be an example (although not always, as non-standard work may be a legitimate choice). In those instances, labour law may be applied to allow individuals to take advantage of the benefits that the global economy can bring. For instance, labour law can be extended to a certain extent to cover those in 'dependent' relationships which do not necessarily conform with the standard employment relationship but which are still deserving of protection. But labour law should not be extended too far in such a way that it interferes with freedom of contract and economic functioning. Rather, the human rights regime should be left to deal with the more dramatic instances of abuse in employment relationships.

In terms of the application of the efficiency view, it can be discerned in the labour law and policy of the UK. The designation of the 'vulnerable worker' in the UK's vulnerable worker policy (2006–10) was an individualistic notion, which blamed the 'lack of capacity' of workers for their vulnerable position. This vulnerability was deemed not to be systemic, and only experienced by a small minority of workers. The proposed solutions were therefore targeted only towards these workers, and involved only incremental changes in the law. Likewise, the Coalition Government's Employment Law Review (2010–2015) was founded on the idea that the majority of workers are not vulnerable. Rather, workers are economic actors involved centrally in the management of their own employment relations. For the majority of employment relationships therefore, the best strategy of the government is to let the parties have the 'freedom to arrange their employment relationships in ways that work for them'.[21] This attitude is particularly in evidence in the creation of the new optional employee shareholder status for workers. The idea is that this new status will allow increased flexibility for employees and employers in the running of their affairs (despite the fact that it will also erode employment protections for those that select it). Interestingly, policies have recently been introduced which are aimed towards the protection of *businesses* as the weaker party to the employment relationship. For example, in the summer of 2013, a new fee structure was introduced to enable employees to 'think more carefully' about whether they should bring an employment tribunal claim which is costly to employers.[22] The aim is to tackle 'vexatious' claims made by employees which threaten to sue businesses 'out of existence'.[23]

At EU level, the efficiency view can be seen in the commitment to the ethos of 'flexicurity' in the design of labour law. 'Flexicurity' represents the notion that individual labour market participants should be able to use the flexibility of work relationships to their own advantage. This requires a level of 'employment' security through a commitment to training and 'life-long learning'. This employment security will support workers by allowing them to easily make the transitions between the more flexible forms of work in the global economy. In the EU, the idea of 'flexicurity' has become pervasive, and was instrumental in the (later) design of the atypical work directives. However, the difficulty is that the association of these directives with the narrow view has undermined their protective elements to a certain extent: arguably the Temporary Agency Work Directive (TAWD) and the Part-time Work Directive were as much about the *promotion* of atypical work, as they were about the protection of workers in these types of relationships. At ILO level, the efficiency view can be discerned in the attempts to strengthen legislation on precarious work through aligning labour rights with 'human' rights. This policy aim was made explicit in the Declaration, and is reflected in the wording of the ILO's Convention on Domestic Work.[24] It has to be questioned, however, what the effect of this policy will be, given that the Declaration

---

[21]   BIS, *Employment Law Review 2013: Progress on Reform* (March 2013) 4

[22]   Ibid 24

[23]   Comments made by George Osborne in a speech to the British Business Leaders Conference in Davos, 28 January 2011 <https://www.gov.uk/government/speeches/speech-by-the-chancellor-of-the-exchequer-rt-hon-george-osborne-mp-at-the-british-business-leaders-lunch-in-davos> accessed 17 July 2013

[24]   In Article 3 of the ILO Domestic Work Convention (Convention 189), it is stated that: 'Each Member shall take measures to ensure the effective protection of the human rights of all domestic workers.'

proceeds by means of the 'soft' enforcement of rights, and there is a lack of political commitment towards the enforcement of standard setting conventions emanating from the ILO.

In terms of the case studies, the efficiency view has been useful in exposing the particular problems faced by precarious workers, and in identifying why they have been excluded from legislation. It has also been useful in suggesting that these workers should be brought within the scope of the law, whether that is labour law or human rights law. However, the efficiency view is inherently conflictual and there are problems with the solutions on the narrow view in practice. On the one hand, the efficiency view recognises that many of the problems faced by precarious workers are a result of the structure of their employment relationships, and the failure of contract law to deal with these issues. However, there is no desire to overhaul the contractual basis of employment relations, because of the fundamental position of freedom of contract in liberal law. This means that in the case of temporary agency work, the status issues which have resulted in their exclusion from labour law have not been addressed systematically, either in legislation or in case law.

It is argued in this book that this dominance of the efficiency view needs to be highlighted, along with the difficulties and contradictions within this view. Particularly problematic is the association of this view with liberalism and the ethos of the 'freedom of contract'. Under the liberal account there is a distinct separation of public and private law, and employment is a determinatively private matter. Employment should follow the scheme of classical private law, and particularly contract law. Under this scheme, the subject of the law are individuals and the role of the state is to create general and abstract rules which allow a framework within which individual free will and freedom of contract can be exercised. The problem is that this doctrine does not recognise inequalities between employers and workers, and is thus problematic for workers who attempt to argue that their contract does not represent the reality of their work relationship. This is particularly a problem for precarious workers who often fall outside contractual protection as a result of the structure of their work relation. This is one of the greatest ironies of the efficiency view. Under this view, precarious work is a result of the restructuring of the global economy and the ability of legal regulation (based on contract law) to deal with this kind of development. However, the solutions to this problem are either based on economic grounds (for example, the ideal of flexicurity) or on adjustments in the contractual system to ensure that those workers excluded by the (labour law) system now fall within it. This is the very contractual system which caused the exclusion in the first place, and can therefore not provide a solution to this problem. Even the reference to the system of human rights within the narrow view is problematic. This regime (in the narrow sense) only protects a certain set of those rights traditionally considered to be labour rights, and it tends only to protect in the most extreme cases of abuse. The human rights regime also has liberal foundations, and as a result, the protections tend to be 'balanced' by reference to government priorities (which may be outside labour rights protection).

7.2.3 Social Law and Regulation for Precarious Work

Social law is extremely critical of liberal theory, and is particularly concerned that jurisprudence based on liberal theory (and classical private law) cannot deliver justice (in employment relationships). According to the social law position, there is nothing 'natural' about the public/private divide. The 'opposition between public law and private law is not based on any thoroughgoing criterion':[25] it is simply a means through which liberal ideologies can be reinforced. The public/private divide operates to maintain (while at the same time obscuring) state power and that of dominant private individuals. As a result, law fails to properly account for power relations between groups, and the institutionalised differential treatment between them. Social law aims to correct these defects by recognising that human action is fundamentally collective, and therefore groups (and the individuals that constitute them) should be the basic subject of the law. Its concern is with what has been referred to as the 'third' function of labour law: the function of labour law to 'influence the distribution of rents, power, rights, resources and economic risks ... between workers'.[26] On the social law scheme, both legal and social protection for vulnerable workers depends on their ability to join groups which represent their interests. Firstly, group associations provide the means to lobby the state for legal recognition in a form which will boost their social position. Hence, the legal protections sought under the middle view tend to go beyond 'formal' equality rights towards more substantive (social) rights. Secondly, these groups provide (further) insurance against the potential commodification processes of capitalism by providing community functions beyond those directly connected to work. The idea on the social law view is that power is placed back into the hands of society to determine the most favourable legal outcomes,

---

[25]   G Gurvitch, 'The Problem of Social Law' (1941) 52 (1) *Ethics* 17, 19

[26]   G Mundlak, 'The Third Function of Labour Law' in G Davidov and B Langille (eds), *The Idea of Labour Law* (Oxford University Press 2011) 317

and it is only when this process is achieved that there will be stability in the social system as a whole.[27]

In a way, this social law view is useful in the consideration of precarious work because it provides a rationalisation for the distinction between groups of 'precarious workers' and the wider working population. The rationalisation for this distinction is the failure of these groups to find access to forms of legal and social protection in the past, and this forms a focal point for the promotion of equality between precarious workers and other groups. Certainly, the visibility of 'precarious work' has meant that a number of equal treatment rights or standards have emerged at all the geographical levels of analysis considered in this study. At ILO level, there are Conventions concerning temporary agency workers, home workers, part-time workers, and more recently domestic workers.[28] At EU level, there are directives concerning part-time, fixed-term and temporary agency work,[29] all of which have been transposed into national legislation at UK level.

However, the question is whether these state guarantees actually function in the ways envisaged by the premises of social law. Social law implies certain assumptions about the nature of equality rights and about the role of law in society generally. The argument is that equality law will function effectively only if the state actively recognises and enforces equality rights, that social groups are given powers of negotiation to ensure those rights, and that the rights go beyond the formal equality of the liberal regime. In practice, the social law scheme has not been realised through the ILO Conventions or the EU atypical work directives because of the failure of these rights to match up to the standards set by

---

[27]   Ehrlich states as follows: 'In reality, therefore, the historical fact that state law is manifestly gaining ground is merely the expression of the intensified solidarity of society. As the conviction grows stronger that everything that is in society concerns society, the idea appears that it would be a great advantage if the state should prescribe a unitary legal basis for each and every independent association in society.' E Ehrlich, *Fundamental Principles of the Sociology of Law* (Harvard University Press 1936 [1913]) 155–156

[28]   Respectively: Convention 181 (PEAC); Convention 177 (HWC); Convention 175 (PWC); Convention 189 and Recommendation 201 (DWC and RDW)

[29]   Council Directive 97/81/EC of 15 December 1997 concerning the Framework Agreement on Part-time work concluded by UNICE, CEEP and the ETUC, OJ [1999] L14/9 (PTWD); Council Directive 1999/70/EC of 28 June 1999 concerning the Framework Agreement on Fixed-term work concluded by ETUC, UNICE and CEEP, OJ [1999] L 175/43 (FTWD); Directive 2008/14/EC of the European Parliament and the Council of 19 November 2008 on temporary agency work OJ [2008] L327/9 (TAWD).

social law. At ILO level, the effectiveness of the Conventions covering precarious work has to be doubted, given the lack of political commitment to their enforcement. Indeed, the most recent Convention concerning marginal workers, the DWC, has so far been poorly ratified by member states. At EU level, the focus has been on the creation of rights for formal equality between atypical work groups and their permanent counterparts. While this may be useful in a liberal regime, this concentration on formal equality is problematic for the social law regime. These rights are individual rights and tend to reinforce the individualised nature of social organisation and discourage the formation of community.

According to the social law view of vulnerability, the formation of community is particularly important for those groups traditionally cast adrift by the legal system (such as precarious workers). This group association gives social power to these groups not just through legal recognition, but in the further functions of these groups as the basis of social life. These further functions allow the negotiation power of the group to be sustained so that the inequalities that they face can be consistently and continually renewed. This is of more than theoretical importance for precarious workers. As has been demonstrated in relation to the case studies, associations of many different types have been successful in negotiating for enhanced rights for precarious workers.[30] Like the professional associations envisaged by the original proponents of social law, these associations have been particularly successful in the context of domestic work when they have taken on further functions which have helped precarious workers in other ways (through the contribution of these association to education and training, and so on).[31] These further functions allow vulnerable workers the means and support to allow them further access to justice for their group.

It can be argued that the influence of the social law view has only been tangential to our current labour law. For example, the ILO Conventions concerning precarious worker groups do set out comprehensive legal protections, but there are real problems with enforcement of these Conventions. The atypical work directives do contain some reference to substantive rights, and there are some associations which have been allowed the space to contribute to the negotiation of protective rights. However, the social law view arguably requires a more fundamental realignment of law, policies and priorities in the field of precarious work

---

[30] For example, the TUC and the Communication Workers Union in relation to temporary agency work in the UK.

[31] For example, the Women United and Active Association in California.

than is currently the case. For example, it might be suggested that, for the social law view to be realised, the nature and form of anti-discrimination law needs to be fundamentally changed to realise the redistributive and substantive elements of this legislation.[32] Furthermore, community organisations need to be given proper (governmental) support to ensure their survival, and must be given proper and sustainable channels through which to attain relevant legal rights. These issues will be considered further in the section on policy suggestions below.

7.2.4   The Vulnerable Subject and Precarious Work

The vulnerable subject theorisations add a further dimension to the claims of social law. They expose liberal theory as based on the 'liberal subject'. That 'liberal subject' is a rational, atomised being which acts autonomously (in the absence of legal intervention). The result is that the notion of vulnerability is hardly considered in the regulation of legal relationships, such as those between employees and employers. Indeed, in the scheme of liberal law, the aim is to stay out of (contractual) relationships, or restrict the application of law to only very narrowly defined categorisations. It is argued on these approaches that it is only in this way that the autonomy of the liberal subject can be sustained and the most efficient allocation of resources can be attained through the market. Where vulnerability is considered in liberal views on regulation, it tends to have negative connotations and to be connected to notions of dependency. Dependency is characterised as both a burden on the state and on efficient modes of economic functioning. There is an underlying assumption that vulnerability is pathological: the aim of the law in this area is to make these elements invisible or to incorporate them to the extent that they can contribute to the economy. Hence, in the area of precarious work, the aim is the achievement of 'formal' equality between precarious workers and the standard employment workforce. Once this formal equality is achieved, precarious workers will be able to achieve a certain level of economic contribution and will disappear from regulatory sight.

The vulnerable subject approach suggests that this view both under-theorises the nature of vulnerability and also creates damaging results for those in particular patterns of vulnerability. The nature of vulnerability is

---

[32]   A Somek suggests that the problem with anti-discrimination law is that it prioritises direct over indirect discrimination. This furthers neo-liberal aims and means that it cannot truly work as a force for group protection. A Somek, *Engineering Equality* (Oxford University Press 2011) 17

under-theorised because vulnerability is viewed as partial and patho-logical, rather than personal and systemic. According to the vulnerable subject approach, the systemic nature of vulnerability means that it can no longer be viewed negatively. Vulnerability is an ever-present potential for all individuals as a result of the position of humans as ontological beings. It cannot be reserved for those who are considered to be making an insufficient contribution to the economy. Furthermore, vulnerability is a *relationship*. That relationship is complex and constituted in the interaction between a number of different social, political, economic and institutional factors. On the vulnerable subject view, the systemic nature of vulnerability means that it must become central to the design of legal institutions (albeit with the recognition that legal institutions can create vulnerability just as they can promote resilience). Those legal institutions must recognise the complexity of vulnerability and consider the constitu-tion of identity. They must also consider how best to promote inclusion and resilience as a way to counteract the negative effects of vulnerability. Although vulnerability can never disappear, the negative experiences of vulnerability can be reduced by institutions which promote autonomy of legal subjects and the building of relationships which contribute to autonomy.

As such, the vulnerable subject approach appears to (re)connect the insights of social law as regards individual and group vulnerability. Vulnerability is a lack of capacity or autonomy which is either reinforced or counteracted by group membership. The law can address this by supporting groups which promote individual development and by ensur-ing basic social rights which allow individuals access to those support mechanisms. This means an attention to issues of agency and identity, but also to wider structures of advantage and disadvantage which allow established patterns of vulnerability to be reinforced. These are important considerations in the law on precarious work. There are a number of examples in the law on precarious work where the law neither reflects actual identity nor promotes (individual) or group identity. In the EU atypical work directives (implemented in the EU member states), the classifications (temporary agency work, fixed-term work, part-time work) neither represent actual inter-group nor intragroup vulnerability. In the case of intragroup vulnerability, the most obvious example is perhaps the notion of temporary agency work. The legislation does not apply to either the most temporary workers (as a result of the 12-week qualification period) or workers deemed 'permanent'. Furthermore, it does not apply to temporary workers generally, despite considerable vulnerabilities within this group (for example, zero-hours workers). A lack of consider-ation is given to mechanisms for building identity in any way which would allow workers to build resilience. Collective bargaining is hardly mentioned. Indeed, in the UK, new proposals have been suggested to allow agency workers to be used to fill the positions of striking workers.[33] This suggests that agency workers are outside the collective representation frame, and are economic elements to be used by employers to counteract collective force. This can only serve to reinforce the vulnerability of temporary agency workers. The law on precarious work remains underscored by liberal structures which disregard the vulnerable subject. In the EU atypical work directives, flexibility is consistently enforced over the security required to allow individuals to build resilience. Lip service is paid to the notion of work quality, but this notion has been consistently undermined in its application. Furthermore, the EU directives and ILO instruments in the field of precarious work remain underscored by the notion of compliance with an 'employment relationship' (under a contract of employment). This kind of employment relationship is extremely difficult for precarious workers to show in a legal sense, particularly as employers deliberately construct their interactions with workers to avoid these legal relationships. Purposive approaches to the law are helpful in this context in order to look 'beyond' the contract to discover the 'true' legal relationship. These kinds of purposive approaches however require individuals to enforce their rights as a matter of common law. Given the real and increasing problems with access to justice for these groups, such purposive approaches can only be a partial solution. The vulnerable subject approach connects with the claims of social law (and to a certain extent classical labour law) to suggest that it is only when these broad structures are tackled that there can be progress for workers.

Indeed, perhaps the greatest benefit of the vulnerable subject approach is in its ability to reignite some of the concerns of social law and classical labour law scholars but without the theoretical and practical constraints of those theories.[34] It brings back to the fore the more sociological emphasis of social law but understands the need for the institutionalisation of rights and democracy as permanent social features.

---

[33]   BIS, *Hiring Agency Staff During Strike Action: Reforming Regulation* (July 2015)

[34]   Indeed, perhaps this is the most that can be expected from the application of a 'new' approach to labour law: 'There is no such thing as a new idea. It is impossible. We simply take a lot of old ideas and put them into a sort of mental kaleidoscope. We give them a turn and they make new and curious combinations. We keep on turning and making new combinations indefinitely; but they are the same old pieces of colored glass that have been in use through all the ages.'

It draws out the liberal critique of social law, but gives that critique a particular focus: the liberal subject of law. In relation to classical labour law, the vulnerable subject approach recognises the classical concern for autonomy in the development of employment relationships (and the need for escape from subordination, exploitation, and so on). But it suggests that autonomy does not adhere to sui generis in the labour subject: it needs to be built by legal and social institutions which recognise its importance. The vulnerable subject approach recognises the need for protection in employment relationships while reflecting that protection alone is not sufficient. Finally, like classical labour law, the vulnerable subject approach recognises the importance of collective representation in employment but is not constrained by a reliance of the institutions of trade unionism (a reliance which has arguably acted as a constraint on the legitimacy of the classical approach).

7.3 POLICY SUGGESTIONS

This section will consider how the focus on the vulnerable subject approach can lead to useful policy suggestions in the field of precarious work. Approaches which start from the vulnerable subject of law (and that includes the insights of social law where these complement this approach) are concerned that labour law should promote mid-spectrum goals: democracy, inclusion and rights. Each of these elements should complement each other. An inclusive approach to the law will promote democracy and allow the building of networks of resilience. Rights will support inclusion and give individuals the tools to be involved in democratic processes. A law which fits this vulnerable subject framework will therefore include all of these elements and it will also consider the interaction between them. The vulnerable subject approach determines that rights cannot be entirely individualistic and formal but must also be substantive and a basis for building democratic networks. It also determines that the notion of inclusion must be broadly defined. Inclusion cannot just concern economic inclusion: the best way for individuals to take 'advantage' of economic processes. Inclusion in this sense is not sufficient for individuals and groups to be able to counteract vulnerability. Inclusion must consider identity and whether the law actually

Albert Bigelow Paine, 'Mark Twain: A Biography 1835–1910', Chapter CCLI <http://www.gutenberg.org/files/2988/2988-h/2988-h.htm> accessed 19 August 2015

includes those who are most vulnerable. Inclusion must also relate to mechanisms through which individuals and groups can (start to) build resilience.

The following section will make policy suggestions in terms of ways in which the law concerning precarious work could be redesigned to meet the premises of the vulnerable subject approach. Three issues will be considered: (1) the scope of the legislation; (2) work quality; and (3) collective rights. It is suggested within each of these sections that improvements can be made within the current law. However, it is also suggested that, for the law to meet the precepts of the vulnerable subject approach, a more radical set of changes may be required. There may be a need for a more fundamental rethink of the structure of our current law and the mechanisms which support it in order for that law to really meet the demands of the vulnerable subject approach (in relation to precarious work). This involves looking at the ways in which our (liberal) law and the structures which support it can perpetuate advantage or disadvantage. For example, the reliance on a narrow personal scope within the atypical work directives and the fundamental reliance on the contract of employment for access to justice can be analysed in terms of its ability to create rather than solve vulnerability. Moreover, there are wider social structures which act alongside the law and which require reconsideration. For example, there is the question of how governments support groups which aim to provide collectivities for workers. This includes trade unions but also goes wider than that. It includes community groups and justice organisations whose remit is to try to improve the experience of vulnerable groups on the labour market. The question is how far these groups are involved in consultation mechanisms and the potential access to justice for these groups within the law.

7.3.1   Legislative Scope

It is clear that legislative instruments concerning precarious work at international and supranational level could do more to promote an increase in legislative scope. At ILO level, derogations from the provisions of Conventions concerning 'atypical work' are permitted on a number of grounds. The PEAC provides that ratifying states can 'exclude, under specific circumstances, workers in certain branches of economic activity, or parts thereof, from the scope of the Convention or from certain of its parts'.[35] The PWC allows the derogation from rights

---

[35]   Article 2 (4)(a) PEAC

where part-time workers are engaged on assignments where the 'hours or work or earnings are below certain thresholds'.[36] The DWC excludes domestic workers who perform domestic tasks 'only occasionally or sporadically and not on an occupational basis'.[37] All of these exclusions should be reconsidered on the basis that they exclude those most likely to be in need of protection. At EU level, a similar point can be made. Under the TAWD there are provisions for member states to insert qualification criteria into the legislation.[38] The insertion of such provisions has proved to be a real problem for temporary agency workers seeking to access rights under the implementing domestic legislation.

There is also a need to think more carefully about the match between these kinds of instruments and those in need of protection. In relation to agency workers, it may be that it is not the temporary nature of the assignment, but the agency structure which create the most vulnerability. It is then difficult to justify the exclusion of any agency workers whose work is not 'temporary'. Likewise, there is no protection for temporary workers per se. These very casual or temporary workers appear to display significant vulnerabilities. A case in point is zero-hours workers who have little or no control over the hours they work or the quantity of work that they receive. They also have considerable income instability and vulnerability, given that they cannot necessarily determine from one week to the next the level of income they will earn. Despite a recent 'consultation' in the UK on the issue of these zero-hour workers and the recognition of their considerable problems, very little action was taken to assure their protection.[39] This needs to be addressed. In the case of domestic work, particular vulnerabilities need to be given greater consideration. Groups need to be specifically included rather than silently excluded. Groups in point might be those operating through (badly funded) social assistance programmes, or those on the edges of the migration system. This kind of recognition might start to allow the legislation to meet the joint mid-spectrum aims of the vulnerable subject approach.

Of course, it may be that a more radical approach is required. There are dramatic problems with the underlying requirement of all the atypical legislation that there must be an employee or worker relationship between the parties. For example, the DWC requires that the domestic

---

[36] Article 8 PWC
[37] Article 1 (c) DWC
[38] Article 5 (4) TAWD
[39] BIS, *Consultation: Zero-Hours Contracts* (December 2013)

worker is engaged under an 'employment relationship'.[40] The atypical work directives only apply to those that 'have an employment contract or employment relationship as defined in the law, collective agreements or practice in each member state'.[41] Showing this kind of relationship is often a real problem for individuals in these situations, precisely because of the 'atypical' nature of their arrangements. Criteria for proving these relationships are defined by the demands of contract law (for example, mutuality of obligation) which tends to be insensitive to inequalities between the parties. These kinds of contractual criteria need to be reconsidered in this context. There is the additional fundamental problem that employers can manipulate the divide between 'employment' on the one hand and 'self-employment' on the other in the design of these kinds of contracts. Although this kind of manipulation is increasingly being shunned in the courts, it remains a problem for a great many individuals working in these kinds of relationships. It is suggested that worker or employee status should be the default position for these relationships and that the idea of self-employment should be reconsidered in this context and more widely. There is also dramatic inconsistency between the legislation in terms of status requirements. In the UK, the FTWR demand 'employee' status, whereas the PTWR require only that the individual is a worker. This creates a further obstacle for one particular group but also demonstrates the falsity of the categories themselves: there is no objective reason why either of these groups should be in one category rather than another.[42]

A vulnerable subject approach requires that labour market participants should be viewed not just as economic beings but as whole persons who have positive contributions to make *as a result of* their vulnerability (that is, vulnerability is inherent but can be channelled effectively). The lifecycle approach suggested in the book *Beyond Employment* is one starting point for reconsidering the value of the contribution of individuals beyond the employment scheme. The suggestion here is that the notion of employment is too restrictive and excludes those most in need

---

[40] Article 1 (b) DWC

[41] Article 2 (1) PTWD and Article 2 (1) FTWD

[42] Indeed, the government in the UK noted this problem and opened up a consultation to clarify employment status in 2014. It was hoped that the review would deliver greater clarity for labour market participants, greater access to rights and greater job stability. However, no direct action was taken as a result of the review. Details of the review are at <https://www.gov.uk/government/news/employment-review-launched-to-improve-clarity-and-status-of-british-workforce> last accessed 7 August 2015

of protection. A looser notion of work is required so that different kinds of work status give rise to different kinds of rights. Under this scheme, four circles of 'social law' are envisaged which take account not only of more casual or temporary forms of work but also of changes in work status during a lifecycle. There are rights inherent in wage-earning work (employment) but these are also complemented by common rights connected with 'occupational activity' (for example, health and safety) and rights ensuing from unwaged work (care for other and training). In addition, there should be a set of universal social rights for all which are guaranteed irrespective of work. Equal treatment rights for men and women apply across all the different circles. It appears that it is only by thinking more positively about the contribution of individuals (and their vulnerabilities) in each of these stages, that individuals can really be viewed as receiving proper institutional support under the vulnerable subject framework.

7.3.2 Work Quality and Substantive Equality

Work quality is stated as an aim in all the atypical work directives and formed part of the Decent Work agenda emanating from the ILO.[43] Indeed, at the time that the atypical work directives were set up in the first phase (the PTWD and the FTWD), there was considerable interest in the idea of work quality and its different dimensions. The Commission produced a Communication setting out its visions for employment and social policies as a 'framework for investing in quality'. Within this framework, quality was seen as the best way to modernise the European Social Model. In this Communication the Commission outlined its concern that 'new and flexible employment patterns may conflict with some of the main dimension job quality' and the 'close link between the level of job quality and social exclusion'.[44] It suggested that, in order to promote the modernisation of the European social model, there should be a set of indicators on quality which should form the basis of cyclical reviews of progress on the promotion of quality in the member states. The notion of quality was broadly defined. Ten indicators of quality were cited, and included not only 'external' elements of work quality (gender equality in the labour market, health and safety and access to social dialogue), but also 'internal' elements of work quality associated with the experience of individual labour market participants. In these internal

---

[43] Clause 1 (a) FTWD, Clause 1 (a) PTWD and Article 2 TAWD

[44] Commission, 'Employment and Social Policies: A Framework for Investing in Quality' COM (2001) 313 final, 9

elements, the question was how far the particular work was compatible with a worker's skills and abilities and his/her ability to develop those skills over time.

This aspiration towards quality has the potential to meet the aims of the vulnerable subject approach advocated in this book. The idea of quality in this broad sense implies that the experience of work is not just directed by externally imposed factors that the individual is powerless to affect. Work quality is a combination of workers' experiences and also institutional support which is given to individuals in the development of their capacities and capabilities (over their lifecycle). Furthermore, work is not necessarily a negative experience, but can act as a positive force where it meets the aims, capabilities and aspirations of workers. The important point is to recognise the role that workers themselves have in the setting of these aspirations and their achievement. To this end, work quality is not just about individual experience, it is also concerned with the quality of relationships that workers establish. For that reason, it is important that workers are given access to networks of collective representation and that these are institutionally supported. This kind of involvement does not act in conflict with the other aims engendering work quality. It is another factor in promoting resilience among workers which acts alongside improvements in (for example) equal treatment rights. The idea of quality is multi-dimensional, just as the idea of vulnerability includes a number of inter-related factors. Quality can be promoted by improvements in law, in society and in the developments in individual capacity more generally. This relies on access to collective support mechanisms and a certain level of basic (social) provision for all.

However, it has been argued in this book that, although work quality was promoted as an aim of legislation pertaining to precarious work, this aim has become narrowly defined and ignored in practice. In relation to the atypical work directives, work quality has become associated with the notion of work security. Those security elements have been lost in the drive to increase flexibility of work. This drive has only accelerated in the wake of the financial crisis. For example, in the FTWD, the provision guaranteeing a permanent contract after a series of successive fixed-term contracts was inserted to meet the aims of promoting both job security and job quality. This guarantee has been eroded in a number of member states by the deregulation of this kind of work following the financial crisis in 2008. Furthermore, narrow definitions of work quality have allowed the collective or institutional issues surrounding quality to be ignored. As a result, the atypical work directives have lost considerable force. Equality has been confined to equal treatment, and there has been little substantive equality achieved in practice. This can be illustrated by the empirical evidence of the experience of part-time workers in the UK. A TUC report published in March 2014 outlined that the PTWRs have not brought about substantive equality for women. In 2014, four-fifths of the net growth of part-time work was in low-paid sectors such as clerical and cleaning work. At the same time, the number of professional jobs fell. It has been argued that the lack of high-quality jobs is the real barrier to equality (for women).[45] Likewise, at ILO level there has been a recognition of the link between broad indicators for quality and those pertaining to decent work.[46] However, in application, the focus has been on measuring country compliance with the Fundamental Rights and Principles at Work rather than broader notions of quality.[47]

The vulnerable subject approach calls for the notion of quality to once again take centre stage. This is a broad, multi-dimensional notion of quality which takes into account individual capacity as well as institutional support. It allows individuals access to collective mechanisms of support and recognises the link between job quality and social inclusion. To a certain extent, this involves looking back at previous indicators of job quality and how these have been promoted in standard employment relationships. It also involves looking forward to capturing the quality elements of more flexible arrangements. That requires looking at the elements of quality which are promoted by or act to promote worker agency. This guards against strategies which simply reinforce vulnerabilities by strengthening employer power.

7.3.3 Collective Representation and Institutional Change

The vulnerable subject approach requires that institutions support worker strategies of resilience. These strategies not only include personal development, but also (and more importantly) the development of collective mechanisms to enhance that development and realise substantive equality. Unfortunately, regulation for precarious work has not effectively recognised this contribution. In the atypical work directives, reference to collective bargaining has been scarce. Wider representation mechanisms

---

[45] IDS, 'Editorial: Part-time Workers' Protection 15 Years On' (2015) 1024 *IDS Employment Law Brief* 1, 2

[46] Report of the Director General of the ILO, 'Sixth Supplementary Report: Measuring Decent Work' (2008) GB 301/17/6, 2 <http://www.ilo.org/wcmsp5/groups/public/–ed_norm/–relconf/documents/meetingdocument/wcms_091183.pdf> last accessed 11 August 2015

[47] Ibid 5

have not been considered. As a result, the effectiveness of these instruments have been compromised, particularly in the face of the strategies of national governments to deregulate collective bargaining mechanisms. Indeed, it is possible to argue that a negative relationship has been forged, and continues to be forged, between precarious work groups and collective bargaining at a national level. Examples of this negative relationship have been explored in Chapter 4 in particular. A further interesting example is that provided by the recent proposals on the deregulation of trade union activity by the UK government. As part of these proposals, it is suggested that Regulation 7 of the Conduct of Employment Agencies and Employment Business Regulations 2003 should be removed to allow agencies to supply temporary staff to cover the absence of permanent workers on strike. This provision puts agency workers in a 'difficult position' because agency workers are forced to act contrary to other (striking) workers.[48] It strips agency workers of any (relational) identity with other workers and with each other: they become merely economic agents whose aim is to further business aims and limit the impact of strike action on employers. Furthermore, these proposals reduce the effectiveness of strike action and thereby weaken other collective means of representation. Workers lose an important way of seeking to achieve quality work and substantive equality. These proposals work in exactly the opposite direction to the preferred mechanisms of legislative response under the vulnerability analysis.

There are further ways in which these new governmental proposals undermine or run contrary to the vulnerability analysis and are symptomatic of current problems in employment regulation (of precarious work). Procedurally, there is insufficient time given to 'stakeholders' to consider the government proposals and formulate a response. The time given for responses is a total of eight weeks, which includes the August holiday period. According to the guidelines produced by the government, consultation should be a total of 12 weeks for proposals involving vulnerable groups, and should take into account holiday periods (four weeks is proposed for the August period).[49] Furthermore, little thought is given to those who might be involved in the consultation (beyond temporary agency workers and their employers). Reference is made only

---

[48]   F O'Grady, 'Trade Unions Bill: Unfair, Unnecessary, Undemocratic' 15 July 2015 <http://touchstoneblog.org.uk/2015/07/trade-unions-bill-unfair-unnecessary-and-undemocratic/> accessed 11 August 2015

[49]   The consultation principles are available at <https://www.gov.uk/government/uploads/system/uploads/attachment_data/file/255180/Consultation-Principles-Oct-2013.pdf> last accessed 11 August 2015

to the 'wider economy and society', and the purpose of the consultation of that group is to 'understand the impact on the wider community who may be affected when industrial action takes place'.[50] There is no recognition that allowing this kind of regulation is a worker rights issue. The result is that, when it comes to a consideration of the responses to the consultation, these rights issues (such as the right to strike) can be brushed over or ignored. Indeed, this was the experience in the construction of the TAWR: employer organisations were more influential than those groups directly supporting workers.

According to the Trade Union Bill,[51] industrial action is presented in an entirely negative way. The focus is on the disruption caused by trade union strike action to business and the 'ordinary people' affected by the dispute. According to the employment minister:

> People have the right to expect that services on which they and their families rely are not going to be disrupted at short notice by strikes that have the support of only a small proportion of union members. These are sensible and fair reforms that balance the right to strike with the right of millions of people to go about their daily lives without last minute disruption.[52]

The reforms downplay the role of collective bargaining in improving or promoting worker rights, and put 'ordinary people' in a contrary position to workers. Workers become the vexatious protagonists of industrial action, which acts directly contrary to the wishes of society. This kind of presentation is dangerous and directly contrary to the vulnerability approach. Labour law becomes not about mid-spectrum goals (democracy, social inclusion and rights), but directly about 'efficiency' and about the efficiency of business. It is not about the resilience of workers in the face of their vulnerabilities.

Labour law, according to the vulnerable subject approach, is not simply about building trade union capacity, but labour law which attempts to dismantle trade union representation does go contrary to the vulnerability approach. If the move towards efficiency-based regulation is to be counteracted, the vulnerability of workers must be recognised.

---

[50]   BIS, *Hiring Agency Staff During Strike Action: Reforming Regulation* (July 2015) 7

[51]   Bill 58, 15 July 2015

[52]   This is quoted in P Wintour, 'Biggest crackdown on trade unions for 30 years launched by the Conservatives', *The Guardian* (15 July 2015) <http://www.theguardian.com/politics/2015/jul/15/trade-unions-conservative-offensive-decades-strikes-labour> last accessed 19 August 2015

However, this is not a permanent vulnerability, and it is not a vulnerability which sets them apart from consumer interests or the interests of society as a whole. Building worker resilience must be seen as achieving mid-spectrum goals that are good for workers and also good for society. The state should be involved in recognising and responding to those goals by ensuring that individuals have the right to collective representation and action and by encouraging that collective representation where it exists. Workers must not be seen as liberal subjects: rational, autonomous and independent beings, but rather they must be viewed as vulnerable agents who build autonomy through relationships of resilience.

Bibliography

Albin E and Mantouvalou V, 'The ILO Convention on Domestic Workers: From the Shadows into the Light' (2012) 41 (1) *ILJ* 67

Alston P, 'Core Labour Standards and the Transformation of the International Labour Rights Regime' (2004) 15 (3) *European Journal of International Law* 457

Anderson J, 'Autonomy and Vulnerability Entwined' in C Mackenzie, W Rogers and S Dodds (eds), *Vulnerability* (Oxford University Press 2014)

Barber B, 'TUC Response to BERR Vulnerable Workers Forum Report' (5 August 2008) http://www.tuc.org.uk/newsroom/tuc-15161-f0.cfm

Barnard C, Deakin S and Hobbs R, 'Capabilities and Rights: An Emerging Social Agenda for Social Policy' (2000) 32 (5) *Industrial Relations Journal* 464

Barnard C, *EC Employment Law* (Oxford University Press 2006)

Barnard C, *EU Employment Law* (Oxford University Press 2012)

Bell M, 'Between Flexicurity and Fundamental Social Rights: The EU Directives on Atypical Work' (2012) 37 (1) *European Law Review* 31

Bell M and Waddington L, 'Reflecting on Inequalities in European Equality Law' (2003) 28 (3) *European Law Review* 349

Bellotti RA, 'Marxist Jurisprudence: Historical Necessity and Radical Contingency' (1991) 4 (1) *Canadian Journal of Law and Jurisprudence* 145

BERR, *Protecting Vulnerable Agency Workers: Government Response to the Consultation* (November 2007)

BERR, *Agency Working in the UK* (2008)

BERR, *Vulnerable Worker Enforcement Forum – Final Report and Government Conclusions* (August 2008)

BERR, *Implementation of the Agency Workers Directive: A Consultation Paper* (May 2009)

Biffl G and Isaac J, 'Globalization and Core Labour Standards: Compliance Problems with ILO Conventions 87 and 98. Comparing Australia and Other English-speaking Countries with EU Member States' (2005) 21 (3) *International Journal of Comparative Labour Law and Industrial Relations* 405

BIS, *Implementation of the Agency Workers Directive: Consultation on Draft Regulations* (2010)

BIS, *Resolving Workplace Disputes: Government Response to Consultation* (November 2011)

BIS, *Employment Law Review Annual Update* (March 2012)

BIS, *Ending the Employment Relationship: A Consultation* (September 2012)

BIS, *Implementing Employee Owner Status: Government Response* (December 2012)

BIS, 'Consultation on Reforming the Regulatory Framework for Employment Agencies and Employment Businesses' (January 2013) <http://www.gov.uk/government/consultations/consultation-on-reforming-framework-for-employment-agencies-and-employment-businesses>

BIS, *Employment Law Review 2013: Progress on Reform* (March 2013)

BIS, *Consultation Principles* <https://www.gov.uk/government/uploads/system/uploads/attachment_data/file/255180/Consultation-Principles-Oct-2013.pdf>

BIS, *Consultation: Zero-Hours Contracts* (December 2013)

BIS, 'Trade Union Membership 2014' (June 2015) <https://www.gov.uk/government/uploads/system/uploads/attachment_data/file/431564/Trade_Union_Membership_Statistics_2014.pdf>

BIS, 'Trade Union Membership Statistics 2014' (June 2015) Table 1.4 <https://www.gov.uk/government/statistics/trade-union-statistics-2014>

BIS, *Hiring Agency Staff During Strike Action: Reforming Regulation* (July 2015)

BIS, *Trade Union Reform: Consultation on Ballot Thresholds in Important Public Services* (July 2015)

Blackett A and Sheppard C, 'Collective Bargaining and Equality' (2003) 142 (2) *International Labour Review* 419

Bogg A, 'Sham Self-employment in the Court of Appeal' (2010) 126 *Law Quarterly Review* 166

Bogg A and Green S, 'Rights Are Not Just for the Virtuous: What Hounga Means for the Illegality Defence in the Discrimination Torts' (2015) 44 (1) *ILJ* 101

Bonner C, 'Domestic Workers around the World: Organising for Empowerment' (30 April 2010) 9 <http://www.dwrp.org.za/images/stories/DWRP_Research/chris_bonner.pdf>

Boulanger O, 'Notes on Social Law' (1920) 40 *Canadian Law Times* 399

Brodie D, 'Employees, Workers and the Self-employed' (2005) 34 (3) *ILJ* 253

Brodtkorb T, 'Employee Misconduct and UK Unfair Dismissal Law: Does the Range of Reasonable Responses Test Require Reform?' (2010) 52 (6) *International Journal of Law and Management* 429

Burchell B, 'The Prevalence and Redistribution of Job Insecurity and Work Intensification' in B Burchell, D Lapido and F Wilson (eds), *Job Insecurity and Work Intensification* (Routledge 2002)

Chen MA, 'Recognising Domestic Workers, Regulating Domestic Work: Conceptual Measurement and Regulatory Challenges' (2011) 23 *Canadian Journal of Women and the Law* 167

Churchard C, 'Ban Swedish Derogation to End Pay Abuses says TUC' (2 September 2013) available at http://www.cipd.co.uk/pm/people management/b/weblog/archive/2013/09/02/ban-swedish-derogation-to-end-pay-abuses-says-tuc.aspx

Coffey A, *Reconceptualising Social Policy: Sociological Perspectives on Contemporary Social Policy* (Open University Press 2004)

Colling T, 'What Space for Unions on the Floor of Rights? Trade Unions and the Enforcement of Statutory Individual Employment Rights' (2006) 35 (2) *ILJ* 140

Collins H, 'Market Power, Bureaucratic Power and the Contract of Employment' (1986) 15 *ILJ* 1

Collins H, 'Independent Contractors and the Challenge of Vertical Disintegration to Employment Protection Laws' (1990) 10 (3) *Oxford Journal of Legal Studies* 353

Collins H, 'Justifications and Techniques of Legal Regulation of the Employment Relation' in H Collins, P Davies and R Rideout (eds), *Legal Regulation of the Employment Relation* (Hart 2000)

Collins H, 'Regulating the Employment Relation for Competitiveness' (2001) 30 *ILJ* 17

Collins H, 'Discrimination, Equality and Social Inclusion' (2003) 66 *MLR* 16

Collins H, *Employment Law* (Oxford University Press 2003)

Collins H, 'Is there a Third Way in Labour Law?' in J Conaghan, RM Fischel and K Klare (eds), *Labour Law in an Era of Globalization: Transformative Practices and Possibilities* (Oxford University Press 2004)

Collins H, 'Theories of Rights as Justifications for Labour Law' in B Langille and G Davidov (eds), *The Idea of Labour Law* (Oxford University Press 2011)

Countouris N, 'The Legal Determinants of Precariousness in Personal Work Relations: A European Perspective' (2014) 34 *Comparative Labour Law and Policy Journal* 21

Countouris N and Horton R, 'The Temporary Agency Work Directive: Another Broken Promise?' (2009) 38 (3) *ILJ* 329

Courtis C, 'Social Rights as Rights' (date unknown) <http://islandia. law.yale.edu.sela.ecourtis.pdf>

Crain M, 'Between Feminism and Unionism: Working Class Women, Sex Equality and Labor Speech' (1993–1994) 82 *Georgetown Law Journal* 1903

Davidov G, 'The Three Axes of Employment Relationships: A Characterization of Workers in Need of Protection' (2003) 52 *University of Toronto Law Journal* 357

Davidov G, 'Collective Bargaining Laws: Purpose and Scope' (2004) 20 (1) *International Journal of Comparative Labour Law and Industrial Relations* 81

Davidov G, 'Who is a Worker' (2005) 34 *ILJ* 57

Davidov G, 'The Reports of My Death Are Greatly Exaggerated: "Employee" as a Viable (Though Over-Used) Legal Concept' in G Davidov and B Langille (eds), *The Boundaries and Frontiers of Labour Law* (Hart 2006)

Davidov G, 'In Defence of (Efficiently Administered) Just Cause Dismissal Laws' (2007) 23 (1) *International Journal of Comparative Labour Law and Industrial Relations* 117

Davidov G, 'The Goals of Regulating Work: Between Universalism and Selectivity' (2014) 64 (1) *University of Toronto Law Journal* 1

Davidov G and B Langille, 'Understanding Labour Law: A Timeless Idea, a Timed-out Idea, or an Idea Whose Time Has Now Come?' in G Davidov and B Langille (eds), *The Idea of Labour Law* (Oxford University Press 2011)

Davidson MJ and Earnshaw J, 'Vulnerable Workers: An Overview of Psychosocial and Legal Issues' in MJ Davidson and J Earnshaw (eds), *Vulnerable Workers: Psychosocial and Legal Issues* (1st Edition, John Wiley and Sons 1991)

Davies ACL, 'The Contract for Intermittent Employment' (2007) 36 (1) *ILJ* 102

Davies ACL, *Perspectives on Labour Law* (Oxford University Press 2009)

Davies ACL, 'The Implementation of the Directive on Temporary Agency Work in the UK: A Missed Opportunity' (2010) 1 *European Labour Law Journal* 307

Davies P and Freedland M, *Kahn-Freund's Labour and the Law* (3rd Edition, Stevens 1983)

Dawson M, *New Governance and the Transformation of European Law: Coordinating EU Social Law and Policy* (Cambridge University Press 2011)

Deakin S, 'Does the "Personal Employment Contract" Provide a Basis for the Reunification of Employment Law?' (2007) 36 (1) *ILJ* 68

Deakin S, 'Contracts and Capabilities: An Evolutionary Perspective on the Autonomy-Paternalism Debate' (2010) 3 (2) *Erasmus Law Review* 141

Deakin S and Wilkinson F, *The Law of the Labour Market: Industrialization, Employment and Legal Evolution* (Oxford University Press 2005)

De Stephano V, 'A Tale of Over-simplification and Deregulation: The Mainstream Approach to Labour Market Segmentation and Recent Responses to the Crisis in European Countries' (2014) 43 (3) *ILJ* 253

De Vos M, 'European Flexicurity and Globalization: A Critical Perspective' (2009) 20 (3) *The International Journal of Comparative Labour Law and Industrial Relations* 209

DTI, *Success at Work: Protecting Vulnerable Workers, Supporting Good Employers. A policy statement for this Parliament* (March 2006)

Dukes R, 'Constitutionalising Employment Relations: Sinzheimer, Kahn-Freund and the Role of Labour Law' (2008) 35 (3) *Journal of Law and Society* 347

Dukes R, 'Voluntarism and the Single Channel: The Development of Single-Channel Worker Representation in the UK' (2008) 24 (1) *International Journal of Comparative Labour Law and Industrial Relations* 87

Dukes R, 'Otto Kahn-Freund and Collective Laissez-Faire: An Edifice without a Keystone?' (2009) 72 (2) *MLR* 245

Dukes R, 'Hugo Sinzheimer and the Constitutional Function of Labour Law' in G Davidov and B Langille (eds), *The Idea of Labour Law* (Oxford University Press 2011)

Dukes R, *The Labour Constitution: The Enduring Idea of Labour Law* (Oxford University Press 2014)

Durkheim E, *The Division of Labour in Society* (Macmillan Press Limited 1984 [1893])

Ehrlich E, *Fundamental Principles of the Sociology of Law* (Harvard University Press 1936 [1913])

Engels F, *The Conditions of the Working Class in England in 1844* (Cambridge University Press 2010)

Epstein R, 'In Defense of the Contract at Will' (1984) 51 *University of Chicago Law Review* 947

European Commission, 'Employment and social policies: a framework for investing in quality' COM (2001) 313 final

European Commission, 'Towards Fundamental Principles of Flexicurity: More and better jobs through flexibility and security' COM (2007) 359 final 6

European Commission, 'Together for Trafficking' <http://ec.europa.eu/anti-trafficking/entity.action?path=percent2FPublicationspercent2FEffective+Protection>

European Economic and Social Committee, 'The Professionalisation of Domestic Work' OJ [2011] C21/39

Ewald F, *L'Etat Providence* (Bernard Grasset 1986)

Ewald F, 'A Concept of Social Law' in G Teubner (ed), *The Dilemmas of Law in the Welfare State* (Walter de Gruyter 1995)

Ewing K, 'The Function of Trade Unions' (2005) 34 (1) *ILJ* 1

Ewing K, 'The Implications of the ASLEF Case' (2007) 36 (4) *ILJ* 425

Eyraud F and Vaughan-Whitehead D, 'Employment and Working Conditions in the Enlarged EU: Innovations and New Risks' in F Eyraud and D Vaughan-Whitehead (eds), *The Evolving World of Work in the Enlarged EU: Progress and Vulnerability* (ILO 2007)

Fineman J, 'The Vulnerable Subject at Work: A New Perspective on the Employment at Will Debate' (2013) 43 *Southwestern Law Journal* 216

Fineman MA, 'The Vulnerable Subject: Anchoring Equality in the Human Condition' (2008) 20 (1) *Yale Journal of Law and Feminism* 2

Fineman MA, 'The Vulnerable Subject and the Responsive State' (2010) 60 *Emory Law Journal* 251

Fineman MA and Greer A (eds), *Vulnerability (Gender in Law Culture and Society)* (Ashgate 2013)

Fredman S, 'Equality: A New Generation?' (2001) 30 (2) *ILJ* 145

Fredman S, *Discrimination Law* (Oxford University Press 2002)

Fredman S, 'Women at Work: The Broken Promise of Flexicurity' (2004) 33 (4) *ILJ* 299

Fredman S, 'Precarious Norms for Precarious Workers' in J Fudge and R Owens (eds), *Precarious Work, Women and the New Economy* (Hart Publishing 2006)

Fredman S, 'Home from Home: Migrant Domestic Workers and the ILO Convention on Domestic Workers' in C Costello and M Freedland (eds), *Migrants at Work: Immigration and Vulnerability in Labour Law* (Oxford University Press 2014)

Freedland M, *The Personal Employment Contract* (Oxford University Press 2003)

Freedland M, 'From the Contract of Employment to the Personal Work Nexus' (2006) 35 *ILJ* 1

Freedland M and Countouris N, *The Legal Construction of Personal Work Relations* (Oxford University Press 2011)

Frenzel H, 'The Temporary Agency Work Directive' (2010) 1 (1) *European Labour Law Review* 119

Fudge J, 'Reconceiving Employment Standards Legislation: Labour Law's Little Sister and the Feminization of Labor' (1991) 7 *Journal of Law and Social Policy* 73

Fudge J, 'Rungs on the Labour Law Ladder' (1996) 60 *Saskatchewan Law Review* 237

Fudge J, 'Beyond Vulnerable Workers: Towards a New Standard Employment Relationship' (2005) 12 *Canadian Labour and Employment Law Journal* 151

Fudge J, 'The Legal Boundaries of Employer, Precarious Workers and Labour Protection' in G Davidov and B Langille (eds), *The Boundaries and Frontiers of Labour Law* (Hart 2006)

Fudge J, 'The New Discourse of Labor Rights: From Social to Fundamental Rights?' (2007–8) 29 *Comparative Labor Law and Policy Journal* 29

Fudge J, 'Global Care Chains, Employment Agencies and the Conundrum of Jurisdiction: Decent Work for Domestic Workers in Canada' (2011) 23 *Canadian Journal of Women and the Law* 235

Fudge J, 'Feminist Reflections on the Scope of Labour Law: Domestic Work Social Reproduction and Jurisdiction' (2014) 22 *Feminist Legal Studies* 1

Fudge J and Owens R, 'Precarious Work, Women and the New Economy' in J Fudge and R Owens (eds), *Precarious Work, Women and the New Economy: The Challenge to Legal Norms* (Hart 2000)

Gearty C and Mantouvalou V, *Debating Social Rights* (Hart 2011)

Giddens A, *Capitalism and Modern Social Theory: An Analysis of the Writings of Marx, Durkheim and Weber* (Cambridge University Press 1971)

Goldin A, 'Labour Subordination and the Subjective Weakening of Labour Law' in G Davidov and B Langille (eds), *Boundaries and Frontiers of Labour Law* (Hart 2006)

Gomez A and Puig IB, 'Domestic Work after Labour Law: The Case of Brazil and Spain' Paper prepared for the Labour Law Research Network Inaugural Conference at Pompeu Fabra University, Barcelona, 13–15 June 2013 <http://www.upf.edu/gredtiss/_pdf/2013-LLRNConf_GomesxBaviera.pdf>

Gomez R and Gunderson M, 'Non-standard and Vulnerable Workers: A Case of Mistaken Identity' (2005) 12 *Canadian Labour and Employment Law Journal* 177, 178

Grimshaw D and Marchington L, 'United Kingdom: Persistent Inequality and Vulnerability Traps' in F Eyraud and D Vaughan-Whitehead (eds), *The Evolving World of Work in the Enlarged EU: Progress and Vulnerability* (ILO 2007)

Gurvitch G, 'The Problem of Social Law' (1941) 52 (1) *Ethics* 17, 21

Harrison A, 'Teachers Announce One-day National Strike' (*BBC News*, 12 July 2013) http://www.bbc.co.uk/education/-23285445

Hart HLA, *The Concept of Law* (Oxford University Press 1961)

Hepple B, 'Restructuring Employment Rights' (1986) 15 (1) *ILJ* 69

Hepple B, *The Making of Labour Law in Europe: A Comparative Study of Nine Countries up to 1945* (Mansell, London 1986)

Hepple B, 'Discrimination and Equality of Opportunity – Northern Irish Lessons' (1990) 10 *Oxford Journal of Legal Studies* 408

Hepple B and Barnard C, 'Substantive Equality' (2000) 59 (3) *Cambridge Law Journal* 562

Hyde A, 'What is Labour Law' in G Davidov and B Langille (eds), *Boundaries and Frontiers of Labour Law* (Hart 2006)

IDS, 'Editorial: Part-time Workers' Protection 15 Years On' (2015) 1024 *IDS Employment Law Brief* 1

ILO, *ILO Declaration of Fundamental Principles and Rights at Work and its Follow-up* (International Labour Office, Geneva 1998)

ILO, Director General of the ILO, 'Decent Work' (1999) <http://www.ilo.org/public/English/standards/relm/ilc/ilc87/rep-i.htm>

ILO, 'Meeting of Experts on Workers in Situations Needing Protection (The Employment Relationship: Scope)' *Basic Technical Document* (International Labour Office 2000)

ILO, *Report V – Scope of the Employment Relationship – Fifth Item on the Agenda* (Geneva 2003)

ILO, *Report V (I) – The Employment Relationship – Fifth Item on the Agenda* (Geneva 2005)

ILO, *Report V (2A) – The Employment Relationship – Fifth Item on the Agenda* (Geneva 2006)

ILO, *Declaration on Social Justice for a Fair Globalization* (2008) <http://www.ilo.org/wcmsp5/groups/public/@dgreports/@cabinet/documents/publications/wcms_099766.pdf>

ILO, Report of the Director General of the ILO, 'Sixth Supplementary Report: Measuring Decent Work' (2008) GB 301/17/6 <http://www.ilo.org/wcmsp5/groups/public/–ed_norm/–relconf/documents/meetingdocument/wcms_091183.pdf>

ILO, *Report IV – Decent Work for Domestic Workers – Fourth Item on the Agenda* (Geneva 2010)

ILO, Report of the Director General, International Labour Conference, 100th session, *A New Era for Social Justice* (International Labour Office 2011)

Jayanetti C, 'Exclusive: More than 2000 Charities and Community Groups Face Cut' (False Economy, 2 August 2011) <http://falseeconomy.org.uk/blog/exclusive-more-than-2000-charities-and-community-groups-face-cuts>

Jeffery M, 'Not Really Going to Work? Of the Directive on Part-time Work, Atypical Work and Attempts to Regulate it' (1998) 27 (3) *ILJ* 193

Jorgensen and Madsen PK, 'Flexicurity and Beyond – Reflections on the Nature and Future of a Political Celebrity' in H Jorgensen and PK Madsen (eds) *Flexicurity and Beyond: Finding a New Agenda for the European Social Model* (DJOF, Copenhagen 2007)

Kahn-Freund O, 'Intergroup Conflicts and their Settlement' (1954) *British Journal of Sociology* 193

Kahn-Freund O, 'Legal Framework' in A Flanders and HA Clegg (eds), *The System of Industrial Relations in Great Britain* (Blackwell, Oxford 1954) 44

Kahn-Freund O, *Labour Law: Old Traditions and New Developments* (Clarke, Irwin and Company Ltd, Toronto/Vancouver 1968)

Kahn-Freund O, 'Hugo Sinzheimer 1875–1945' in R Lewis and J Clark (eds), *Labour Law and Politics in the Weimar Republic* (Basil Blackwell, Oxford 1981)

Kennedy D, 'Three Globalizations of Law and Legal Thought: 1850–2000' in D Trubek and A Santos (eds), *The New Law and Economic Development: A Critical Appraisal* (Cambridge University Press 2006)

Lalani M, *Ending the Abuse: Policies that Work to Protect Domestic Workers* (Kalaayan, May 2011) <www.kalayaan.org.uk/documents/Kalayaan Report final.pdf>

Langille B, 'Core Labour Rights – The True Story (A Reply to Alston)' (2005) 16 (3) *European Journal of International Law* 409

Langille B, 'Labour Law's Theory of Justice' in G Davidov and B Langille (eds), *The Idea of Labour Law* (Oxford University Press 2011)

Laws J 'Public Law and Employment Law: Abuse of Power' (1997) *Public Law* 455

Leighton P, 'Problems Continue for Zero-Hours Workers' (2002) 31 (1) *ILJ* 71

Leighton P, 'Temporary Agency Working: Is the Law on the Turn?' (2008) 29 (1) *Company Lawyer* 7

Leighton P, Syrett M, Hecker R and Holland P, *Out of the Shadows: Managing Self-employed, Agency and Out-sourced Workers* (Butterworth-Heinemann 2007)

Lewis R, 'Kahn-Freund and Labour Law: An Outline Critique' (1979) 8 *ILJ* 202

Littlefield NO, 'Eugen Ehrlich's Fundamental Principles of the Sociology of Law' (1967) 19 (1) *Maine Law Review* 1

Lopez J, De La Court A and Canaldo S, 'Breaking the Equilibrium between Flexibility and Security: Flexiprecarity as the Spanish Version of the Model' (2014) 5 (1) *European Labour Law Journal* 18

McCann D and Murray J, 'Promoting Formalisation through Labour Market Regulation: A Framed Flexibility Model for Domestic Work' (2014) 43 (3) *ILJ* 319

McCrudden C, *Buying Social Justice: Equality, Government Procurement and Legal Change* (Oxford University Press 2007)

McGaughey E, 'Should Agency Workers Be Treated Differently?' LSE Law, Society and Economy Working Papers (July 2010) <http://papers.ssrn.com/sol3/papers.cfm?abstract_id=1610272>

McHarg A and Nicolson D, 'Justifying Affirmative Action: Perceptions and Reality' (2006) 33 (1) *Journal of Law and Society* 1

Mackenzie C, 'Relational Autonomy and Capabilities for an Ethics of Vulnerability' in C Mackenzie, W Rogers and S Dodds (eds), *Vulnerability* (Oxford University Press 2014)

MacNaughton G and Frey D, 'Decent Work, Human Rights and the Millennium Development Goals' (2010) 7 *Hastings Race and Poverty Law Journal* 303

Mangan D, 'Employment Tribunal Reforms to Boost the Economy' (2013) 42 *ILJ* 409

Mantouvalou V, 'Work and Private Life: Sidabras and Dziautas v Lithuania' (2005) 30 (4) *European Law Review* 573

Mantouvalou V, 'Servitude and Forced Labour in the 21st Century: The Human Rights of Domestic Workers' (2006) 35 (4) *ILJ* 395

Mantouvalou V, 'Labour Rights in the European Convention on Human Rights: An Intellectual Justification for an Integrated Approach to Interpretation' (2013) *Human Rights Law Review* 529

Marshall S, 'Shifting Responsibility onto Labour: How the Burden of the European Financial Crisis Shifted Away from the Financial Sector and onto Labour' (2013–2014) 35 *Comparative Labor Law and Policy Journal* 449

Marx K, *Das Kapital: A Critique of Political Economy* (Pacifica Publishing Studio 2010)

Massimiani C, 'Flexicurity and Decent Work in Europe: Can They Co-exist?' (2008) Working Paper of the Centro Studi di Diritto Lavoro Europeo 'Massimo D'Antona', Universita degli Studi di Catania No 65/2008 <http://www.lex.unict.it/eurolabor/ricerca/wp/int/massimiani_n65-2008int.pdf>

Maupain F, 'New Foundation or New Façade? The ILO and the 2008 Declaration on Social Justice for a Fair Globalization' (2009) 20 (3) *European Journal of International Law* 823

Mundlak G and Shamir H, 'Bringing Together or Drifting Apart? Targeting Care Work as "Work Like No Other"' (2011) 23 *Canadian Journal of Women and the Law* 289

Mundlak G and Shamir H, 'The Third Function of Labour Law' in G Davidov and B Langille (eds), *The Idea of Labour Law* (Oxford University Press 2011)

Neaşu D, 'The Wrongful Rejection of Big Theory (Marxism) by Feminism and Queer Theory: A Brief Debate' (2005) 24 *Capital University Law Review* 125

NHS, 'Vulnerable Adults' <http://www.nhs.uk/CarersDirect/guide/vulnerable-people/Pages/vulnerable-adults.aspx>

Office for National Statistics, 'Temporary Employees' (November 2011) <http://www.ons.gov.uk/ons/rel/lms/labour-market-statistics/december-2011/tableemp07.xls>

Office for National Statistics, 'Temporary Employees' (May 2013) <http://www.ons.gov.uk/ons/rel/lms/labour-market-statistics/july-2013/tableemp07.xls>

Office for National Statistics, 'Labour Market Statistics' (July 2013) <http://www.ons.gov.uk/ons/dcp171778_315111.pdf>

O'Grady F, 'Trade Unions Bill: Unfair, Unnecessary, Undemocratic' (15 July 2015) <http://touchstoneblog.org.uk/2015/07/trade-unions-bill-unfair-unnecessary-and-undemocratic/>

Paine AB, 'Mark Twain: A Biography 1835–1910', chapter CCLI <http://www.gutenberg.org/files/2988/2988-h/2988-h.htm> accessed 19 August 2015

Peacock L, 'Protests Begin Over Agency Workers Cheated on Pay', *The Telegraph* (16 January 2013) <http://www.telegraph.co.uk/finance/jobs/hr-news/9803866/Protests-begin-over-agency-workers-cheated-on-pay.html>

Perulli A, 'Fundamental Social Rights, Market Regulation and EU External Action' (2014) 30 *International Journal of Comparative Labour Law and Industrial Relations* 27

Prosser T, 'Regulation and Social Solidarity' (2006) 33 (3) *Journal of Law and Society* 364

Ratti A, 'Agency Work and the Idea of Dual Employership: A Comparative Perspective' (2008–9) 30 *Comparative Labour Law and Policy Journal* 835

Rawls A, 'Conflict as Foundation for Consensus: Contradictions of Industrial Capitalism in Book III of Durkheim's Division of Labour' (2003) 29 *Critical Sociology* 295

Risak M and Warter J, 'Decent Crowdwork: Legal Strategies for Fair Employment Conditions in the Virtual Sweatshop', Paper presented to the Regulating for Decent Work 2015 Conference <http://www.rdw2015.org/uploads/submission/full_paper/373/crowdwork_law_Risak Warter.pdf>

Rodgers G, 'Precarious Work: The State of the Debate' in G Rodgers and J Rodgers (eds), *Precarious Jobs in Labour Market Regulation: The Growth of Atypical Employment in Western Europe* (ILO 1989)

Rodgers G, Lee E, Swepston L and van Daele J, *The ILO and the Quest for Social Justice 1919–2009* (ILO 2009)

Rogowski R, 'Industrial Relations, Labour Conflict Resolution and Reflexive Labour Law' in R Rogowski and T Wilthagen (eds), *Reflexive Labour Law: Studies in Industrial Relations and Employment Regulation* (Kluwer Law International 1994)

Schlachter M, 'Transnational Temporary Agency Work: How Much Equality Does the Equal Treatment Principle Provide?' (2012) 28 (2) *International Journal of Comparative Labour Law and Industrial Relations* 177

Sciarra S, 'Notions of Solidarity in Times of Economic Crisis' (2010) 39 (3) *ILJ* 223

Shaw J, Hunt J and Wallace C, *European Social Law of the European Union* (Palgrave Macmillan 2007)

Simpson B, 'The National Minimum Wage Five Years On: Reflections on Some General Issues' (2004) 33 *ILJ* 22

Singer JW, 'The Player and the Cards: Nihilism and Legal Theory' (1984) 94 (1) *The Yale Law Journal* 1

Sinzheimer H, 'Das Rätessytem' (1919) in H Sinzheimer, *Arbeitsrecht und Rechtssoziologie: Gesammelte Aufsätze und Reden (Band 1)* (Otto Brenner Stiftung 1976)

Sinzheimer H, 'Rätebewegung und Gesellschaftsverfassung (1920)' in H Sinzheimer, *Arbeitsrecht und Rechtssoziologie: Gesammelte Aufsätze und Reden (Band 1)* (Otto Brenner Stiftung 1976)

Sinzheimer H, 'Grundzüge des Arbeitsrechts (1927)' in H Sinzheimer, *Arbeitsrecht und Rechtssoziologie: Gesammelte Aufsätze und Reden (Band 1)* (Otto Brenner Stiftung 1976)

Sinzheimer H, 'Zur Frage der Reform des Schlichtungswesens (1929)' in H Sinzheimer, *Arbeitsrecht und Rechtssoziologie: Gesammelte Aufsätze und Reden (Band 1)* (Otto Brenner Stiftung 1976)

Sinzheimer H, 'Die Reform des Schlichtungswesens (1930)' in H Sinzheimer, *Arbeitsrecht und Rechtssoziologie: Gesammelte Aufsätze und Reden (Band 1)* (Otto Brenner Stiftung 1976)

Sinzheimer H, *Grundzüge des Arbeitsrechts* (2nd ed Gustav Fischer Jena 1927)

Smismans S, 'The European Social Dialogue in the Shadow of Hierarchy' (2008) 28 (1) *Journal of Public Policy* 161

Smit N and Fourie E, 'Extending Protection to Atypical Workers, Including Workers in the Informal Economy, in Developing Countries'

(2010) 26 (1) *International Journal of Comparative Labour Law and International Relations* 43

Smith P, 'Organizing the Unorganizable: Private Paid Household Workers and Approaches to Employee Representation (2000) 79 *North Carolina Law Review* 45

Smith P, 'The Pitfalls of Home: Protecting the Health and Safety of Paid Domestic Workers' (2011) 23 *Canadian Journal of Women and the Law* 309

Somek A, *Engineering Equality* (Oxford University Press 2011)

Spector, 'Philosophical Foundations of Labor Law' (2005–2006) 33 *Florida State University Law Review* 1119

Stone KVW, 'Legal Protections for Atypical Employees: Employment Law for Workers without Workplaces and Employees without Employers' (2006) 27 (2) *Berkeley Journal of Employment and Labour Law* 251

Supiot A, 'The Transformation of Work and the Future of Labour Law in Europe: A Multi-disciplinary Perspective' (1999) 138 (1) *International Labour Review* 31

Syrpis P and Novitz T, 'Economic and Social Rights in Conflict: Political and Judicial Approaches to their Reconciliation' (2008) 33 (3) *European Law Review* 411

TUC, 'The EU Temp Trade: Temporary Agency Working Across the European Union' (2005) http://www.tuc.org.uk/extras/eu_agency.pdf

TUC, 'Hard Work Hidden Lives: The Full Report of the Commission on Vulnerable Employment' (7 May 2008) http://www.vulnerableworkers.org.uk/files/CoVE_full_report.pdf

TUC, 'Vulnerable Workers Project Final Report. Informing Strategies for Vulnerable Workers' (April 2009) <http://www.vulnerableworkersproject.org.uk/wp-content/uploads/2009/04/vwp_final_report_final.doc>

Turner B, *Vulnerability and Human Rights* (Pennsylvania University Press 2006)

Ungerson C, 'Whose Empowerment and Independence? A Cross-national Perspective on "Cash for Care" Schemes' (2004) 24 *Ageing and Society* 189

UNISON Scotland, 'Briefing 50: February 2014: Legislation Update TUPE 2014' <http://www.unison-scotland.org.uk/briefings/b050_BargainingBrief_LegislationUpdateTUPE2014_Feb2014.pdf>

Van Gierke, *Die Soziale Aufgabe des Privatsrechts* (Berlin 1889)

Van Wanrooy B, Bewley H, Bryson A, Forth J, Freeth S, Stokes L and Wood S, '2011 Workplace Employment Relations Study' <https://www.gov.uk/government/uploads/system/uploads/attachment_data/file/210102/13_1010-WERS-first-findings-report-third-edition-may-2013.pdf>

Vosko L, 'Decent Work: The Shifting Role of the ILO and the Struggle for Global Social Justice' (2002) 2 (1) *Global Social Policy* 19

Vosko L, *Managing the Margins: Gender, Citizenship and the International Regulation of Precarious Employment* (Oxford University Press 2009)

Wedderburn Lord, 'Collective Bargaining or Legal Enactment: The 1999 Act and Union Recognition' (2000) 29 (1) *ILJ* 1

Wedderburn Lord, Lewis R and Clark J, *Labour Law and Industrial Relations: Building on Kahn-Freund* (Clarendon Press, Oxford 1983)

Weiss M, 'Re-inventing Labour Law?' in G Davidov and B Langille (eds), *The Idea of Labour Law* (Oxford University Press 2011)

Wintour P, 'Biggest Crackdown on Trade Unions for 30 Years Launched by the Conservatives', The Guardian (15 July 2015) <http://www.theguardian.com/politics/2015/jul/15/trade-unions-conservative-offensive-decades-strikes-labour>

Wynn M and Leighton P, 'Will the Real Employer Please Stand Up? Agencies, Client Companies and the Employment Status of the Temporary Agency Worker' (2006) 35 (3) *ILJ* 301

Zambioni M, 'The Social in Social Law: An Analysis of a Concept in Disguise' (2008) 9 *Journal of Law and Society* 63

Index

agency work *see* temporary agency
   work
Alston, P. 104–5
Australia
   trade union codes of ethics 193
Autoclenz v. Belcher [2011] 145
autonomy
   classical labour law theory 48–9
   temporary agency workers 157–9
   vulnerability 37–40
   vulnerable subject theory 154, 157–8,
      188, 211

bargaining power inequalities 4–6, 10,
      12, 35, 196
   capitalism 20–23, 46
   classical labour law theory 43, 45–6
   collective bargaining 43, 45–6, 136–7
   economic efficiency 61–3, 203–4
   employment contracts 22–3, 61–3,
      136
   market failure 63
   opportunism 63
   temporary agency workers 8, 127–8
   trade union ballot thresholds 127–8
Belgium
   domestic worker trade unions 192
Bicknell, Mrs S v. Miss I Hughes [2007]
      186–7
Brazil
   domestic worker trade unions 171

capabilities approach
   efficiency theory 73–4
   vulnerable subject theory 90
capitalism
   bargaining power inequalities 20–23,
      46

class influences 21–2, 34–5, 39–40,
      78
classical labour law theory 11–12, 43,
      45–7, 194
   commodification 20–21, 23, 62–3
   economic constitutionalism 47
   economic efficiency 62–3
   price *vs.* dignity 23
   worker vulnerability 15, 18–23, 78–9
care responsibilities 7
   cash for care schemes 185–7
   division of labour 30–31
   domestic work protections 185–7
childcare *see* care responsibilities
classical labour law theory
   autonomy, role of 48–9
   background 43
   capitalism 11–12, 43, 45–7, 194
   collective bargaining 43, 45–6, 55–6
   criticisms of 139–42, 172–4, 197
   domestic work 163, 167–74, 194
   economic constitutionalism 47
   efficiency theory challenges to 62,
      203–4
   function of law, and 48–50, 55
   gold collar workers 139–40
   historical influences on 55–6
   homogeneity of interest or status
      55–7
   ILO Conventions 96
   industrial relations, role of 47, 50–54
   labour as property 46–7
   limitations 47, 55–8, 92–3, 139–42,
      196–7
   market forces controls 58–61
   public interest 48–50
   selective goals 45–7, 55–8
   social law theory, and 45, 75, 77

237